JANET RENO

Doing the Right Thing

Paul Anderson

John Wiley & Sons, Inc.
New York • Chichester • Brisbane • Toronto • Singapore

To my wife, Janet L. Fix,
and our son, Tate

Excerpt from "Janet Reno" from "Capitol Steps" parody lyrics. Copyright © 1993, Strauss and Newport.

This text is printed on acid-free paper.

Copyright © 1994 by Paul Anderson
Published by John Wiley & Sons, Inc.

Library of Congress Cataloging-in-Publication Data
Anderson, Paul
    Janet Reno : doing the right thing / Paul Anderson.
      p.   cm.
    Includes index.
    ISBN 0-471-01858-9 (cloth : acid-free paper)
    1. Reno, Janet, 1938–   . 2. Attorneys general—United States—
Biography. I. Title.
KF373.R45A53 1994
353.5′092—dc20
  [B]   94-4262

Printed in the United States of America

10 9 8 7 6 5 4 3 2 1

Acknowledgments

Janet Reno didn't want this book to be written—at least, not yet.

Her reaction when I first told her about it in August of 1993 was to laugh one of her big, deep laughs. "Oh, c'mon," she said. "I haven't even been here six months yet. This still seems so ephemeral to me."

I am grateful to her for the cooperation, albeit limited, she subsequently gave me. She decided to give me no greater access than she gives any other journalist who writes about her and the activities of the Department of Justice. But she allowed family members and friends to be interviewed, if they wished, and she agreed to answer specific questions when I needed to clarify facts about her family history and career.

Dozens of people have graciously provided time and recollections, during my ongoing reporting both for the *Miami Herald* and for this book. Among them are the following:

Charlotte M. Acquaviva, Julie Anbender, Caroline Aronovitz, Ernest Brown, Bob Butterworth, Tom Cash, Michael Chmura, Bill Clinton, Sandy D'Alemberte, Marie Driscoll, Sam Dubbin, Bettina Dudley, Dante Fascell, Roy Furman, Jeanine Jacobs Goldberg, Bob Graham, Erwin Griswold, Lani Guinier, Lisa Hardeman, Philip Heymann, Webster Hubbell, Maggy Hurchalla, Patricia Ireland, Tom Jipping, Harry Johnston, Marcia Kanner, Dan Kavanaugh,

Ron Klain, Gerald Lewis, Buddy MacKay, Bob McDiarmid, Carrie Meek, Charles R. Nesson, Hazel Nowakowski, Patsy Palmer, Arva Moore Parks, Robert Reno, Hugh Rodham, Lula Rodriguez, Katherine Fernandez Rundle, Patricia Schroeder, Ricki Seidman, Buddy Shorstein, John Edward Smith, Sara Smith, and Sally Wood Winslow.

I am also grateful to my *Herald* colleagues for their assistance, encouragement, and patience with this project, most especially executive editor Doug Clifton, national editor Frank Davies, political editor Tom Fiedler, Liz Donovan, Margaret Kempel, Gene Miller, and Peter Slevin.

Also, this book couldn't have been written without relying on the outstanding work that so many at the *Herald* and the late and lamented *Miami News* performed in covering Reno and her office over the years.

Other writings I found helpful were Sidney Blumenthal's excellent article about Zoë Baird in the *New Yorker,* February 15, 1993; Glenn R. Simpson's story of lobbyists spreading rumors about Reno in *Roll Call, The Newspaper of Capitol Hill,* March 4, 1993; *Capitol Games,* Hyperion, 1992, by Timothy W. Phelps and Helen Winternitz; *The Florida Handbook 1993–1994,* Peninsular Publishing Co., by Allen Morris; *The FBI: Inside the World's Most Powerful Law Enforcement Agency,* Pocket Books, 1993, by Ronald Kessler; *Knights of the Fourth Estate,* E. A. Seemann, 1974, by Nixon Smiley; *Miami,* Pocket Books, 1987, by Joan Didion; *Miami, City of the Future,* The Atlantic Monthly Press, 1987, by T. D. Allman; and *Miami, The Magic City,* Centennial Press, 1991, by Arva Moore Parks.

I had a lot to learn about the difference between writing for a daily newspaper and writing a book. I am grateful to my editors, Jan Cook and Hana Lane, for their extremely patient guidance in that learning experience. In a pinch, Jan also proved that former *Herald* staffers never lose their reporting skills.

Finally, I am forever grateful to my wife, Janet L. Fix, whose savvy, suggestions, and support made this book possible. She, too, helped with some reporting. I only hope that someday I can make up to her the long hours I spent at the computer terminal in our spare bedroom while she prepared for the birth of our first child. Tate Perry Fix Anderson's early arrival on December 30, 1993, caused a deadline or two to slip, but not too badly.

Paul Anderson
Bethesda, Maryland

CONTENTS

PROLOGUE

Substance, Not Spin

Janet Reno's long, purposeful strides carried her across the courtyard and up the steps to the plain stone platform. It was just after noon on Tuesday, April 6, 1993. Barely spring, the day was overcast and chilly, and most of the cheering audience wore wool and topcoats. Reno wore only a lightweight navy knit suit and a simple red blouse, the kind of understated outfit she favors.

She stepped behind a podium emblazoned with the Justice Department seal, an American bald eagle in flight. Around her in the drab brick courtyard at the center of the Justice building, nearly a thousand employees had gathered to hear the first speech from their new boss. Others were watching from the surrounding office windows.

It was her twenty-fifth day on the job. She started to speak, then paused as her amplified voice echoed off the granite walls around her.

"I'm the new kid on the block, and I thought I should let you know my hopes and dreams and how I do things," Reno began. "While I'm the attorney general, we will address each issue with one question: What's the right thing to do? . . .

"Let us leave here today resolved to ask that of ourselves and others as we seek justice, remembering that sometimes doing the right thing is very politically unpopular. Sometimes it will be painful, for it will, of necessity, hurt someone. But with strength and courage, let us face that question unafraid and together seek justice for all."

The eleven-minute speech carried the emotional wallop of the coach's talk at a homecoming pep rally. Cheers and applause rang through the courtyard. A confident, smiling Reno stepped down from the platform and walked through the crowd to shake hands. Barbara Burley, a short, stout woman from the Antitrust Division, squeezed up next to the towering Reno to have a picture taken by a coworker. Reno smiled broadly and paused for a pair of shots. Burley quivered with delight after Reno moved on to greet other workers.

"She's EX-cel-lent," Burley said, enunciating each syllable. "After all the talk about the 'Year of the Woman' in Washington, this makes it real. She'll bring a different touch. It's good for the department."

Reno won the hearts of her audience that day with a simple statement of what she believes. As her words forecast, the year ahead would at times be painful. She would find that standing on principle can be lonely. And she would learn some hard truths about political reality in the nation's capital.

Janet Reno is a remarkable woman whose intelligence, conscience, and capacity for work are all too rare in American politics, even in Washington, D.C. As a prosecutor from an ethnically and racially diverse city at Ground Zero in the war on drugs, she is uniquely qualified to serve as attorney general. She has captured the public imagination with her legendary intransigence on matters of personal principle. But integrity can be an inconvenient attribute in the political world, one that could spell her downfall.

Her place in history was assured the moment she was sworn in. During a visit to an elementary school early in her tenure, a young girl asked Reno how many women had served as attorney general of the United States. "I'm it," Reno replied. "No!" the girl said, her jaw dropping.

Reno feels a responsibility to other women. At the end of her confirmation hearing, Reno declared: "I will set an example that will enable people to understand, if a woman can be attorney general of the United States, she can do anything."

But Reno is exceptional for more than blazing a trail for women. As a politician, she is decidedly atypical, more concerned with substance than style. She was one of the nation's foremost prosecutors, despite the fact that she had once declared she would never be a prosecutor because they were "more interested in securing convictions than in seeking justice."

She is totally honest, brutally frank, uninterested in what is fashionable or trendy, unimpressed with wealth. A handsome woman with a resolute jaw and camp-counselor hairdo, she no more softens her appearance than she softens her views. Her only makeup is light red lipstick; her blunt-cut fingernails are polished with a clear gloss. She rotates through a small stock of discreet earrings, which never dangle between her abbreviated haircut and her broad shoulders. Her only other jewelry is an occasional gold locket and an old-fashioned gold watch. She alternates between two pairs of glasses, one gold-rimmed, the other a red-tinted plastic.

She makes use of her legendary height—six feet one and a quarter inches in bare feet, six two in her customary low heels—when she seeks to intimidate. Otherwise, she leans forward to speak to people and leans down for children.

For her solid frame, Reno prefers understated suits with clean lines and simple detailing, often the selections of a personal buyer at Saks Fifth Avenue who chooses off-the-rack professional apparel. The buyer was a concession to Miami friends who nagged her about updating her image some years ago. But no high-fashion Christophe for her; she hasn't changed her wash-and-run hairstyle, trimmed high above the ears and low across her forehead, since the pageboy days of her early career.

Reno would rather hike the Everglades or sail Biscayne Bay than attend a White House ball. She is devoted to family and reverent about its importance, but she has never married. She is a caring, fun-loving friend, yet has not had a romantic relationship in years. She loves and is loved by children but has never had her own.

Reno walks to work. She also flies tourist-class and rides Washington's subway as circumstances permit. She vows that when President Clinton no longer needs her services, she will leave her furnished rental apartment in downtown Washington and return to the rustic Miami home she has lived in since 1949.

Somehow, one can't imagine her easing into a plush berth at a genteel Washington law firm, earning an enormous salary as a prize rainmaker, the partner who attracts new clients.

Rather, one can read Reno by understanding her heroes—every one an iconoclast, a risk taker, a visionary. As personal heroes, she chooses her mother, Jane Wood Reno, her father, Henry Olaf Reno, and her maternal grandmother, Daisy Sloan Hunter Wood. Political heroes include Abraham Lincoln, Thomas Jefferson, Franklin Roosevelt, Harry Truman, Robert Kennedy, and former Florida Governor LeRoy Collins, who led a courageous fight to desegregate public schools, lunch counters, and other institutions.

Most of her heroes were Democrats, as is she, a political heritage she accepted without much analysis—like most lawyers, she is a linear thinker, approaching problems logically rather than creatively—or subsequent doubt. "I don't think I ever decided I was a Democrat. I've always been a Democrat, and certainly it was my parents and my grandparents that influenced me. As time went by, I would question, and each time I questioned I came out on the same side as my parents."

Her patriotism verges on the sappy but is unquestionably sincere, as friends can attest who attended a party she gave in late March 1993. Reno had returned to Miami to pack up for Washington, and she invited her former staff from the Dade State Attorney's Office to a Bring Your Own Everything party at her home. More than four hundred people—employees and their families and some friends—showed up.

Her staff presented her with a sheet cake decorated with the American flag. As the crowd pressed close around her, Reno began to sing "America, the Beautiful." People joined in, tears welling in many eyes.

On her return to Washington, she acknowledged how her life would change. In Miami, she had daily contact with constituents and often nightly as well, since they could call her at home. "It was nice to walk around in my bare feet and pick up the phone when it rang and not think of myself as attorney general," she said later. "Somehow or another I've got to blend Washington with all of America and try to be accessible."

Reno has addressed that concern with a daunting schedule of personal appearances. Unlike her predecessors, she prefers speaking to "real people" in schools and community halls rather than to other lawyers who populate bar associations and other legal groups. She knows the spotlight follows her wherever she goes, so she uses each public appearance to drive home her personal agenda about the holistic causes of crime, the significance of family, the importance of community involvement.

Reno learned about community relations in Miami. In the conflagration that accompanied the 1980 riots, she read the anger of people who felt ignored and discounted. She emerged from that experience smarter and stronger and—eventually—with the respect of those who had blamed her for the acquittal of the police officers who murdered Arthur McDuffie. But it was not the last time she would be held accountable for a deadly inferno.

It is 1,057 miles between Washington and Miami. On tough days, Reno feels every mile.

Her mother once said, "She doesn't love prestige as much as she loves pressure." Reno applies the same pressure to those around her. She holds her employees and even her friends to the high expectations she has for herself. One friend says Reno will "get in a mood, a snit, about something" and treat even her closest friends brusquely. "We've all been on the receiving end of an abrupt Janetism."

She has a prickly sense of principle and has thrived politically because she is seen by voters as uncompromising and willing to accept the responsibility for her decisions. That's what catapulted her to stardom after the horror of the inferno at the Branch Davidian compound near Waco, Texas. But when she chooses to dig in her heels, she faces inevitable conflict with those politicians who are willing to sacrifice principle for expediency. In her first year, she stood up to White House aides who attempted to cut corners, such as in the travel office affair, in pursuit of an ill-considered goal.

Through all the turmoil, Reno has brushed aside the whining of anonymous White House staffers and insists that she is comfortable in the support she receives directly from the Oval Office. President Clinton promised her independence in exchange for her best legal advice, and that's what she says she intends to provide.

At some point, though, that means that Clinton—a man known to seek "wiggle room" when it suits his political ambitions—could become Reno's worst friend. She wouldn't be fired; she is too popular for that. Rather, she would follow the course of Elliot Richardson, the attorney general who resigned rather than execute Richard Nixon's order to fire Watergate special prosecutor Archibald Cox.

Reno came to Washington as a true outsider, both to the city's entrenched power structure and to the Clinton administration. For all the talk of change during the 1992 campaign, she personifies it as much as anyone brought to Washington by the election. Yet Reno wasn't involved in the Clinton-Gore campaign, nor is she a longtime "Friend of Bill."

Indeed, she was the president's third choice for attorney general and the last person to join his cabinet. Clinton needed Reno to overcome his fumbles with his first two selections, Zoë Baird and Kimba Wood. Although that gives her a certain independence, it also means she has no old friend as an ally in the White House.

What she relies on is her belief that Clinton, too, wants to do the right thing. He promised her independence and a chance to reinvigorate the Justice Department. She believes in that promise.

She treasures a photograph of the president and herself that was taken on his first visit to the Justice Department. It's a black and white that was shot in her private office as she and Clinton gazed admiringly at the painting of Robert F. Kennedy that hangs over her fireplace.

Clinton inscribed the photo, "To Janet." Across the bottom, he wrote, "Someday people will look at your picture like this."

PART ONE

Early Years

CHAPTER 1

Growing Up a Reno

Kendall Drive begins near glistening Biscayne Bay, just south of Miami, then heads due west toward the vast saw-grass sea that is the Everglades. Flanked by shopping centers, apartment complexes, gas stations, and discount stores, it could be any six-lane highway in America. But it's not.

Travel far enough west on Kendall Drive and you might catch sight of an incongruous oasis of pine trees behind a funeral home. Locate a narrow dirt driveway behind a fence, unmarked since a vandal made off with the mailbox stenciled "Reno," and you've found passage into the singular domain of Janet Reno.

Three and a half acres of scrub pine and palmettos remain of what was once a twenty-one-acre refuge. When Janet's parents, Henry and Jane, purchased the property in 1947, it brushed the eastern reaches of the sprawling Everglades. That same year the federal government had the same idea, but on a different scale. It laid claim to 1.4 million acres fifteen miles west of the Reno outpost, creating Everglades National Park, an area larger than Delaware.

Until she was appointed attorney general in March 1993, Janet Reno lived in a rustic cypress-beamed home built, board by board, by her mother at the end of that dirt road. That quirky, slant-roofed bungalow, not the furnished apartment Reno rents within walking distance of the Justice Department, remains her home.

Reno's home, like her family, occupies a special place in her heart. During her confirmation hearing before the Senate Judiciary Committee, she told a hushed audience how the house was built in 1948 and 1949, and how much it means to her:

"There were four children a year apart, and we were outgrowing [our previous] house. Daddy didn't have very much money. One afternoon, Mother picked us up at school, and she said, 'I'm going to build a house.' We said, 'What do you know about building a house?' And she said, 'I'm going to learn.'

"And she went and talked to the brickmason and the electrician and the plumber, and she learned how to build a house. She dug the foundation with her own hands with a pick and shovel, she laid the blocks, she put in the wiring, she put in the plumbing, and Daddy would help her with the heavy work when he got home from work at night.

"I have lived in that house ever since, and as I come down the driveway through the woods at night, with a problem, with an obstacle to overcome, that house is a symbol to me that you can do anything you really want if it's the right thing to do and you put your mind to it."

Janet Reno treasures her remnant of primeval Florida, but it was a far different place—gaudy, raucous, outrageous—that attracted her grandparents to Miami during the boom years of the 1920s. Thanks to Henry Morrison Flagler's railroad, tourists and settlers could travel from Jacksonville to Miami. South Florida real estate was as golden as the sunshine. To appease the exotic tastes of wealthy newcomers, Addison Mizner, architect to the superrich, spun Alhambran architectural fantasies in Palm Beach, and real estate developer George Merrick interlaced his idyllic community of Coral Gables with waterways patterned after Venetian canals.

An Indiana headlight manufacturer named Carl Fisher launched the land-buying frenzy. In 1915, Fisher dredged up muck from Biscayne Bay, transforming a mangrove swamp into Miami Beach. There weren't many nibbles from land buyers, however, until he took to promoting his creation with bathing beauties, boat races, pink flamingos, and a giant thermometer erected in Times Square to beam Miami's tropical temperatures to the frigid natives of New York.

Fisher's strategy worked. At the peak of the boom, sun-hungry northerners streaming into Miami created such a housing demand that 481 hotels and apartment buildings rose along the beach in one year.

The Florida fantasy captivated a pair of Danish immigrants, Robert and Louise Reno, who were still looking for their American dream. Robert Marius Rasmussen had owned a photo studio in Denmark but longed to provide a better life for his family. He joined the massive influx of Europeans who poured into the United States early in the century, and after working for a year at a midwestern tire factory he had saved enough money to bring his family over.

In 1913, Rasmussen returned to Denmark for his wife and two sons, Henry Olaf, eleven, and Paul, seven. But they would start their new life with a new name, Robert decided, to avoid the prejudice he had felt from second-generation Scandinavian immigrants. Looking for something suitably all-American, he turned to a map of the United States and settled on Reno, which was short and easy to pronounce.

On arriving in their new home in Withee, Wisconsin, the Reno boys spoke no English. Henry later told his children he got teased for his funny accent and odd clothes. But after four years, he spoke English well enough to become editor of his high school newspaper.

When Robert's effort to open a photo studio failed, the Renos answered the clarion call to Florida, their hopes bolstered by friends who had gone ahead.

College-age Henry had dreams of being a farmer. He studied agriculture at the University of Tennessee and the University of Wisconsin. His education ended after two years when money ran out. Henry followed his family to Miami, where his father had become chief photographer for the *Miami Herald.*

While his father told stories with pictures, Henry decided to do it with words. He became a police reporter for the *Herald* in August 1924, a beat he would own for forty-three years.

Crime was a growth industry in those wide-open days of Prohibition. Henry quickly made a name for himself by covering the bootleggers and rumrunners who thrived in South Florida. One of Reno's most memorable stories, *Herald* editor John Pennekamp once recalled, was written on a sunny Sunday afternoon when federal agents chased down the speedboat of a notorious liquor runner named Red Shannon. The agents got their man—shot him dead, in fact—in front of a stunned crowd of thousands gathered on Miami Beach for a boating regatta.

The excitement of Miami also captivated the Wood family of Sunnyside, Georgia. George, a lawyer, and Daisy, his genteel Southern bride, decided to relocate George's law practice after the collapse of the state's cotton-based economy. Their roots ran deep in Georgia soil; George's father, George Washington Wood, had been a railroad stationmaster as well as a circuit-riding Baptist preacher. According to his tombstone, "He served the churches of Central Georgia. He preached Jesus."

George and Daisy's five children were born in Sunnyside, just outside Macon. Their first, Jane, born in 1913—the year that Henry Reno arrived in the United States—was quickly pegged as precocious. In fact, Jane's dazzled teachers had her intelligence tested at age nine.

"There was a story in the *Macon Daily Telegraph* with a headline I remember: 'Jane Wood Declared Genius.' I found out there was nothing like being declared a genius to make people hate you," Jane Wood said later. She reacted with the spunk she passed on to her own children. "I had to go out and fight some of the boys on the block to prove I was still me."

In 1925, the Woods packed up Jane and her younger siblings, Dorothy (known as Dolly), Daisy, Winifred, and George, and headed for the bright southern horizon. They settled in Miami Beach, the heart of the action. But it took a terrifying storm for the Wood children to appreciate life as Floridians.

"I thought, at first, South Florida's just poor, flat country, compared to my Georgia's pines and hills," Jane said. "To me, it was just dull, dumb, and flat.

"It was the Hurricane of 1926 that changed my feelings. We

were living on Miami Beach in a house a block from the ocean. That hurricane had winds of two hundred miles an hour. We rode it out in our house, and when we went out we thought it was over. Miami Beach was completely covered with water, inundated. We found a great big snapper trapped in the middle of the street and caught him.

"Then the wind started again. We didn't know the calm was just the eye coming right over us. What did we know about hurricanes? But we got home all right, and later we cooked the snapper on an open fire.

"To me, it was very exciting. I saw the hurricane as a great vandal, and that appealed to me. There's something of the vandal in all of us. The storm was a great wrecker. I'd never seen anything like it. After that, I loved Florida because the hurricane was part of it; it wasn't dull and dumb. It had force, all that great power. It was something I could feel."

Just across Biscayne Bay in Miami, Henry Reno was also caught up in the infamous hurricane. Few on the *Miami Herald* staff had experienced a hurricane, and many assumed the city was somehow immune to tropical storms. As the killer storm bore down on South Florida, editors debated whether to alert residents and risk raising undue alarm. Finally, when gale winds and heavy rain snapped phone lines to the newsroom at three A.M., the news editor decided to add a bulletin to the city edition then on the presses. He sent Henry out into the storm to get an update from the weather bureau.

Henry grabbed a flashlight and raincoat. He had to battle the wind just to open the door onto Miami Avenue. The scene he met was astonishing. Bracing himself against the roaring gale, he edged along the buildings. Around him, signs and awnings crashed to the ground, electrical wires snapped and arced sizzling blue flames. He took refuge in an arcade, where for two hours he watched the destruction in growing fear.

With the first gray light of dawn, the wind dropped, then stopped completely. The eerie silence made Henry's ears ring. He tentatively stepped into the street, ankle-deep in water. As far as he could see, the city lay in ruin. One of the city's proud new skyscrapers was twisted, its floors exposed where wind had ripped away the outer walls. To his horror, he saw human forms amid the rubble, then realized they were mannequins blown through shop windows. Gradually, other people emerged, looking ghostly in the dawn. Overhead, sea birds soared against patches of blue sky.

Henry continued toward the weather bureau when one of the forecasters raced into the street, shouting at people to return to shelter, that this was just the eye of the storm. Henry raced back to the *Herald.* Many of the 242 people killed that day were swept off causeways by rising water or trapped without shelter amid the furious winds of the storm's back edge.

The Hurricane of 1926 marked a turning point for Miami. In the wake of its horrifying destruction, the South Florida boom went bust. Three years later, the stock market crash put the finishing touches on an era of excess.

The Wood family, however, prospered. Jane got hooked early on newspaper writing. She started filing school sports stories for the *Miami News* when she was just fourteen. She graduated from Miami High a year later, after skipping three grades, and entered the University of Miami.

There she flunked her journalism courses because, she said, she was too busy learning to drink home brew to concentrate on her writing. But she sailed through physics and graduated with a bachelor's degree. Her plan was to attend graduate school at Columbia University in New York, but she first took a job with the *Herald* at the lowest rung on the journalistic ladder—as an obituary writer.

Jane met someone at the *Herald* who captured her eye, Henry Reno, the tall, dapper police reporter twelve years her senior. As Jane later recounted it, Henry mentioned in the newsroom that he was going to take his boat out the next day to dive for Florida's clawless lobsters on the first day of crawfish season. "Take me, take me," she pleaded, adding a lie that she knew how to catch the critters.

The seas and the sips of his Cobb's Creek whiskey did her in. After she got seasick, Henry took her home, let her nap, and served his catch with melted butter when she awoke.

"I didn't think he'd ever ask me anywhere again. But he did," Jane said. He was thirty-six, she was twenty-four when they got married and moved into a small house in Coconut Grove, an enclave of lush vegetation and wooden bungalows that attracted Miami's pioneer families and the likes of poet Robert Frost and Marjory Stoneman Douglas, author of *The Everglades, River of Grass*.

Within a year, Henry and Jane started their family. Janet Reno was born on July 21, 1938, at Jackson Memorial Hospital. She was given no middle name. Jane claimed that labor took so long that she was too exhausted to come up with one. The earliest photo of Janet, from 1939, shows a chubby tot with blond curls and a big grin getting an outdoor bath in a tin washtub.

Three other children followed Janet in rather rapid succession, and Jane gave up full-time newspaper work to tend her flock. Robert Marius, named for his grandfather, came eighteen months after Janet. He was followed a year later by Margaret, and a year after that came Mark. The siblings and their closest friends still use their childhood nicknames: Janny, Bobby, Maggy, Marky.

In one of Janet's earliest memories, the children accompanied their father each morning to his bus stop a few blocks away, riding in a long wagon built by Henry to hold all four kids. It was named the Markomobile in honor of the youngest. Their route took them past the Plymouth Congregational Church, constructed in 1897 to resemble a Spanish mission, complete with twin belfries. Each trip was a bit frightening, because the kids convinced themselves that wolves lived behind the stone wall surrounding the church. Neither Henry nor Jane, tickled with the imaginations of their children, did anything to refute the notion.

In 1943, the family moved to a house in rural South Miami, far from the development along the shores of the Miami River and Biscayne Bay. The once-sleepy town that only snapped to life during the winter tourist season now hosted thousands of soldiers and bustled with year-round importance. In postwar years, so many of those GIs would return to settle that Dade County's population nearly doubled by decade's end.

World War II shortages revived Henry's long-deferred dream of farming, at least on a limited scale. The Renos populated their spacious lot with cows, goats, turkeys, ducks, and eventually hundreds of chickens. Selling broilers, eggs, and butter (Henry and Janet milked, Jane churned) helped make ends meet.

The war years meant saving tin cans and counting gas ration coupons for their 1938 Ford V-8 coupe. Occasionally, the children thrilled to see an open army truck roaring down U.S. 1, bringing German soldiers to a barbed wire–encircled POW camp on Kendall Drive.

The war brought news from Denmark. The Renos talked about the courageous Danes who rescued Jews from the deadly grasp of the Nazis. Henry, whose mother, Louise, didn't live to see the war's end, stayed in touch with relatives in Denmark and told his children stories about their Danish kin.

The Reno menagerie flourished, thanks to Henry's love for animals. One night, he came home from a bar leading two donkeys, Felix and Pedro. And for Christmas of 1943, Janet got a pinto pony that she named Tony.

From the first day, Tony showed spunk. That Christmas morning, Janet was told to look outside for her present. She came back inside and announced: "Santa brought me a pony, but he's run away!" She guessed her gift from the rope and droppings left behind.

Over the years, Janet often would have to track Tony down when angry neighbors called to say he had galloped through their flower gardens or tomato patches. But once a year Tony redeemed himself, when he provided pony rides for neighborhood youngsters at the South Miami Carnival. Later, Janet purchased a young horse, named Betty, for $125 earned doing chores.

Lisa Reno, oldest daughter of Henry's brother Paul and two

and a half years older than Janet, recalled how exciting it was to spend a week each summer "on the farm" with her cousins.

As small girls, they were treated by their grandmothers to tea parties with dolls. But they grew to prefer horseback riding and outdoor games. "We were all tomboys," Lisa said of herself, Janet, and Maggy. "We rode horses all over, climbed trees, got dirty just like the boys."

The girls frequently went topless, like Henry and the boys. As Janet neared puberty, her mother mandated a T-shirt. "Do I have to wear shoes, too?" Janet asked. The answer was usually no.

Most mornings, Janet awoke at about six to the sound of her father on the telephone: "Hi, this is Reno of the *Herald*. Do you have anything going?" Henry would start calling police departments—what reporters call "cop shops"—at five-thirty A.M., checking on overnight arrests, burglaries, the occasional murder. When he reported to work, it was to the Miami police headquarters, not the *Herald* newsroom, preferring to have his desk among the cops.

A photo from the era shows a decidedly proper-looking man with slicked hair, a carefully trimmed mustache, wire-framed glasses, a starched collar, tightly cinched tie, and double-breasted suit. Although he may not have looked like a cop, he knew how to court valuable sources and lasting friendships by bringing fresh doughnuts to the police station on Sunday mornings and sharing his homegrown sweetheart roses and gardenias with secretaries.

Reno was known for his flowers. Years later, he shipped roses and gardenias to his daughters at their far-off colleges by wrapping them in damp tissue inside cigar boxes. "The first time I got one, I saw these little holes in the lid and thought Daddy had sent me an animal," recalled Maggy, who attended Swarthmore. When family members arrived in Washington for Janet's confirmation hearings, they brought her fresh blossoms from Florida wrapped in damp tissue in a cigar box.

Twice a year, Henry took his oldest daughter and son on his rounds, where he introduced them to the lawyers and judges he often told stories about at home. Along with grandfather George Wood, known as "Pooh," those lawyers helped plant the idea of a legal career in Janet's mind. None were women, but her grandmother and mother, and other strong females in the family, provided ample evidence that women could become anything they wanted.

Janet's maternal grandmother, Daisy Sloan Hunter Wood, had worked as a legal secretary until she got married. She encouraged her daughters to do whatever they wished; they became a battlefield nurse, a pilot, and a journalist, and her son became a doctor. In each, Daisy instilled a sense of duty to family and community. Her fourteen grandchildren adored her and called her "Dai-Dai."

"She was a strong woman," said Sally Wood Winslow, daughter of Daisy's namesake, known in the family as "Daisy Junior." "She had a great sense of self-confidence, a purpose in life, and a strength. She was a very strong figure in all our lives. I grew up thinking all women were that way."

Two of Daisy Wood's daughters shouldered wartime duty. Daisy was an army nurse with General George Patton's troops in North Africa and Italy. As a Women's Air Service Pilot (WASP), Winnie flew military planes from factories to air bases and taught flying while male instructors were overseas.

"When they came home in their uniforms, they were heroines to me, and I thought they were magnificent," Janet recalls.

Early in her tenure as attorney general, Reno joined her Aunt Winnie at the dedication of a statue honoring WASPs for their wartime service. At the ceremony in Sweetwater, Texas, Reno pinned to her brightly flowered dress a button that read, "Write Women Back into History." When she returned to Washington, Reno put a four-inch replica of the statue on the mantel in her private office.

But of all the women in Janet's life, none had a more profound influence than her hurricane-loving mother. Outspoken, outrageous, absolutely indifferent to others' opinions, Jane Reno was truly one of a kind. She drank beer like it was soda, eschewed a bra, and wore flowered housedresses and sneakers everywhere she went. Later, Jane would jazz up her outfit with a floppy hat with flowers when she accompanied her daughter to political affairs.

Jane lavished on her children the kind of love that empowered, not enslaved. Yet she maintained such a lifelong hold on Janet's loyalty that not even the possibility of a presidential appointment could lure Janet from her ailing mother's side. Reno declined to be considered for a job in the Clinton administration until after her mother's death.

"She taught us to play baseball, to bake a cake, to play fair," said Janet. "She beat the living daylights out of us sometimes, and she loved us with all her heart. She taught us her favorite poets. And there is no child care in the world that will ever be a substitute for what that lady was in our lives."

Asked once if she considered herself a feminist, Reno answered, "My mother always told me to do my best, to think my best, and to do right and consider myself a person."

According to Maggy, "What gave us our self-confidence was the absolute certainty that every adult in our world loved us absolutely. They weren't always perfect, and we weren't always perfect. But we could count on that love."

Jane and Henry didn't play favorites among their children, according to family members and friends. "They were all considered equally," said cousin Sally. "They were all encouraged to be leaders, and they all had skills and talents beyond any age limits." Each of her Reno cousins displayed a remarkable sense of independence and self-confidence, Winslow said. "And you can't stand out so much when everybody has it."

Jane read aloud to the kids daily, everything from *Swiss Family Robinson* to classical poetry. Janet's favorite book was Kenneth Grahame's children's classic, *The Wind in the Willows*. She delighted in the tales of Rat, Mole, and their friends, who captured the magic and mystery of nature that she experienced in her daily explorations. But it was in the independent-minded Toad that the Reno children found lessons in morals and ethics—and the personification of their mother. Toad is so taken by fancy motor cars that he steals one and ends up in prison. He is clever enough to escape but can't return home until he learns to rely on his friends to battle his enemies.

The children saw themselves in the whimsical Mole and Rat, but it was their mother who most resembled the impossible Toad, who was "irresponsible and difficult, but he was not bad," said Maggy. "He was convinced in the ultimate rightness of everything he did."

Later in life, Janet would give copies of the book to adult friends who had never read it. And when, as attorney general, she was invited to appear on the tenth-anniversary broadcast of the public television show "Reading Rainbow," she read to a group of children from the book that meant so much to her. She assumed a different voice for each character and her face glowed as she returned to the Wild Wood . . . and to happy days at her mother's knee.

In 1947, Henry and Jane decided to flee still farther westward, in search of more space, more privacy. They invested their savings in twenty-one acres "as far west as they could go before the land gets squishy," said South Florida historian and family friend Arva Moore Parks. The land, costing five hundred dollars an acre, was at the southwestern corner of Kendall Drive (Southwest 88th Street) and 112th Avenue.

They moved into a small frame house on one corner of the property, but roughing it didn't faze the Renos. Henry and Jane had introduced their children to the quiet wonders of the Everglades and the Florida Keys. The family loved camping, hiking, fishing, swimming, and, later, skin diving. That summer, when Janet turned nine, Henry's pal, horse breeder Eddie Padgett, helped give the kids a vacation to remember. He loaned Henry a horse van, and the kids helped clean it out. They installed bunk beds, a fifty-gallon water drum, and an old icebox. Then Henry, Jane, and the three oldest kids roamed around Florida for three weeks, visiting beaches on the west coast, touring the state capitol in Tallahassee, and floating in old inner tubes down a stretch of the Suwanee River.

At home, the kids were free to roam the acreage with their assortment of pets, including a devoted black-and-white mongrel named Liza. One afternoon, walking back from a small rock pit where limestone had once been quarried, Liza ran ahead of the gang and rushed barking into a clump of palmetto bushes. She backed out with a yelp and dropped dead before reaching the house. She had scared off a rattlesnake, but not before it sank its fangs into her. Janet staged a funeral and wept for days.

Growing up, Maggy said, "We had very few rules except that we couldn't do what was wrong. We could be wild, adventurous, enthusiastic about anything we chose. But we couldn't be mean, and we couldn't be dishonest."

Recalling childhood visits to what she calls the Reno ranch, Winslow said, "We were wild young kids. Not wild like crazy, but adventurous, constantly adventurous. We knew every square inch of the property and played on it."

The Reno children relied on each other as playmates since they were far from any neighbors. The nearest store was five miles away. At night, one could stand in the middle of Kendall Drive, then a two-lane road, and see no light in any direction. The school bus didn't even come out that far; Henry dropped the children off at school on the way to work, and Jane picked them up at day's end.

Education was in Jane's thoughts when she planted an avocado grove. She expected the revenues to finance college for the children. But another hurricane dashed that hope. The 1947 storm flooded the property, along with 80 percent of Dade County and Broward County to the north. The kids delighted in the opportunity to swim and catch tadpoles in the yard, but most of the avocado trees died.

The children were well tanned and healthy, their only medical problems caused by accidents. Janet suffered a mild concussion when she was eleven by falling off her pony, which kept her home from school for a few days. She read books and asked if her pony could visit her room.

Jane surprised the children one spring by tucking peacock eggs under the chickens, who hatched an exotic brood. Each bird, cock or hen, was named Horace. One unfortunate Horace came tumbling down the chimney into a roaring fire one chilly morning—an oft-told family tale. Horace progeny still roam the property, their raucous cries reverberating through the neighborhood that has closed in around them. Janet keeps a spray of Horace feathers in her Justice Department office.

Ultimately, no adventure was more typically Jane than building the house on Kendall Drive. It took two years, first to learn and then to build. The experience, Jane later said, taught her, "You can learn to do anything you want, if you aren't hurried." Some of her tutors, like tile maker Travers Ewell, became lifelong friends.

Some materials, like the bricks used in the fireplace, the hearth, and the steps, were scavenged from demolished buildings. Henry and Jane sold off ten acres and Jane wrote freelance articles at twenty-five dollars apiece to finance what building supplies she needed.

The kids were allowed to help with some tasks. They moved dirt and rocks, creating a pile on which they played king of the hill. As the oldest, Janet often was given more responsibility, earning the envy of her siblings, Maggy said.

In an era still innocent of air conditioning, the completed house was sited and designed to take advantage of breezes. Jane wouldn't hear of fans, as they created unnatural wind currents. A fifty-foot screened porch—half the house's area—ran along the front of the house. Inside, there were no ceilings, the better to let the hot air rise to the sloping, cypress-beamed roof. For a classical touch, the pitch of the roof matched that of the Parthenon, which Jane had visited while on a college trek to Greece.

Inside, there were three bedrooms, a kitchen, and a bathroom. For years, none had doors. They were only installed when guests complained of the lack of privacy. "The Chinese say, if you finish your house, you die. I had the bathroom doors, but I hadn't hung them," Jane once explained. The porch, which served as living room and dining room, featured a swing, benches made from split logs, a couch and chairs, and a large table that Jane also used as her desk. For years there was no telephone, and certainly no television.

"The house rises up out of the land," Parks said. "It looks like it belongs." Surrounding the house is a typical South Florida thicket of palmettos and pines, sea grapes and gumbo-limbo trees.

The outside doors were never locked, and family and friends drifted in and out at will. Jane occasionally brought home a hitchhiker for lunch or dinner. She often paraphrased Tennessee Williams's line, delivered by Tallulah Bankhead at a Coconut Grove Playhouse production of *A Streetcar Named Desire:* "I've always been able to trust in the kindness of strangers." To which she added her own admonition: "If you can beat them up, pick them up."

On Sunday afternoons, the Reno ranch was a popular stopping place for the Renos' wide circle of friends. Journalists, cops, and relatives would sit under shade trees, drinking coffee and talking politics. Everyone had an opinion about local judges, county commissioners, or the latest news from Tallahassee and Washington, D.C.

In 1948, Harry Truman and Thomas Dewey waged a memorable battle for the presidency. Henry and Jane, both die-hard Democrats, allowed ten-year-old Janet to stay up all night for the first time in her life as the radio broadcast returns. Politics was a favorite topic among the Renos, described by a friend as a clan of "omnivorous readers, omnivorous talkers, and omnivorous communicators."

"We are a campfire family. We talk about everything," said Maggy. "And we all talk at once, because we each believe that our opinion is as valid as everyone else's. The way you get heard is to yell, 'Shut up, I'm talking!' "

Education was highly valued, and good teachers became family friends. At a PTA meeting in the late 1940s, Jane told her children's instructors, "Thank you for sending them home with stars in their eyes."

Reno developed a lifelong admiration for teachers because of her own classroom experiences. "I can remember my sixth-grade class at South Miami Elementary and learning about Beethoven for the first time and learning about geology for the first time." Her teachers "opened up horizons that I still find marvelous. I didn't know anything about music, and they could teach me music. I didn't know anything about Rome, and they could teach me about Rome."

Janet stood out as a student. Literally. Both Woods and Renos were tall, and the Reno kids inherited from both sides. By age eleven, she was five feet eleven inches tall. She remembers herself as "scraggly."

But she wasn't particularly self-conscious, according to Hazel Nowakowski, who taught physical education and conducted after-school cotillion classes for seventh-, eighth-, and ninth-graders to learn manners and ballroom dancing.

"She was taller than everybody in class. She was even taller than me," Nowakowski remembers. "But Janet wasn't affected by her height. She wasn't concerned about how she looked or what people thought. She never walked slumped over."

At school, classmates respected Reno's size and judgment. "The other kids looked to her on whether a ball was fair or foul. Once she decided, that was it. The kids respected her leadership," Nowakowski said. In her private classes, Reno was "a good dancer, not exceptional. She was comfortable with boys."

Nowakowski believes that cotillion "was one of the things she dearly loved because it was so different from life at home." The Reno household was "unstructured," according to Nowakowski. "Jane couldn't care less how the table was set. But she wanted nice things for her kids. She was a wonderful mother who let them grow up to be themselves."

Janet had another place to turn for exposure to the finer things—grandmother Daisy, whom she often visited after school. The Woods lived in one of the original Coral Gables houses, built by George Merrick directly across Castile Street from his own home. Constructed of coral rock, it had polished oak floors, high ceilings, and Spanish tile on the porch.

"Janet's love for lavender-scented, ironed sheets came from

her grandmother," said old family friend Sara Smith. Daisy was "very blueblood" and always had a maid.

At home, Janet still sleeps in a four-poster bed that she got from her grandmother.

Dai-Dai's home offered another illicit appeal: television. In 1952, millions of American were laughing at the antics of Lucille Ball and Desi Arnaz. By 1955, thirty-two million Americans had TV sets. But not the Reno household.

"My mother wouldn't let us have a television. She said it contributed to mind rot," Janet said.

Henry Reno's children learned at an early age that journalism took patience. Years later, Janet would learn that dealing with journalists also took patience. As a child, she and her siblings spent many a Saturday morning waiting in the car while Henry visited with one of his primary sources, Eddie Padgett. Henry would bring the fidgety kids Cokes and potato chips to buy himself more time to talk.

Padgett was a former bolita operator—bolita is the Latino version of "numbers"—who proved to be a rich source of tips about Miami's thriving illegal gambling. For years, Henry conscientiously reported on gambling, noting when the roulette tables opened at Little Palm or dice games sizzled at Club 86. The clubs would shut down briefly, then reopen, protected by widespread corruption and the common belief that gambling was essential to sustain the booming tourism industry.

When Al Capone and his Chicago mob started muscling in on Miami Beach bookmaking, the *Herald* focused the bright light of public scrutiny on the underworld. So blatant was the grip of gambling that Senator Estes Kefauver chose Miami as the site for the first hearings of his Special Committee to Investigate Organized Crime in May 1950. The *Herald* waged a six-year crusade against gambling until the Mafia finally abandoned Miami for the more congenial environment of Havana.

For Henry Reno, dogged legwork and years of carefully

cultivated sources paid off. Reporting by Reno and Wilson "Red" McGee earned the *Herald* its first Pulitzer Prize in 1951, for public service journalism. Reno and McGee split a five-hundred-dollar bonus.

Senator Kefauver returned to Miami in 1955, this time to investigate baby-selling practices in Miami. Now it was another Reno who stepped into the spotlight.

Jane had gone to work for the *Miami News* after the children were in school and the house completed. At the request of the subcommittee's special counsel, Jane went undercover to investigate local doctors suspected of selling babies. Wearing a floppy hat and a fake diamond ring, Jane posed as a wealthy New Yorker eager to adopt a baby. Her testimony about her experiences helped shed light on the practice of baby brokering.

As a reporter, Jane worked on exposés about child welfare, institutional care of the aging and mentally ill, and political intrigue. When her stories dealt with subjects her editors deemed more appropriate for male reporters, she wrote under the pseudonyms of Sam Hawkins or Richard Wallace. Her talent as a storyteller often imbued her writing with emotion, a sense of caring about people that her children knew well.

Her most touching story, Jane often said, documented the attempt by a fifty-two-year-old lawyer to set a world record for a deepwater dive. She was among the witnesses when Hope Root lowered himself over the side of a boat on December 3, 1953. He was trying to reach 430 feet. He hit it, passed it, and kept going. The bottom lay about 750 feet down.

"Hope Root dived into the most beautiful world he knew and died in the royal blue Gulf Stream yesterday," she wrote through tears.

> Somber reporters and photographers, seasick and heartsick, felt like buzzards while an awfully nice little guy went out of this world before our eyes and cameras.
> Divers know what his death was like: A long plunge through beauty, ecstasy—that would be the nitrogen narcosis—blank, the end. Gone for sure, but no body, no burial, no coffin.

Do you think he was crazy to literally find heaven down under the water? You ought to go and look. There isn't anything ugly down there. Everything's quiet, every movement is smooth, every color is quite perfect. Only down there is just one color, the perfect blue of evening.

You can go down into that world and live for a while in your eyes, be completely satisfied just to look. You are cradled, weightless, down there in the home all life on this earth came from.

Jane also chronicled the efforts of Miccosukee Indians to get a school on their reservation in the Everglades and became close to this small tribe living along the Tamiami Trail west of Miami. In a special show of friendship and trust, tribal elders invited Jane to bring her children to private rituals such as the Green Corn Dance, celebrating the Miccosukees' sacred bond with the land. She was given an Indian name, Princess Apoongo Stahnegee—"rumor bearer."

The Reno family adopted two sayings of the Indians. One was overheard at an all-night Green Corn Dance during a discussion of oddities in modern society: "When the world gets old, you see strange things."

The other saying originated at a Miccosukee alligator-wrestling attraction. As a young wrestler attempted to subdue an agitated gator, the animal snapped its jaws, severing the youth's finger in front of a horrified crowd of tourists. "These things happen to Indian boys," the announcer said.

The Renos relished both lines, repeating them whenever something strange or unexpected happened.

In 1951, when Janet was thirteen and had finished Ponce de Leon Junior High School, Henry and Jane decided to send her to school in Europe for a year. She stayed with an uncle of Jane's, Roy S. Wood, a U.S. military judge with the Allied High Command who lived in the old Danube River town of Regensburg. He had been impressed by his great-niece during a visit to Miami in 1950 and had invited her to visit.

"Among my vivid memories will be a spy trial over which my uncle presided," Reno wrote the summer she returned. "The dignity of the court, the entire atmosphere and the conduct in the rooms made me very proud of my uncle as a representative of my country in a conquered land."

Of all Germany, she continued, "it was Berlin that most quickened my heart, and was the most exciting city, and Berliners were the Germans who moved me to respect and admiration. You could see the Russian propaganda in the Eastern sector of Berlin, and there I first in all my life felt Russia as really menacing. There I felt that Russia was afraid of us, was a frightened country grabbing everything she could out of a grab bag, and in her fright she is dangerous."

During school holidays, Janet traveled around Europe. In Italy, she strolled the Appian Way. "I could love to live in Rome, because there was so much of today and yesterday all tied together."

In Paris, she attended the opera. "There I heard Gounod's *Faust,* which I enjoyed much more than the Folies Bergère. But I enjoyed Wagner more than any opera, because his music is stirring and exciting like Berlin, he sweeps you up."

She wrapped up her trip with a visit to her father's godmother and aunts in Denmark. "They made me feel part of their family, a wonderful thing to feel. Danes are such a buoyant, gay people, they know how to have nice parties and be so sweet. It was much the loveliest country in Europe to me, most like America, and the people were handsome and dressed as though they are somebody."

Her father helped polish the writing and managed to have the report published in the *Herald* on July 13, 1952, as an early present for Janet's fourteenth birthday. The headline said: "14-year-old Miamian Writes Own Story of 9 Months in Europe; Finds Reds Menacing, Faust More Fun Than Folies Bergère."

Janet closed her piece with these observations: "Besides learning to love opera and enjoy history even more than I used to,

Europe also taught me how to knit and manage my money and speak a little Deutsch."

In 1952, Janet entered Coral Gables High School, a largely upper-class school with a good academic reputation and about twenty-five hundred students. That November, the first hydrogen bomb was exploded on Eniwetok, and prefab bomb shelters soon appeared on the market. During her freshman year, Janet's major social studies project was to produce a "career notebook" filled with news clippings, pictures, and professional journals. The career Janet selected was nuclear physicist.

Janet was a serious student, active with the Girls Athletic Association, French Club, National Honor Society, and Future Teachers of America. She lettered in both softball and basketball. But her favorite activity was the National Forensic League, the debating club, whose faculty sponsor, a caring and thoughtful English teacher named Werner Dickson, coached Reno for three years. In her senior year, Reno won the state extemporaneous speaking contest.

Her mother said it was only natural. "She can give you a few thousand words—a few thousand well-chosen words—on just about anything." Members of the Gables High senior class took up a collection to send Janet to the national competition in San Jose, California, but she didn't win.

Like all southern schools, Gables High was segregated. During Janet's senior year, Rosa Parks refused to give up her seat in the front of a bus in Montgomery, Alabama, the spark that ignited the civil rights movement. Within months, blacks would boycott segregated buses in Tallahassee.

Henry and Jane Reno were outspoken integrationists who had cheered the Supreme Court's landmark *Brown v. Board of Education* ruling in 1954. At that time in Miami, "black and white worlds did not meet," said Arva Moore Parks.

For most Coral Gables students, social life revolved around

high school football games, then played in the Orange Bowl, and drive-in burger stands like Jimmy's Hurricane and the Big Wheel. For Janet, who lived fifteen miles from school and usually didn't have a car available, social opportunities were limited. Yet she was well liked.

"Janet was always very friendly," said classmate Nancy Leslie. "She was terribly bright, but she was low-key about her ability. She was not an egghead. She was very easy to talk to."

According to one friend, Janet's height "must have made social relationships difficult. I don't remember her dating or going to dances that everyone went to."

As a senior, Janet's classmates voted her "most intelligent," and she was featured several times in her yearbook, the 1956 *Cavaleon.* One photo showed her in a scoop-necked dress with puffy sleeves, her grandmother's pearls around her neck. Her hair was cut in a page boy and she wore lipstick. The caption read: "Janet Reno . . . debater and scholar. In both, extraordinary."

In the group picture of the French Club, a simply dressed Janet stood off to one side in the back row, towering over the other students.

She was bound for the Ivy League and adventures she could hardly imagine.

CHAPTER 2

Ivy League Ambitions

Well liked by classmates and teachers, an excellent student and a top athlete, Janet Reno would have had her choice of colleges. Most Coral Gables students went on to college, many to state schools, but Janet chose Cornell University in Ithaca, New York, a demanding Ivy League school more than a thousand miles from home.

Cornell had several virtues that appealed to Reno: she wanted a school outside the South; its diverse student body meant it was Ivy without being exclusive; and it had been coeducational for almost a century. (Cornell founding president Andrew White had decided to admit women after first surveying other coeducational institutions to determine if mixing the sexes risked producing "strong-minded" women and "unmanly" men.)

Henry and Jane sold a chunk of their homestead to pay the tuition, a practice they continued as each child entered college. While she received some scholarship money, Janet also helped with expenses by working at college and during summer breaks as a clerk with the Dade County Sheriff's Department, a job arranged by her dad. Henry Reno also had a hand in Bob's summer job as a *Miami Herald* copy boy during his college years at Tulane.

Janet's position with the Sheriff's Department installed her in a favorite spot, the county courthouse she had often visited with Henry.

"I would sneak down at lunchtime, or just before lunchtime, to watch the great lawyers in action," she told the Association of Trial Lawyers of America years later.

"The courtrooms of the Dade County Courthouse, of that beautiful old federal building [in downtown Miami], were like magical places to me when I went with my father as he covered trials, both criminal and civil. And I thought that one of the most wonderful things that anybody could do was to be a lawyer."

When she left for Cornell that fall, Reno wanted to enroll as a prelaw major. But, bowing to the wishes of her mother, who wanted her daughter to become a doctor, Reno majored in chemistry.

She left home in 1956, the year that Elvis Presley delivered the music industry to a teenage market and a musical identity to a new generation. In blatant defiance of their scandalized elders, well-groomed, middle-class young men and women succumbed to the rockabilly beat laid down by the sultry-faced Memphis truck driver.

Elvis held sway over musical tastes, but teenage dress conveyed consummate conventionality. Indifferent to fashion, Reno conformed to the conventional uniform—tailored skirts and demure white blouses, cardigan sweaters and bobby sox. But what brought her real distress was the campus dress code that didn't allow women to wear pants. In the Finger Lakes region of New York, winter temperatures plunged below zero. Reno, accustomed to the steamy tropics, told friends that she had never imagined such cold.

During her sophomore year, Reno met Bettina Corning, now Bettina Dudley, the daughter of a wealthy and socially prominent New York family. An unlikely pair, Bettina, whose father was mayor of Albany and who had received her education at genteel boarding schools, and Janet, the product of two South Florida journalists who lived at the edge of a swamp, nonetheless became lifelong friends.

"Janet would work all night on papers," Dudley said. "She worked a lot harder than I did. We spent hours just sitting around and talking. And we went for long walks all over the campus. It's a beautiful campus with gorges and trees and a lake. We both have a strong interest in the environment, although it wasn't called that then. It was 'nature.' "

Reno didn't date or socialize with Cornell's fraternity crowd. Instead she bolstered her credentials as a fledgling workaholic with her attention to demanding courses and part-time jobs, including waiting tables and working as a dormitory monitor. She sat at the front desk of her dorm in the evening, checking in and out the girls who pursued more active social schedules. Yet she was no shrinking violet; Reno was later elected president of her dorm.

During Reno's sophomore year, Cornell was unexpectedly catapulted into the national spotlight by a student demonstration that foreshadowed the turmoil that rocked campuses a decade later. Student outrage at an administration attempt to ban female students from the off-campus apartments of male students culminated in a raucous demonstration outside Reno's dorm, Sage Hall, followed by rock-throwing and name-calling at the home of the university president. Student leader Richard Farina, later a well-known folksinger and husband of Joan Baez's sister Mimi, wrote a fictionalized account of the incident in his book *Been Down So Long It Looks Like Up to Me.*

Largely ignored during the controversy was the inherent discrimination—common to campuses in the 1950s—that required only female students to live in dormitories and abide by a dress code and a curfew.

Such sexism was so ubiquitous as to be invisible. When Dudley met with a professor to discuss her interest in studying veterinary medicine, the man ("a little twit," Dudley called him) told her, "Go ahead and apply, but we don't accept women. They're not strong enough."

"I crept away," said Dudley, who stood almost as tall as Reno's six feet two inches. "In those days, that was sort of ordinary. We didn't make a big deal out of it. If someone told me something like that today, of course, I'd probably get physically violent."

Reno was elected president of the Women's Student Government Association during her senior year and had her pick of dorm rooms. She chose well, selecting a room in Balch Hall with a beautiful view of a gorge. Already interested in politics, Reno was delighted to be invited to introduce one of her political heroes, Harry Truman, to a student gathering. She stayed up late researching and writing her introduction, Dudley remembered, then "shone" when presenting the former president.

Inspired by a teacher, Reno stayed with chemistry, even after abandoning thoughts of becoming a doctor. But a summer job convinced her that she wasn't "cut out to be a scientist."

"Between my third and fourth year, I worked at the Howard Hughes Medical Research Institute [in Miami] on a project to determine the correlation between emphysema and the percentage of certain proteins in human lung tissue," Reno recalled. "I really was not that good at it."

That year, Reno decided to pursue a law degree. She applied to the largest, most prestigious school in the Ivy League, Harvard, which had admitted women only since 1950. Janet labored over her application, then waited.

The day the response arrived from Cambridge, it was Dudley who collected the mail.

"Remember the old rule that a thick envelope means good news and a thin envelope means you've been turned down?" Dudley said. "Well, I remember opening the mailbox and finding a thick envelope from Harvard."

Reno was ecstatic. Dudley insisted they celebrate with a fancy dinner. They went to a nearby steakhouse and feasted on porterhouse steaks and wine, a meal that cost less than ten dollars in those days. "It was a wonderful evening because she was so thrilled," Dudley recalled.

Still worried about her mother's legendary distaste for lawyers, Reno nervously called home with her news. But when she announced that she had been accepted, her mother whooped with delight.

Reno graduated with a bachelor's degree in chemistry in May 1960. The expense of the trip kept Henry and Jane from the graduation, but Maggy and her fiancé, Jim Hurchalla, represented the Reno clan.

A sense of history pervades Harvard Yard, the tranquil, ivy-shrouded heart of the nation's oldest institution of higher learning. Established in 1636, Harvard University can stagger incoming students with the daunting burden of its intellectual accomplishment. The law school, founded in 1817, has graduated far more Supreme Court justices than any other law school, one U.S. president and a president of Ireland, 28 percent of all deans of accredited U.S. law schools, and uncounted members of Congress.

At the same time, critics have charged the school with decades of sexism and racism and with pitting students against each other in an orgy of competition. It has been accused of neglecting public service law in the interest of filling the ranks of corporate law firms. In his autobiography, consumer advocate Ralph Nader, class of 1958, charged that his alma mater provides students with only "the freedom to roam in their cages."

Attending Harvard Law School was a dream come true for twenty-two-year-old Janet Reno, but intimidating as well. In September 1960, Reno walked into Austin Hall to hear Dean Erwin N. Griswold welcome the class of 1963. "I don't think I've ever felt so lost as I did then," she told the class of 1993 at its commencement. "I wondered what it would be like. Contracts and torts were confusing, I didn't understand the perspective of the law, criminal law was boring."

As one of just 16 women in her class, Reno faced challenges decidedly different from those encountered by the 509 male students. With this class, Harvard Law School launched its second decade of coeducation, yet little had changed since 13 female students were first admitted in 1950.

The law school campus still offered only one women's rest room, and it was tucked away in the basement of Austin Hall, where relatively few classes were held. The trek could be a long one.

Professors like W. Barton Leach made little secret of their

disdain for women. Leach, who taught property law, declared that "he wouldn't call on women in the big classrooms. He said their voices weren't powerful enough to be heard," recalled Charles Nesson, one of two Reno classmates who now teach at the law school. "So he scheduled Ladies' Day, and he made the five women in my section sit in front. Then he sat down close to the male students and questioned them.

"And we sat through that and laughed, without the thought ever occurring to us that something totally wrong was happening," Nesson said. "It had to have had some powerful effects on Janet and the others."

Ladies' Day infuriated American Red Cross President Elizabeth Hanford Dole, class of 1965, who served as Secretary of Transportation in the Reagan administration and Secretary of Labor in the Bush administration.

"Charles W. Kingsfield [the infamous law professor of the novel, movie, and television series *The Paper Chase*] at his most perverse could not have devised a more public humiliation," Dole later wrote.

Some women took Ladies' Day good-naturedly. "We had fun with it," recalled Reno classmate Marie Driscoll, a trademark attorney in New York. "We made our presentation in verse."

"And it was a relief in a way," said Charlotte Acquaviva, an attorney at the Connecticut Insurance Department. "When it was over, we knew we likely wouldn't be called on again for the rest of the year. We could relax a little."

Even Dean Griswold, who had presided over the initial admission of women, told Reno and her female classmates that "he did not know what we were going to do with our legal educations," Reno remembered.

Griswold's comment came at a dinner he hosted for women of the class in the fall of 1960. The dean had just finished telling the women "he wanted us to feel at home . . . and he didn't want the law school to discriminate," Reno said. She took no offense at Griswold's remark and has remained close to the dean and his wife.

Class member Florence Wagman Roisman, who became an

attorney at the National Housing Law Project and a member of the faculty at Georgetown University Law School, recalled that Harvard women "put up with an incredible amount of shit. There was an aversion to having us there, if not an outright hostility, from a lot of the faculty." But at the time, she admitted, "We didn't really know any better."

Reno and her classmates were pioneers, the vanguard for women who would benefit from the social and political revolutions that began in the mid-1960s.

Classmate Roy Furman, who became a Wall Street investment banker and served as finance chairman of the Democratic National Committee, believes most male students respected Reno and the other women.

"They had to be special in intellect and in wanting a career in the law just to be here. But that was true of everyone," Furman said. "The women had a special character, a willingness to work that much harder. They had a 'firstness' about them, I guess you could call it."

They were also lightning rods for male prejudice.

According to U.S. Senator Bob Graham, who grew up north of Miami and graduated from the law school in 1962, "The pervasive attitude was that a woman in law school just took a position that should have been filled by a man who was going to practice the law and provide for a family."

Despite the obstacles, Reno was exhilarated. In letters home, she described herself as "awed and inspired and happy," Maggy noted. She was impressed "not with the personality of the place, but its intellect and history."

Bettina Dudley and her new husband visited Reno at Cambridge and found her "very, very happy. She seemed to love law school."

Harvard taught its students to think critically, to analyze a problem carefully, then to argue a viewpoint aggressively. The school exposed them to great minds on the faculty and among visiting lecturers. A talk at Memorial Hall by Eleanor Roosevelt, another of her heroes, will stay with her, Reno says, "as long as I live."

The pace was grueling and the stakes were high. Students labored the entire academic year before they learned where they stood. The only comprehensive tests were given in June.

Reno got her best grade in her tax class. Shortly after her swearing-in as attorney general, she met the acting chief of the Justice Department's tax division during her initial round of staff meetings. "I mentioned that I hadn't thought much about tax matters since law school, where my tax professor was Ernest Brown. He started chuckling and said, 'Do you realize that Professor Brown now works for you?' "

Reno walked down a floor to the tax division to say hello to Brown, a senior consultant to the department. "He greeted me not as if I was the attorney general, but as if I were still in his class," Reno said.

Brown was "delighted," he said, to have Reno as his boss. He restrained an impulse to quiz her on tax law. "I didn't feel that I was in the position to pose any tax questions to her that day."

Like others who knew her at Harvard, Brown said he hadn't recognized Reno as a potential attorney general—but neither did he recognize the future Supreme Court justices and other prominent legal scholars he taught over the years.

The commitment of many Harvard professors to the relentless questioning used in the Socratic teaching method meant that students faced daily the possibility of being publicly humiliated. Reno remembered fumbling for an answer in her contracts class one day.

She had been "a little bit hung over," she admitted years later, when Professor Jack Dawson asked her a question about a complicated jurisdictional dispute involving a Native American.

Knowing of Dawson's background in Democratic politics, Reno quickly crafted a response to divert him: She couldn't answer the question, she said, because "I haven't decided whether I'm a Goldwater Republican or a Stevensonian Democrat."

The hoots from her classmates got her off the hook. "It brought the house down."

Reno struck classmates as bright, studious, and quick-witted. She occasionally indulged in late-night conversations and political debates over drinks. She got involved in the campus Democratic Club and, like many others, spoke with admiration of the Harvard graduate just elected to the White House, John F. Kennedy.

"She was a straight arrow," said Jeanine Jacobs Goldberg, who practices law in Los Angeles. "She cared deeply about things like equal application under the law."

Nesson recalled Reno as "a very solid, realistic person. She didn't get swept up in the bullshit of law; she saw it as a way of resolving real problems."

"She was always very engaging. She was interested and interesting," said Bob McDiarmid, now a partner in a Washington law firm.

Reno's classmates also remember her as somewhat of a loner. She didn't live in Wyeth Hall with many of the other women but shared off-campus apartments with friends. One year Reno lived in the garret of a professor and his family. She was known to take long, solitary walks through historic neighborhoods and cemeteries. Twice, she hiked from Lexington to Concord.

"Law school is a fairly lonely time for most people," McDiarmid remarked. "It's not structured to encourage camaraderie or long-lasting friendship. It's much more work-centered."

Despite their minority status, women didn't develop a close-knit clique, said Roisman, who also lived off-campus.

"None of the women were particularly friendly, it seemed to me," she said. "Having women friends was déclassé. You had achieved something to be 'one of the boys.' Every woman who made it through Harvard came out very self-reliant and independent. You had to be."

Reno graduated from Harvard Law School in June 1963, "certainly not near the top" of her class, she admits. Two months earlier, a

U.S. Supreme Court ruling mandated that states provide counsel for all criminal defendants; two months later, Martin Luther King, Jr., led the massive March on Washington for equal rights.

"I made a promise to myself when I graduated from law school that I would never do anything that I didn't enjoy doing," Reno told the graduating class of 1993. "And almost every day of the year since that June of 1963, I have awakened glad that I was going to work, glad that I was going to court, glad that I was going to grapple with a problem."

Reno soon concluded that Harvard Law School provided "the best educational experience I ever had," she said. "Those classes that I often anticipated with trepidation really taught me how to think. And I believe that the way I approach problems—taking them apart and putting them back together again—is due to the training I got from some extraordinary professors."

Six months after her appointment as attorney general, Janet Reno returned to Harvard Law School for her thirty-year class reunion. A survey done in advance of the reunion revealed the career paths classmates had followed. A relative handful worked as attorneys in government agencies, including the Justice Department under Reno. An even smaller number of classmates practiced public-interest law.

Some classmates, like Gordon Baldwin, assistant curator of photographs for the J. Paul Getty Museum in Malibu, California, had given up the law to pursue other careers. A few had retired early. Thirty-six had died. The vast majority of the class was in private practice, holding partnerships in big firms on Wall Street and in large cities.

Reno missed a reunion of another sort three weeks earlier when women gathered on campus to mark the four decades since the first women earned Harvard law degrees. "Celebration 40" participants recalled the demise of Ladies' Day when feminism swept Harvard and other college campuses. They noted that newer classroom buildings have equal numbers of men's and women's rest rooms. And they cheered the news that the law school's 1993–94 enrollment was just over 40 percent female.

"How grand it has been to see those barriers fall," newly sworn-in Supreme Court Justice Ruth Bader Ginsburg said. When she entered the Harvard Law School in 1956, she was one of nine women in a class of more than four hundred. She transferred and graduated from Columbia in 1959.

At her reunion in October 1993, Reno mingled for about three hours with former classmates during a reception at the Boston Museum of Fine Arts. She walked through several galleries to view a splendid exhibit of paintings by Peter Paul Rubens and seventeenth-century contemporaries. Classmates approached to introduce themselves as she paused in front of huge canvases like the dramatic *Prometheus Bound,* which shows an eagle tearing out the liver of a struggling mortal who had offended the gods.

When she strolled into a hall where cocktails were being served, Reno shook hands, chatted easily, and smiled for snapshots with classmates and their spouses. One classmate she did not see was Florence Wagman Roisman, who boycotted the reunion to protest Harvard's failure to hire women of color for its faculty.

Serving in the cabinet "has been an extraordinary adventure," Reno said again and again. She recalled being asked during the nomination process whether she felt prepared to serve as attorney general. "I thought to myself, 'Perhaps three years at Harvard Law School and fifteen years as chief prosecutor for Dade County could prepare you for anything.' "

When it was time for Reno to speak, her classmates were ushered into a long gallery with a vaulted ceiling and marble walls and floor. She stood between two seventeenth-century Flemish tapestries and lectured her well-dressed audience. Lawyers, she told them, are too concerned about their own incomes and don't do enough to make the legal system reach the poor and children.

"The law is not reasonable to the great majority of the poor and working poor," Reno said, citing the example of a single mother who struggles to get off welfare and finds a minimum-wage job, only to be told she is making too much money to continue receiving Medicaid coverage for her children's health care.

"Lawyers for too long have stood by and let it happen again and again and again. . . . If we value our democratic form of government, we're going to have to find a way to make the law a lot more real to a lot more people than it has been."

Earlier that day, before Reno's arrival, about one hundred classmates had debated a proposal that the law school impose a public-service requirement as a condition of admission. Some argued for mandatory service as a way to change the public perception of lawyers as selfish and greedy. Others contended that they voluntarily gave back plenty, as they had served in the military or were now serving on the boards of hospitals, foundations, and the United Way.

The proposal was voted down overwhelmingly.

Janet Reno's family had instilled in her the values of integrity and fairness and the courage to stand alone. College and law school trained her to love the law and respect its power. At age twenty-five, Reno took her Ivy League education and returned to Florida, drawn by compelling ties to home and community.

PART TWO

Building a Reputation

CHAPTER 3

Janet Reno, Attorney-at-Law

A Harvard Law School degree may open many doors, but for Janet Reno, it didn't win her the job she wanted.

In 1962, during her second year at law school, Reno applied for a summer job at Steel, Hector & Davis, a well-regarded corporate law firm in Miami. The firm appealed to her because its senior partners were well known locally; one had been Dade County attorney.

Reno got turned down flat. The firm had no female lawyers and saw no reason to change. While Reno felt the sting of discrimination, she expressed no emotional outrage. In a characteristic response, she simply refused to take the rejection as a personal rebuff.

She considered the turndown "disappointing but not shattering," according to sister Maggy. "Our mother had given us a sense that a great deal of the world was stupid—not antifemale, but just stupid."

Reno spent the summer of 1962 with a smaller but similarly well-regarded firm, Brigham & Brigham. Considered a good training spot for young lawyers, the firm specialized in civil work, especially property law.

She returned to Brigham & Brigham as an associate after graduation in June 1963, handling a variety of real estate work. Over the next four years, she became a specialist in eminent domain,

47

defending property owners against government attempts to take land through condemnation.

Reno appeared frequently in court, where, even though she was handling low-profile cases, she began to gain experience, build her confidence, and make contacts in the legal community she so admired. She had only one criticism of private practice: "I always had trouble charging a person to protect their rights."

While Reno was establishing herself professionally, profound winds of change were blowing through Miami. Like the Hurricane of 1926, they ushered in a new era.

On New Year's Day 1959, news that a charismatic young revolutionary named Fidel Castro had crushed Cuban President Fulgencio Batista sparked celebration in Miami's Cuban exile community. Soon, Batista supporters seeking safe haven arrived in Miami, crossing paths at the airport with joyous Cuban exiles heading for home.

Within months, however, the picture changed. Despite his democratic pronouncements, Castro embraced Marxism. He set up a totalitarian regime, seized factories, and silenced opposition with firing squads. By the summer of 1960, disenchanted Cubans seeking refuge in Miami were filling six flights a day. Many of the newcomers were professionals fleeing their homeland with little more than the clothing on their backs. They settled in run-down neighborhoods where rents were cheap and scrambled for what jobs they could find.

On April 17, 1961, President Kennedy watched in horror as the U.S.-backed attempt to overthrow Castro ended in disaster. Castro's forces killed 80 CIA-trained exiles who attempted to land at the Bay of Pigs on Cuba's south coast; another 37 drowned when their boat sank, and 1,180 were captured. Families and friends in Miami felt betrayed by the U.S. government, which hadn't sent troops to support the freedom fighters.

Eighteen months later, the Cuban missile crisis brought the

world to the brink of nuclear war. U.S. reconnaissance planes had discovered Soviet missile and bomber bases in Cuba, just ninety miles from Key West. In a message to Soviet Premier Nikita Khrushchev on October 22, Kennedy demanded that the Soviets remove the installations and ordered a naval blockade of Cuba. The U.S. military mobilized, sending a cavalcade of army trucks rolling into Miami. Missiles were positioned in South Dade tomato fields, and tent cities housing combat-ready troops blossomed around the county.

For Americans, and especially Floridians, the crisis assumed frightening proportions. Residents stockpiled bottled water and canned foods. Schoolchildren practiced air-raid drills as the nation awaited Khrushchev's response.

It came on October 28. The Soviets would dismantle the bases in return for a U.S. promise not to invade the island. Although the standoff ended peacefully, a hundred thousand Cuban exiles in Miami were forced to abandon their dreams of returning home.

Castro freed the imprisoned Bay of Pigs invaders in late 1962, and President and Mrs. Kennedy welcomed them home at an emotional ceremony in the Orange Bowl. Later, negotiations with Castro accelerated the exodus of disillusioned Cubans. Between December 1965 and April 1973, two "Freedom Flights" a day brought in about 150,000 refugees, doubling the Cuban exile population in Miami and transforming Reno's hometown into an international city.

Congress agreed to give the exiles special immigration status, which let them stay in the United States indefinitely, obtain work permits, and collect government benefits. Within a few years, they could become American citizens and register to vote.

Cuban-American success stories abounded in those early years of exile, testimony to the newcomers' energy and industry. Miamians developed a taste for the tiny cups of cafe Cubano sold by sidewalk vendors in "Little Havana," where Southwest Eighth Street became Calle Ocho.

People like Reno who worked downtown couldn't miss the increasing number of Spanish-language signs on storefronts and the accents heard in courthouse corridors and elsewhere. But real contact with Cuban exiles was slow to develop in the business and legal communities, which were still dominated by white, American-born men.

Accommodating the enormous influx of refugees—one of the largest peacetime migrations in modern history—created tensions as Cubans competed for jobs with blacks who had long staffed the hotels, restaurants, and other service industries. Black frustration finally erupted in rioting and looting in Liberty City, the city's black ghetto, in August 1968. A little more than a decade later, blacks would again take to the streets in outrage. In 1980, however, their rage would be directed at Janet Reno.

Police and National Guard troops quelled the 1968 riot as Richard Nixon accepted his party's presidential nomination at the Republican National Convention in Miami Beach and hippies and yippies smoked marijuana in Coconut Grove's Peacock Park. It was a summer for the history books.

Years after the tumultuous decade, Reno noted that she was born too early and worked too hard to be a 1960s radical. While younger Americans were raging against the establishment, she was establishing her career.

Yet she shared a youthful admiration for John F. Kennedy and his brother Robert that fell just short of worship. She respected their commitments to civil rights and public service. Like most Americans, she was shocked and saddened by their assassinations.

She vividly remembers learning of JFK's death. "I was in the small law office that I had in Miami at 846 Brickell Avenue, and I had just come back from a court case. And the investigator came in and told me, and we stood there and listened on the radio and finally heard it confirmed. I went home about two hours later and watched it with my mother and grandmother."

The days-long spectacle that riveted the nation also riveted Reno: "I'll never forget it."

Soon after, Miami whispered of its own surreal connection to the assassination of President Kennedy. The Cuban exile community, for whom the Bay of Pigs remained a fresh and painful memory, buzzed with rumors linking Castro to JFK's murder. Reno put no stock in the talk and channeled her political interests along traditional lines.

She joined Miami's chapter of Young Democrats, where she met rising young professionals who would later be instrumental in her career. And she volunteered in a political campaign that would change her life.

Reno met Gerald Lewis at a Harvard alumni lunch, then worked with him in Young Democrats. A native of Birmingham, Alabama, Lewis had attended Harvard as an undergraduate, spent two years as an army paratrooper, and then enrolled at Harvard Law School. He graduated in 1960 and settled in Miami, where he joined a large firm, Blackwell, Walker & Gray.

Politics appealed to Lewis. A gregarious guy with a warm smile, he decided to run for an open seat in the state house in 1966. It was a rare opportunity. Districts for Florida's state legislature were being redrawn by court order after years of battles for political control between urban and rural interests. Back-slapping, tobacco-chewing politicians from the northern reaches of the state, known as "pork choppers," had held the reins for years. The new plan used population, not geography, to allocate districts, creating dozens of open seats in Dade County and other urban areas and opening the floodgates to a wave of young, progressive lawmakers.

Lewis invited Reno to an early campaign strategy meeting at his home and was impressed with her commonsense approach to politics. While others offered "a lot of grandiose ideas" for his campaign, Reno took a legal pad around the room getting people to sign up for specific jobs.

"She was very nuts and bolts," he remembered. "While others talked about a lot of foolishness, she focused on what needed to be done." Reno immediately worked up a schedule for volunteers to accompany Lewis to the huge airline maintenance hangars at Miami International Airport, where candidates traditionally shook hands with union workers during six A.M. and three P.M. shift changes.

Although there was an official campaign manager, Reno and Lewis's wife, Ann, were "de facto co–campaign managers," Lewis said. The two women remained friends even after the Lewises were divorced a few years later. Ann Lewis went on to become political director of the Democratic National Committee and a well-known consultant.

Lewis won the election and shortly after attended a thirtieth wedding anniversary party for Henry and Jane Reno at their home. Late in the evening, Reno told Lewis that she was considering striking out on her own and starting a small law firm. "We should talk about it," she said.

Reno didn't know that Lewis had already taken that leap—or had been pushed. Blackwell, Walker & Gray didn't let its lawyers hold public office, and, following the lead of Earl Faircloth, a partner who had been elected state attorney general in 1964, Lewis resigned after his election.

Lewis called Reno the day after the party. "We're both sober now," he told her. "Do you remember what you said? Were you serious?" "Absolutely," she replied.

Within days, the partnership of Lewis & Reno had signed a lease for office space on the seventh floor of the City National Bank Building. There were three desks; the two lawyers shared a secretary. The first set of law books on their shelves, a first edition of the *Southern Reporter*, had belonged to George Wood, Janet's grandfather.

Lewis quickly corrected sexist friends who surmised that he would do the real work while Reno did research and handled office chores. In fact, she ran the firm while he went to Tallahassee for spring legislative sessions, campaigned for reelection in 1968, and ran successfully for the Florida Senate in 1970.

Lewis & Reno's general practice included wills, real estate closings, and sundry business transactions. They got referrals from friends at larger firms, even Steel, Hector & Davis. Reno also had some carry-over work from her old firm, Brigham & Brigham.

Lewis described Reno as "one of the best attorneys I've ever known. You've never met a more organized person."

He recalled that a client wanted Lewis and Reno to fight a county zoning decision, saying the change would ruin his residential neighborhood. The client had already lost before the zoning board and county commission, and he assumed he would lose in court. "But it was worth it to him just to fight to delay the project as long as possible," Lewis said.

Reno didn't win, but she kept the case tied up in court for months. At one point, the county attorney's office claimed there was no transcript of a disputed hearing. Reno found an old case that had ruled that the court could rely on an affidavit from her client, saying that his version of events was what happened.

"The other side spluttered and argued, but you better believe they found that transcript," Lewis said. "I always told people who had cases against her, you better be prepared."

A later law partner, Talbot D'Alemberte, described how Reno once cut down an opponent's expert tax witness with unrelenting questioning that left him seeming uncertain and confused on the stand. She used her size to intimidate leaning in close and getting tougher and meaner in her queries. "She left no wiggle room," he said.

Lewis and Reno stayed busy and solvent. "We thought it might be tough in the beginning, but we did OK," Lewis said. They once had a chance to make some easy money, but Reno refused it. They were hired to probate a sizable estate, and the rules of the Florida Bar would have allowed them to take a percentage of the estate for their work. "I don't remember exactly how much it would have been, but I know it would have taken care of our overhead for a year," Lewis said.

But Reno decided the job was going to be simple, since a will had been drawn years earlier and a trust had already been established. "I don't see how we in good conscience could take a percentage," she told Lewis. They billed on a hourly basis for the work performed.

Lewis related that story to White House aides and FBI investigators who were scrutinizing Reno's background as President Clinton contemplated nominating her as attorney general.

"I honestly don't know of another lawyer who would have

done that," Lewis said. "But Janet just did not feel right about it. That's the kind of integrity she has."

At her parents' invitation, Reno had moved back home when she finished law school. The house had gotten quieter since her three younger siblings had moved out.

Her mother was working in public relations. Jane had quit the *Miami News* in 1958 to accept a job from hotshot publicist Hank Meyer, who lured her to his firm by doubling her salary. With four kids in college at the same time, she couldn't refuse. Meyer got his money's worth.

Jane made a name for herself concocting clever stunts to publicize such clients as the Miami Seaquarium. She won international headlines for the Seaquarium when she arranged to ship a male porpoise to Italy to console a female porpoise whose mate had died. Palooza was flown to Lalla by National Airlines, another client of Jane's firm, and they immediately fell in love. Lalla-Palooza. Or so her story line went.

It was National Airlines that made Jane's hard-earned reputation as an alligator wrestler. Jane had learned the technique, akin to reptile hypnosis, from the Miccosukee Indians, who taught her to flip the gator over and stroke its belly to put it in a sleepy stupor. Jane said she never handled anything over three feet.

When Jane wanted to promote National's inaugural Miami-London flight, she arranged for the mayor of Miami Beach to offer the mayor of London an alligator for the London Zoo. Her Miccosukee friends caught one, taped its jaws shut, and dropped the critter off at the house. But the tape came loose, and Jane got nipped. She left to get help.

Janet and Bob arrived home to find a trail of blood and a note of warning on the door. Wielding brooms and chairs, they corralled the reptile in the fireplace until Jane returned with reinforcements.

Middle age failed to dampen Jane's enthusiasm for adventures. In May 1965, at the age of fifty-two, she took a bedroll and six days of vacation and set out alone to hike 104 miles of east-coast beach, from Jupiter to Patrick Air Force Base, just south of Cape Kennedy. When she chronicled the audacious trek for the newspaper, she revealed that the beaches were so deserted she went skinny-dipping each day.

Henry Reno's health had not been good. A heart attack in 1960 permanently damaged his heart and left a weak spot, an aneurysm, in his aorta. Henry didn't dwell on it. He returned to work, continuing to prefer the police station to the newsroom. When the *Herald* moved from downtown into a massive new building beside Biscayne Bay in 1963, Henry wouldn't visit the office until the editors insisted.

When he finally did show up, he was delighted that an officious young security guard turned him away. Henry identified himself as "Mr. Horace Greeley," and no one in the fifth-floor newsroom would allow him to come up.

After more than forty years on the police beat, Henry continued to have better sources than any other cop reporter in town. He knew the people who made the system work—clerks in the medical examiner's office, fingerprint technicians, dispatchers—and they passed him the nitty-gritty details of the most interesting cases.

But when faced with a story that put the police in a bad light, Henry found it tough to confront his friendly sources. Gene Miller, who won a Pulitzer Prize for stories that rescued two men wrongly condemned to death row, said Henry would pass tips on controversial stories to Miller and other reporters, asking them to keep his name out of it.

"His information was always good, but his loyalties were mixed," Miller said.

Henry made his last visit to the newsroom on December 16, 1966, for his retirement party. A battalion of law-enforcement officials and the whole Reno family attended, including Bob, who had worked his way up from copy boy to *Herald* reporter—the third generation to work at the paper. Less than two years later, Bob left the *Herald* and Miami to become a columnist for *Newsday* in New York.

Henry may have retired, but he kept up his Sunday-morning doughnut runs to stay in touch with his friends at the police station.

He was ready for a quieter life, though; some friends suggested he was finally overwhelmed by Jane's eccentricities. So he moved some books and clothes and his five dogs to a secluded cabin in a hardwood hammock—an elevation of dry land with trees—about fifteen miles southeast of Immokalee in the Everglades.

Henry had fallen in love with that part of the Glades when he visited son Mark, who worked as a game warden in the area. The cabin had enough dry ground around it to plant a vegetable patch. Mark and Bob hoisted a fifty-gallon drum onto cypress logs and rigged a pump so Henry could take showers. He cooked his meals on a propane stove.

His children said he still loved Jane and had not abandoned his family. He would come home on weekends, and he delighted in his thirtieth wedding anniversary celebration. What had it been like to spend three decades with Jane Wood? he was asked at the party. "Has it been thirty years?" Henry replied. "Thirty years with such a woman! Well, to tell the truth, I wouldn't have missed it for a million."

Henry returned home for the last time at the end of July 1967. Shortly after, just eight months into his retirement, he suffered another heart attack. On August 12, 1967, a group of hunters found his body slumped over a table in the secluded cabin. He had been dead for days; his casket was closed at the funeral.

At her confirmation hearing, Janet remembered her father fondly, showing off a badge that made him an honorary Miami policeman. "I still have police officers who come up to me and tell me how accurate he was and how fair he was in his reporting," she said. "But as he reported on all that was going on that was bad in the community, he was never mean."

Recalling his stories about being an awkward immigrant boy, she added, "I think he remembered what it was like to be teased, and he always looked at people with respect, with dignity. He tried to see the best in people."

Reno said she was shocked at one point to learn that her father had a reputation as a "fixer," someone who could get traffic fines rescinded for friends and poor folks. In truth, his obituary revealed, he always took the tickets, then stopped by the court clerk's office and paid them out of his own pocket.

Henry's funeral was held at an Episcopal church in Coconut Grove. The Reno ranch was now Jane and Janet's, and they would share it for another twenty-five years.

During the 1960s and early 1970s, the marriages of Maggy, Bob, and Mark produced seven children. Jane was delighted and loved their visits. "Grandchildren are the reason you have children," she said. "You can give them ice cream for breakfast."

She and Janet also "adopted" other broods, including Gerald Lewis's three daughters, Susan, Beth, and Patty. The girls were four, six, and eight when Gerald and his wife, Ann, split up, and Gerald routinely took them and their two dogs to the Reno house on weekends.

Janet became a surrogate mom. "They worshipped her and spent a lot of time with her," he said.

Many evenings, Reno also dropped by Lewis's house after work to check on the girls. "She was super with them at a crucial time," he said. "I'll always be grateful."

Patty Lewis was the political writer for the *Star* in Anniston, Alabama, when Reno was nominated to be attorney general. She recalled in a column that Reno was "the first grown-up I remember knowing outside my relatives. The attorney general–designate taught me how to dig for fishing worms when I was nine years old, and how to iron my clothes when I was eleven."

At the Reno home, "we spent countless hours, adults and children alike, playing capture-the-flag games. . . . We kids were treated well, but we were far from spoiled. We knew enough to listen to the grown-ups. There was an almost unspoken arrangement: We were treated like people as long as we acted right. We could listen to the talk and even take part, as long as we followed the rules.

"One reason I have such fond memories, I'm convinced, is

that those rules were not always the same as the rules outside. No one ever told me or my sisters we couldn't do something because we were girls. Janet didn't teach me to iron because of my gender, but because she saw it as a simple survival skill like fishing, chopping wood, and cooking."

For years, Reno accompanied Gerald Lewis to political functions, and they often socialized together. Some friends suggested they were romantically involved. "It was nothing serious," Lewis insisted. "We were good friends. Sure, we'd often go out to dinner, and sometimes to a ball game or a movie."

Like Lewis, other friends tell of Reno's fondness for their children and her warmth and caring. Dale C. Webb, a single mother who met Reno through civic activities, said Reno often dropped by her house in Coral Gables for quick suppers and chats with her children. Later, when Webb quaked at the prospect of teaching her teenagers to drive, Reno volunteered. She would take them to a community college campus on Sunday afternoons and let them get behind the wheel in vast, deserted parking lots where nothing could be damaged.

"I went along once and thought it was an awful experience," Webb recalled. "She told me to get in the backseat and shut up."

Reno was "the world's greatest aunt" to her nieces and nephews, said Maggy. "To suggest Janet is childless is ridiculous. She has changed more diapers and burped more babies than many women have. She has rocked them to sleep and taught them to read."

Bettina Dudley, Reno's Cornell roommate, recalled how "wonderfully alive" the Reno house was on her annual visits to Miami, where Jane would greet Dudley with a warm, "Hello, my darling." On almost every trip, Janet would take Bettina for an afternoon sail on Biscayne Bay. It became a tradition between them to finish the sail and toast the sunset with gin and tonics.

In 1971, Reno was profiled in a *Miami News* story with the headline, "Drafting Laws a Snap for Lady Legal Eagle." The article quoted Reno, then thirty-two, as saying, "I'd like to get married and have four children. I wouldn't mind at all trading a political career for that. I'd probably get involved anyway and be out batling pollution or trying to save the beaches."

One frequent guest at the house, lawyer Dan Kavanaugh, fondly remembers an intergenerational game called "sardines" as the capstone of each busy day. Janet says her mother taught her kids the game, but she wasn't sure who invented it.

After dinner on the porch, young and old would line up in the backyard facing the house. While the crowd counted aloud to fifty, one person, designated as "it," would run off into the twilight and hide.

Then everyone would scatter and try to find the hiding place. A discoverer would not reveal the spot, but crouch down and join the hider in the palmetto thatch or other location. As successive players came upon the hiding place, they, too, squeezed in. The resulting crush gave the game its name.

Eventually, there would be so much whispering, giggling, and shushing that even the youngest child would find the spot. The game ended when the last person checked in.

"It was wonderful. The kids loved it. There were never any distinctions between adults and children," Kavanaugh said. "And it was certainly Janet's favorite." On one of her quick trips home after becoming attorney general, Reno invited a group of friends to the house and insisted on playing sardines after dinner.

Kavanaugh met Reno at a campaign rally in 1964. He made an unsuccessful bid for the legislature that year, and she was beginning to get involved in politics. He, too, attended Harvard Law School, graduating two years ahead of Reno. After working for a congressional committee in Washington for a few years, he returned to Miami and joined what was then the state's largest law firm, Fowler White.

Their shared experiences from Cambridge and interest in politics drew them together. Reno and Kavanaugh, who is six feet four inches tall, dated seriously—or "went together," as he puts it—for a decade. "Janet was an interesting person with a strong personality. She was smart, attractive, outdoorsy, lots of fun to be with," he said. They went hiking, canoeing, sailing. "We had a good time together."

At one point, friends thought they would be married, but their career demands—especially hers—kept them from making a commitment. "We just went our separate ways" but remained good friends, said Kavanaugh, who is now married and has a daughter.

Reno's interest in politics grew out of the stories her parents told, the issues they debated, and the strong opinions everyone shared, according to Kavanaugh. "There was nothing fancy or contrived about the discussions around that big table on the porch. There was straightforward talk about the big issues of the day. Everybody was generally well read and outspoken. You had to have a big voice to get heard."

In March 1971, with Lewis's support, Reno launched her public-service career. A major rewrite of the Florida Constitution had been approved by the voters in 1968. But its sponsors had left the unwieldy court system untouched, saying it was too complicated to take on all the issues at once. In truth, they also feared a political backlash from municipal judges, justices of the peace, constables, and small-town lawyers that could kill the rest of the package.

Representative Talbot D'Alemberte, a Miami lawyer known as Sandy, assumed leadership of the House Judiciary Committee in 1971 and decided to make court reform his major project. He knew both Reno and Lewis, having signed on to manage Lewis's campaign in 1966 before deciding to run for an open house seat himself.

D'Alemberte, already a friend, would become a major influence in Reno's life. As tall as Reno and athletically built, Sandy had a perpetual smile and bubbled with energy and ideas. He was a private pilot, an accomplished sailor, and a vigorous racquetball player. His slight stammer suggested his tongue couldn't keep up with his nimble mind.

D'Alemberte hired Reno as general counsel to the House Judiciary Committee at $17,500 a year. Lewis was vice chairman of the counterpart committee in the senate and would be working with her.

In a matter of months, Reno authored Florida's no-fault divorce law and tackled the constitutional amendment to reform Florida's courts. She studied the often conflicting ideas of committee members, judges, academics, and others, then sorted reality from rhetoric.

When a workable compromise emerged, she drafted the legal terminology that abolished municipal courts and created a uniform two-tiered trial system: county courts for small cases; state circuit courts for large civil cases and major crimes. Under the plan, appeals would be heard by state district courts and then the state supreme court. Judges would be elected to the county and circuit benches in nonpartisan contests; the governor would appoint judges to the appellate benches.

Legislators approved the plan during a special session that November. Voter approval was next. D'Alemberte and his allies assured taxpayers that they would get better service from a less fragmented and less confusing court system. Reno spent weekends traveling the state to build support among lawyers and judges and was occasionally invited to spend the night in their homes.

Voters ratified the amendment in March. Reno had earned a reputation as the consummate legislative staffer—someone who did the hard work but let the politicians take the glory.

Success in Tallahassee boosted Reno's confidence in her political skills. Her name surfaced as a possible candidate in January 1972 when a state representative from Dade County resigned after being indicted in an insurance scam.

She decided to wait until fall to see how Dade's districts might be redrawn based on 1970 census figures. In early summer, she jumped into a crowded field for an opening in District 113.

Reno went at campaigning full bore. She walked door to door, armed with reports full of facts and figures about state government. She attended every neighborhood meeting and civic club she could find. She sought guidance from old family friends with political experience. The most valuable advice, she often said later, came from Jack Orr, who had lost his legislative seat after supporting a 1956 resolution to end the segregation of public schools. He was attempting a comeback in 1972 by running for mayor of Dade County.

Orr told her: "Just keep on doing and saying what you believe to be right. Don't pussyfoot, don't talk out of both sides of your mouth just to be popular. Say what you believe and you will wake up the next morning feeling good about yourself. But if you pussyfoot and equivocate and try to be Miss Popularity, you will wake up the next morning feeling miserable."

The legislative campaign focused largely on criminal-justice issues. "People have told me they're not 'law and order' types, but are concerned because every house on their street has been broken into in the last two or three months," Reno said in a newspaper interview. "The state's primary responsibility is to protect people in their homes and on the streets."

She touted her experience as a legislative staffer in Tallahassee and said she could "hit the ground running up there."

When she beat five other Democrats in the party primary in September, everyone predicted the seat was hers. She had to face a Republican opponent, John Cyril Malloy, a forty-two-year-old patent attorney, in the November general election, but the district's voters were heavily Democratic. Malloy and Reno found little to disagree on; like Reno, he talked tough on crime and called for better education.

Much to his own surprise, Malloy narrowly beat Reno. He had joked just days before the election that he hoped she wouldn't beat him too badly. People credited the long coattails of Richard Nixon, who had trounced George McGovern at the top of the ticket. Malloy didn't gloat, but repeatedly complimented Reno on running an honest, issue-oriented campaign.

Lewis lost as well. He had given up his senate seat to run for the state Public Service Commission, which regulated utilities, and was defeated by Republican Paula Hawkins. The proconsumer reputation Hawkins built serving on the PSC helped get her elected to the U.S. Senate in 1978.

Reno and Lewis gathered to watch election returns with family and many of their old friends. "What an awful night," Lewis recalled. "Janet and I cried on each other's shoulders."

Two years later, Lewis made a comeback, winning election to the state cabinet as comptroller, an office he still held when Reno went to Washington.

Looking back, Reno said she learned a valuable lesson from her first loss. "Well, I did not feel exactly good the morning after my election, but I remembered what Jack Orr told me, and that is what I have tried to follow ever since."

She also took consolation from history. "Somebody, some kind soul, I suspect my brother Bob, put a biography of Abraham Lincoln on my bedside table, and it was helpful to learn that Lincoln lost his first election, too. It's good to know how to lose."

The day after the election, Dade State Attorney Richard Gerstein decided to offer Reno a job in his office. He had been impressed by her work on court reform and by her campaign.

Gerstein was a legend. Though popular for being a tough prosecutor, he also was dogged by allegations that he had been soft on organized crime during his early years in office. In the late 1960s, Republican Governor Claude Kirk accused Gerstein of protecting racketeers and sent several special prosecutors to Dade County to investigate. They found nothing, and voters repeatedly returned Gerstein to office.

Gerstein would gain a national reputation in 1973 when he won the first conviction in the Watergate case. The trial of Bernard Barker on charges of laundering money through a Miami bank proved the link between the Nixon White House and the 1972 burglary of Democratic National Committee headquarters in Washington.

Gerstein's job offer surprised Reno, whose father was among

those who thought Gerstein was on the take. "You don't want to offer me a job," she told Gerstein. "I've been one of your biggest critics."

"That's why I want you," he replied.

Reno remained unconvinced. "For the first nine years of my legal career, I swore I would never be a prosecutor because I thought they were more interested in securing convictions than seeking justice," she said later. She finally agreed when Gerstein "persuaded me to go to work for him by saying I could change that perception."

Her credo became: "The first objective of a prosecutor should be to make sure innocent people do not get charged. The second objective is to convict the guilty according to due process and fair play."

Reno's work in Tallahassee helped define her new duties. The constitutional amendment she had written gave additional responsibilities to Florida's state attorneys, and Gerstein assigned her the task of developing administrative systems to handle them. One task had a profound impact on her: State attorneys would begin prosecuting those under age eighteen who were charged with a crime. From December 1972 to February 1973, Reno's chief duty was to set up a Juvenile Division.

During Reno's frequent appearances before judges handling juvenile cases, she saw dramatic evidence of the relationship between children's backgrounds and the crimes they committed.

"I looked at the sixteen- and seventeen-year-olds I was prosecuting, and I looked at their presentence investigation," she recalled. "They had never known their father. They didn't see their mother very often. They had dropped out of school. They had become the drug dealer's gofer. They didn't have any structure or order in their life."

During 1973, Reno often traveled to Tallahassee to serve as a consultant to the senate committee that was revising the state criminal code. When that was done, she returned to Gerstein's office full-time as his chief assistant.

In April 1975, her name briefly surfaced as a possible candidate for a vacancy on the Florida Supreme Court. One account said Gerstein had "given his blessing," but nothing came of it.

That December, Reno led a successful effort to open records of the Florida Parole Commission to public scrutiny. The effort was prompted by Gerstein's outrage when three commission members voted to parole the leader of a notorious home-robbery gang after he had served only nine years of two life sentences. James Clyde Kish and his gang had received stringent sentences because they would terrorize their victims, often with heated butcher knives, to learn where jewelry and other valuables were hidden.

Reno also prosecuted bingo-hall operators who were ripping off their charity sponsors. "Very sophisticated gamblers," she called them.

In the office, her biggest gains were administrative reforms. Her predecessor as chief assistant, Seymour Gelber, had always thought of the post as "the hire-and-fire SOB job." Reno improved the personnel process by establishing an employment screening process.

Continuing her parents' tradition, Reno's home remained a popular gathering spot. It was the site of the annual picnic for the state attorney's office. Highly competitive volleyball matches were staged in the yard. It was a matter of hot debate who was the better player, Gerstein, who was six feet five inches tall, but blind in one eye due to a war injury, or the six-foot two-inch Reno, with her tremendous reach.

Jane retired in February 1974, at age sixty, "just because I had enough money to do it," she told a friend. Devoted to her own mother, Dai-Dai, she wanted to spend time with her. Dai-Dai lived another year, to age ninety-one.

Her kids gave Jane a chain saw, which she used to keep her

yard clear of Brazilian pepper trees and other fast-growing intruders. During the week, Jane ran the household while Janet worked. On weekends, they often went canoeing or hiking together. Jane occasionally treated herself to a vacation, sometimes taking along a niece, nephew, or grandchild. This time, when she sold another acre of her land, she could finance trips to Australia and New Zealand, the Galapagos Islands, and Greece and Persia.

After three and a half years with Gerstein, Reno decided to leave the state attorney's office in May 1976. "I want to practice law," she explained. She was making thirty thousand dollars a year. Gerstein was sorry to lose her. "I hope public service has not seen the last of Janet Reno," he said.

She signed on as a partner with Steel, Hector & Davis, the firm that had rejected her fourteen years earlier. The firm had grown from eleven lawyers in 1962 to more than twenty, and the newer partners were younger and more progressive. They included her old boss D'Alemberte and another outspoken liberal and good friend, John Edward Smith.

The firm's clients included some major corporations: Florida Power & Light Company, National Airlines, Southeast Banking Corporation, and WPLG-TV, a local ABC affiliate owned by the *Washington Post*. (The call letters of WPLG are the initials of Philip L. Graham, the publisher of the *Post* and the older half-brother of Bob Graham.) Jane loved to tease Janet by referring to the clients as "the big crooks."

Reno settled into a businesslike routine. In a year and a half, she tried four civil suits to verdict or judgment and handled some regulatory work. Her weekends were free for her beloved hiking and canoeing and scuba diving in the Keys. There were regular Sunday-morning racquetball matches on a court behind D'Alemberte's house.

Steel, Hector & Davis also encouraged its partners to get involved in community work on a free, or pro bono, basis. John Edward Smith recruited Reno for the board of directors of the Greater Miami Legal Services Corporation, where she helped make policy decisions about budgets, caseloads, and priorities. The experience made her a lifetime supporter of legal aid for the poor.

Indeed, when she returned to Harvard Law School to deliver

the 1993 commencement address, she pointedly lectured the young graduates that 80 percent of America's poor could not afford legal assistance. Four months later, she leveled a challenge at her own class during its thirtieth reunion: "Why don't we each adopt a block of families at risk? And if their landlord's being an SOB and won't fix the plumbing, go after him."

Unexpectedly, Reno's comfortable life changed. In late 1977, Gerstein shocked the city by announcing that he would resign effective January 20, 1978. After twenty-one years in office, he wanted to return to private practice. A longtime fan of the horses, he also accepted an unpaid post as a director of Hialeah Race Track. Horse racing, he said, was the last vice he could physically tolerate.

The governor would appoint a replacement until an election could be held in November. In a letter to Governor Reubin Askew, Reno recommended Ed Carhart, her friend and her successor as Gerstein's chief assistant. Gerstein himself recommended Reno and Carhart equally. But others recommended Reno over Carhart and the other fifty applicants.

The governor's deliberations dragged on for more than a month. He finally called Reno from Tallahassee on a Tuesday evening in early January and began chatting about the job and about the need for closer working relationships between local law-enforcement agencies, an obvious reference to Gerstein's long-running feud with E. Wilson Purdy, the chief of the Metropolitan Dade County police department.

"He spoke for about ten minutes about what he thought the role of the state attorney involved," Reno recalled. Then there was a pause, and he asked whether she might be interested. "Governor, I'm honored," she said.

At age thirty-nine, Reno became the first female state attorney in Florida's history. Florida law gave her substantial power. She could subpoena any witness she chose and file charges directly, except in a murder case, which required her to seek a grand jury indictment.

At the time, the state attorney's office had 286 employees, including 91 attorneys, and a budget of nearly $4.5 million. It handled forty thousand misdemeanors and fifteen thousand felonies a year.

The job, which paid $41,000, meant a pay cut for Reno, who was earning between $50,000 and $60,000 at Steel Hector. Asked if she would enjoy the job, Reno said, "I've never worked at something I didn't like."

Gerstein praised the selection. "She's one of the best-organized persons I've ever seen. Her capacity for work is unlimited, and her attention to detail is unusual," he said.

On the day she was sworn in, Askew—beginning the last year of his second term—wanted to put to rest rumors that he turned to Reno only after male candidates turned down the job.

"I asked only one person to take the job, and that was Janet," the governor stated. "I did not appoint her because she was a woman, but because she stacked up better than the others." [*her qualifications were*]

Askew, a deeply religious man, didn't realize what he'd said until the crowd began to titter; then he turned a bright scarlet. For years, Reno delighted in repeating the story.

Reno, wearing an orchid corsage, spoke briefly to about a thousand well-wishers gathered in a college auditorium. "My number-one goal is to make the streets safe, and I pledge every effort for the prosecution of crimes of violence," she said.

"Whoever you are, whatever color you are, whatever language you speak, I want you to feel at home here and part of the community."

CHAPTER 4

Cracking Down on Miami Vice

Janet Reno slipped rather quietly into the role of state attorney, offering little more than the customary sentiments about fulfilling the public trust. But she had no interest in stepping into the shoes of her colorful predecessor. For more than two decades, Richard Gerstein had stamped Dade County with his vision of justice. Reno had some changes in mind.

During her first weeks in office, she ruffled feathers among Gerstein loyalists with her personnel and organizational changes. Over the next fifteen years on the job, she would stir up more than feathers, arousing both vehement animosity and unshakable loyalty.

Critics would blast her for a higher-than-average felony acquittal rate; champions would cheer as she brought the authority of her office to bear on a broad range of social issues. Throughout the tempest, she steered a steady course, her compass locked on a bedrock commitment to a sense of fairness.

First, Reno wanted her team in place. Of her three new chief assistants, only Tom Petersen was a Gerstein holdover. He would oversee administrative chores and civil and juvenile courts. She filled the other slots with former prosecutors Hank Adorno and William Richey, whom she lured back—at a cut in pay—from private practice. She offered Adorno the high-visibility Criminal Division and Richey the challenging investigations and public corruption cases.

Though the three division chiefs often would go into court-rooms to handle major cases, Reno herself rarely appeared before a judge. She would be administrator and policy setter, not hands-on prosecutor. In other words, she stayed out of "the pits," as the criminal prosecutors under Adorno called their courts.

She also established a more formal chain of command, re-aligning the division directors who reported to Adorno, Petersen, and Richey, and holding chief assistant and division directors responsible for what happened under them.

Within the first four months, twenty of her ninety-one pros-ecuting attorneys left the staff. Most departures, however, could be attributed to normal turnover; young lawyers often gain experience on a prosecutor's staff, then depart for better-paying jobs. Reno once complained that the base salary for a lawyer at the U.S. At-torney's Office was almost twenty thousand dollars more than she could pay.

But at least a half-dozen lawyers left because either they or Reno were unhappy. Edward Carhart, the friend whom Reno had recommended, then bested, for the state attorney's job, left shortly after she took office. He would soon reappear on the other side of the aisle during the most important criminal case of Reno's career.

To fill vacancies, Reno reinvigorated the recruitment program she had developed for Gerstein six years earlier, adding one step to the process: She would interview each job finalist. She delighted in asking applicants unexpected questions, such as, "Who's your favorite U.S. Supreme Court justice? Why?"

Half of her first group of sixteen hires were women.

On the cool, pale-blue wall behind her desk in her office on the sixth floor of the Metro Justice Building, Reno hung a calming scene of her beloved Everglades painted by South Florida artist Beanie Backus. But the decor belied her intensity. From her first day as state attorney, Reno showed an amazing capacity for work.

She would rise at six A.M., drink a cup of tea, then begin her thirty-minute commute before rush hour. She drove an eight-year-old green Ford Mustang—she saved the state-issued Chevrolet sedan for official business—arriving at the office in time for a seven-thirty session with her Spanish tutor. Like many Miamians, Reno resolved to master Spanish, which had increasingly become the language of the streets. She practiced with Spanish-speaking staff and occasionally gave speeches in Spanish.

Reno then set the day's agenda with her assistants, who updated her on the most important pending cases. For lunch, she often dined on yogurt and orange juice at her desk. The afternoon was taken up with staff meetings, constituent meetings, and telephone calls.

Because she wanted to stay in touch with the community, she spoke to a civic club, a homeowners' group, or a school almost daily. When there was an evening meeting, it might be midnight before she got home. If work demanded, she would return to the office, where she kept a sleeping bag handy for all-nighters.

The relentless pressure reduced her need for caffeine, but she developed a taste for a shot of cafe Cubano at three o'clock each afternoon. After Reno moved to Washington, Lula Rodriguez, a Cuban-American from Miami whom she hired as her executive assistant, installed an espresso machine in the tiny kitchen just off Reno's private office so the midafternoon fix could continue.

Reno honed a highly efficient working style. Long before Americans began orchestrating their lives with Filofaxes, Reno tracked all meetings and major cases in a small black notebook. When someone promised her a memo in three days, it was duly noted. If the third day appeared without the memo, she would ask for it. Her assistants used to joke about making "that damn black book" disappear.

The woman who as a girl had towered conspicuously over schoolmates now used her height to maximum advantage. Reno would capture her listeners' full attention by leaning forward, then speak in low, flat tones that forced some to strain to hear. When provoked, she could raise her voice and pepper her assault with profanities. But most often, she would simply glare at her hapless victim, set her jaw, and, spitting out each word in a measured tone, express her "disappointment." A stabbing right index finger provided dramatic punctuation while her left hand poked her gold-rimmed, aviator-style eyeglasses back up her nose. The object of her ire usually withered.

When a case was mishandled—in the early days, her office suffered the acute embarrassment of a string of singular mistakes—she would demand an explanation. In writing. Quickly. Assistant state attorneys dreaded getting the request, "Miss Reno would like to know exactly what went wrong."

"If you do something wrong, the worst thing you can do with Janet is to not say, 'I goofed. I made a mistake.' If you admit your mistake and promise not to do it again, she'll accept it and say, 'OK, let's move on,' " said Katherine Fernandez Rundle, who rose through the ranks to become Reno's top assistant and was appointed to succeed her. "If you try to make excuses or blame someone else, she can just write you off."

Rundle learned from experience. She had to admit her responsibility once when charges were dropped against an illegal bingo operator because Rundle missed a filing deadline and again in 1984 when, from her office, she called lawyers to seek endorsements for Reno's reelection campaign. Rundle made the calls on her lunch hour, but she left her office number for calls to be returned.

But for all her intensity, Reno inspired loyalty from her staff with her motherly concern for their families and her habit of writing notes to those who had done a commendable job or suffered a personal loss.

As state attorney, Reno had to navigate the daunting bureaucracy of Dade County's criminal-justice system. Under home rule, Metropolitan Dade County police had arrest powers countywide, an area larger than Rhode Island, but many municipalities, including Miami, also chose to keep their own police forces.

As a result, Reno's office reviewed every arrest by twenty-six police agencies, deciding within 30 days whether to prosecute each case. State law then required prosecutors to bring a case to trial within 180 days, or 60 days if the defendant demanded it.

In addition to jurisdictions "going in twenty-six different directions with different priorities," as Reno complained, everyone in the system had a special concern. Some judges wanted to crack down on career criminals; others wanted to go after drug cases. Corrections officials worried about overcrowding at both the county jails and state prisons.

And each year the state legislature launched a new attack on a real or perceived crime problem. The state imposed minimum mandatory sentences for violent criminals and large-scale drug dealers in 1980; three years later, it mandated a full set of sentencing guidelines.

For Reno and her staff, each shift in the political winds meant new demands, new training, new strategies, all within tight budgetary constraints.

In her first year, Reno set a frenetic pace. Her eye was on the calendar: Her interim appointment by Governor Askew would expire in November, when a special election would determine who would complete the final two years of Gerstein's term.

Those first months were a roller-coaster ride as she launched new initiatives while keeping up with cases carried over from Gerstein's tenure.

In February 1978, she renewed the crackdown on illegal bingo operations that she had initiated years earlier when she was Gerstein's assistant. Scams infuriated Reno. Bingo patrons, often retirees on fixed incomes, loved their Wednesday night bingo games, spiced with the thrill of a modest jackpot. Churches, civic groups, senior-citizen associations, and Boys' and Girls' Clubs relied on income from the games to finance good works. Yet sophisticated bingo operators were skimming the profits. In two months, police, backed by Reno's prosecutors, arrested sixteen people at a half-dozen locations for gambling violations.

In March, she demonstrated her holistic approach to crime prevention by spending a Saturday at a conference with county librarians. She was an enthusiastic supporter of library programs. Children who feel welcome in libraries, she said, won't wind up on street corners and in county jails.

In April, Reno ordered Assistant State Attorney Robert Godwin to pay the full fine, plus penalties, on 116 overdue parking tickets, setting a scrupulous ethical standard that she would maintain for herself and her staff. Godwin got the five-dollar tickets for overtime parking at meters around the Metro Justice Building, where parking was tight, and had attracted the media spotlight—and Reno's attention—when he negotiated a reduced fine of seventy-five dollars with a sympathetic judge. Miffed over the issue, Godwin later left the staff to join the public defender's office.

Reno's reputation for ramrod rectitude grew over the years with tales of her insistence on paying full price, whether for a pizza or a new car.

In May, Reno got called for jury duty. She refused the opportunity to be excused and served for two days in a civil trial. "It's kind of humbling and it gives you a touch of pride," she said.

News broke in May that Reno's office had subpoenaed more than seven hundred people listed as holding jobs at federally funded training agencies. Petersen and his assistants interviewed about three hundred fifty workers, but many others couldn't be found, leading investigators to conclude that payrolls were padded and funds were being skimmed. Criminal charges were filed against local administrators of the Comprehensive Employment and Training Act (CETA) program.

Reno's office suffered its first public-relations nightmare that month, involving, of all places, the Juvenile Division Reno had established under Gerstein. Twenty cases against youths arrested for shoplifting, burglary, and strong-arm robbery were dropped when her office didn't file charges within the thirty-day time period set by state law. Blame fell on a new secretary. A supervisor was replaced, and Reno reorganized the division.

In July 1978, she had to head off a potential conflict of interest and resign from the board of Floridians Against Casino Takeover

(FACT), a blue-chip group organized to defeat a referendum to legalize casino gambling. Every major politician in the state, including Governor Askew, opposed the measure, which raised the specter of a major invasion by the Mafia.

But when procasino forces accused FACT of election-law violations, they sagely filed their complaint with Reno's office rather than the state Division of Elections, neutralizing the state attorney while her office conducted its investigation. Voters overwhelmingly rejected the referendum that fall.

Reno understood the importance of staying tuned to voter moods and built a reputation for being accessible to the public. She often answered her own phone at the office, and she listed her home number—although not her address—in the metro-area telephone book. People called 271-2963 at all hours. One irate citizen woke Reno at one A.M. to complain that his neighbor's roosters were keeping him awake.

"Listen, you can hear those roosters crowing right now," he said, holding out the phone for a cock-a-doodle-do. Reno promised to get a zoning inspector to check the situation the next day.

Some lower-level assistant state attorneys, expected to follow the chain of command at the office, would mutter that a member of the public had easier access to Reno than they did.

Reno later got a second line at home, giving out that number only to family and closest friends. After a particularly tough day, she might unplug the first line and answer only the second. But she despised answering machines and never put one on either line.

Reno spent the late summer and early fall of 1978 fending off a noisy challenger, fellow Democrat Richard Friedman, who had made his name the previous year by leading a futile battle to block construction of Dade County's long-awaited elevated mass transit system.

It turned out to be not much of a challenge. Reno won 76 percent of the vote in the party primary in September. Since no Republican contender had filed, she won a two-year extension of her occupancy of her pale-blue office.

Reno barely had time to savor her triumph, however, before Miami was plunged into an eighteen-month nightmare that threatened to put a swift end to her political career. The African-American community, which had long suffered the vestiges of racism in Dade County's criminal-justice system, would soon use the name "Reno" as an epithet.

On February 12, 1979, five white Metro-Dade police officers armed with a search warrant raided a house they suspected of harboring a stash of drugs. Its two occupants were beaten when they resisted arrest, and the house was ransacked.

It was the wrong house. Nathaniel LaFleur, a well-known black schoolteacher, and his twenty-year-old son Hollis had resisted because they thought the plainclothes detectives were robbers. The police officers had used racial slurs, the LaFleurs charged. Pictures of the older LaFleur, his bruised head swathed in bandages, filled television screens and newspaper pages. The state attorney's office embarked on an investigation.

Two months later, Reno announced that her office couldn't prosecute the cops. "They made a mistake," Reno contended. "They went to the wrong house by mistake. There was no criminal intent. There was no crime of trespass."

The black community was outraged. The Community Relations Board (CRB), established by the county to ease racial tensions, and other groups lambasted her decision. Blacks "are wondering if they will get a fair shake if they come to your office," CRB member Annie Love told Reno at a gripe session. CRB member Alvin Rose accused Reno of conducting a superficial investigation.

"Tell me where I've gone wrong," Reno responded angrily. "You tell me what I should have done that I didn't."

Tempers had barely begun to cool when Reno's office charged several widely respected black officials with corruption or theft. County Commissioner Neal Adams was arrested in November for running illegal bingo games at the Northside Amusement Hall.

Two charities Adams had named as the beneficiaries had never received any money. Adams served two years of probation and was out of office for good.

Then, a few months later, Dade School Superintendent Johnny Jones was charged with diverting nine thousand dollars in public funds to construction of his weekend home on Florida's west coast, some of the money used for gold-plated plumbing fixtures. Solomon Barnes, a black high school principal and close friend of Jones, also was charged. Jones later faced additional charges of taking seventy thousand dollars in kickbacks from a school-supplies salesman.

After Jones was convicted of grand theft, Garth Reeves, the black publisher of the *Miami Times,* declared that Reno "is to the black community what Hitler was to the Jews." To that and other complaints, an indignant Reno responded: "I don't care who you are, what color you are, where you come from. When a crime is committed, I'm duty-bound to prosecute." Jones's sentence on the felony charge was later overturned on appeal; two misdemeanor counts stuck.

The worst was yet to come. The case that would shatter Dade County began at 1:51 A.M. on December 17, 1979, with an early morning motorcycle ride. Arthur McDuffie, a thirty-three-year-old black insurance executive—a former Marine and father of three—was traveling well over the speed limit when he roared past a police cruiser on his cousin's Kawasaki, launching a high-speed chase that lasted eight heart-stopping minutes.

When McDuffie finally pulled over, he was instantly hand-cuffed and surrounded by a phalanx of white Metro-Dade police officers. Officer Charles Veverka, Jr., landed the first blow, but the ensuing melee was a blur of fists, metal flashlights, and nightsticks. "They looked like a bunch of animals fighting for meat," one witness recalled. McDuffie's helmet was torn off and the blows "shattered his skull like an egg," the medical examiner said. Shortly after he arrived at the hospital, McDuffie fell into a coma. He died five days later.

Metro-Dade police smashed the motorcycle and helmet in an attempt to portray the incident as a traffic accident, but city of Miami officers had witnessed the scene and reported it to their supervisors. Reno's office hurried to investigate.

Special engineers were hired to study the damage to McDuffie's helmet and the motorcycle. Investigators interviewed or tried to interview every officer who was on the scene. Three officers were given immunity to tell their stories, including Veverka, who was the son of a high-ranking police official.

On December 29, five white police officers, including two sergeants, were charged with manslaughter and falsifying their reports to cover up the crime. Reno called it "one of the most tragic events in the history of this county."

Although there was no videotape of the incident, as there would be a dozen years later in the Rodney King case in Los Angeles, the two cases had parallels. Reno and her top assistants would build their case on testimony from police officers on the scene, both participants in the beating and witnesses. And they decided to try the five officers at the same time.

The community looked on as the state attorney's office hunkered down to prepare for its most important case. Hank Adorno, head of the Criminal Division, would lead the team. For five months, Reno committed more staff, time, and effort than had ever been devoted to a single case during her tenure.

Judge Lenore Nesbitt agreed to a defense motion to move the case out of Miami, and it was set for Tampa. The first task, to seat a jury, took three weeks.

The jury pool contained just eight blacks. All were eliminated by defense lawyers, who could strike thirty-four prospects without explanation. The jury ultimately empaneled was all male and all white. Adorno had hoped to seat women on the jury but saw the defense strike all of them as well.

The jurors were described as "hard-headed businessmen, not sick rednecks" by defense lawyer Ed Carhart, the former assistant state attorney who represented Sergeant Herbert Evans. The defense strategy was to undercut the state's case by charging that

Veverka and the two other officers testifying under immunity were motivated by self-interest.

The surest sign that prosecutors were in trouble came when one defendant won a directed verdict of acquittal even before the case went to the jury. The judge said the state hadn't built a strong enough case.

On Saturday, May 17, 1980, the four remaining defendants were acquitted on all charges. The news hit the Associated Press newswire at 2:42 P.M. Before sunset, Liberty City, Miami's largest black neighborhood, erupted in anger. Rioters chanted "Reno! Reno! Reno!" as they torched cars, smashed windows, and looted businesses. At least three unsuspecting whites were pulled from their cars and battered to death.

The unrest spread into Overtown and the black section of Coconut Grove. Gunfire crackled through the night. Sections of the elevated expressways, sources of controversy when they first cut across Miami's established black neighborhoods, were closed to traffic.

The disturbances spread south toward Jackson Memorial Hospital, the county's largest public hospital. As ambulances delivered the injured and dying, paramedics and doctors could hear gunshots just a block away.

Reno was horrified. From her office windows at the Metro Justice Building, she and Adorno watched plumes of smoke rise over the city early Sunday morning. "I just couldn't believe it," Adorno said.

Reno consoled Adorno. She knew how hard he had worked on the case. "People who were there said it was one of the finest closing arguments they ever heard. I don't think a man does that, puts that much energy into a case and is so bitterly disappointed as he was when I saw him that morning at the Justice Building, unless he believes in his case, believes in his cause."

She set to work organizing teams of prosecutors to process those arrested during the riots. Two courtrooms opened on Sunday at two A.M. and ran around the clock for days. Charges included arson, looting, burglary, and worse.

For four days, the city was at the mercy of snipers and mobs. Miami police broke up a crowd of thousands who surrounded the Metro Justice Building while Reno, judges, and other officials hunkered down inside. National Guard troops enforced blockades in an attempt to contain the violence. A countywide curfew was imposed.

When the fury finally was spent, sixteen people were dead, hundreds were injured, and more than a thousand were arrested on riot-related charges. Damage estimates reached two hundred million dollars.

Literally overnight, Reno went from being castigated as "anti-police" for prosecuting the McDuffie defendants to being vilified as "antiblack" for losing the trial.

"I don't recall the emotion so much as just thinking that I must put one foot in front of the other," Reno said later. "It continued like that into the summer."

Some legal experts were quick to attack Reno's handling of the McDuffie case. Carhart said Reno and her prosecutors overreached and "went for the home run" by putting all the officers on trial at once. He called it a "total lack of judgment." Other former prosecutors concurred that the officers should have been tried separately and immunity offered only to those who had been at the scene but had not participated in the beating.

At an emergency meeting of the Community Relations Board, black sociologist Marvin Dunn and other community leaders called for Reno to resign. "Janet has become a symbol to blacks of everything that is wrong with the criminal-justice system," Dunn said.

"Janet Reno's office is racist," black lawyer H. T. Smith said flatly.

Reno refused to consider quitting, saying, "If a relatively small number of people can riot and force an elected official from office, that is anarchy and the destruction of the democratic process."

Since she was up for reelection in November, she reminded her critics, "You have a perfect opportunity to get rid of me then."

Jesse Jackson, who flew to Miami to meet with black leaders, added his voice to the chorus of criticism: "There is a growing consensus that her office is a source of humiliation to black people, and she has become a symbol of oppression to all of us."

Day after day, Reno defended herself and her office. She argued her prosecutors "did everything possible." She decided to stay out of the riot areas until they cooled. "I am a force for anger." When anonymous callers made death threats, she sent her mother to stay at her sister Maggy's house in Martin County. For a few nights, Reno moved in with friends. "I'm trying to take sensible precautions," she said.

But friends feared for her safety. "She was amazingly blasé about it," said Dan Kavanaugh. "She took some small precautions, but she refused to be intimidated or change her lifestyle."

"I think this is a time when everybody has to keep cool," Reno said. "Once you're in a situation like this, you don't have any choice. You stay cool, and most of all you continue what you're doing to ease the situation."

Despite the vilification from some quarters, Reno got quiet support from many. Friends and family rallied around her. She received a call from Erastus Corning II, the mayor of Albany and father of her Cornell roommate, Bettina Corning Dudley, who urged Reno to hang tough. He advised her to do the right thing, and she would survive.

Years later, Reno said the charges of racism by blacks "hurt deeply. I felt I had always had a strong commitment to civil rights. . . . I felt more strongly about the prosecution in that [McDuffie] case than any other matter we had handled.

"If the state attorney could control jury verdicts, the verdict would have been guilty. But I, of course, could not."

After a few weeks, Reno began to go into black neighborhoods to talk about the case. She spoke to community groups and sat for extended question-and-answer sessions with newspaper editorial boards. She offered to open her files to anyone who wanted to review the case; other than journalists, only one person accepted. She went on radio talk shows, including one hosted by Dunn. He asked her to list the problems confronting the community as it recovered from the riots. Reno looked squarely at him and said, "Frankly, Marvin, one of the biggest problems is you."

"The woman comes back swinging, and I respect her for that," Dunn said later.

What she would not do was apologize. She stubbornly repeated that she, Adorno, and her staff had done the best they could with the facts they had.

It would take time, but Reno was determined to satisfy her critics. "To explain peremptory challenges, immunity, change of venue, and other concepts—to enable the public to understand— has been one of the most difficult and demanding aspects of the job," she said.

"It made her even more focused," said Katherine Fernandez Rundle. "She was determined to do whatever it took to restore confidence in herself and her office."

Reno promised to talk with her critics "anytime, anywhere," so she would meet people at night in dangerous neighborhoods, even stand at street corners where she would be met and escorted to meetings. Her aides worried about the personal risk, but she refused to wear a bulletproof vest or take a deputy. Nor did she carry a gun, although she had proudly qualified with a police revolver at a state gun range in November 1979. She insisted, "I have to go."

Reno made sure her audiences knew that she had hired seven black lawyers for her staff and three more would join the office that summer, so nearly 10 percent of her attorney positions were filled by blacks. "And considering the percentage of black lawyers available throughout the country, it is extraordinary representation."

When she heard a concern or suggestion that she could follow up on, she did. And she went back to the community and reported on her findings.

"People thought, 'Is she crazy?' But it worked. They could see she cared," said Carrie Meek, a state legislator who in 1992 became the first black elected to Congress from Florida since Reconstruction.

H. T. Smith, who previously had criticized Reno, said she "was everywhere. She became the most accessible public official in Florida, bar none." Recalling that he had called on her to quit, Marvin Dunn said, "I'm glad she didn't take my advice."

Investigations into the causes of the riot spread the responsibility wider than Reno's office, although she got her share of blame.

A report issued by a special citizens' committee appointed by Governor Bob Graham suggested that although the McDuffie verdict triggered the riots, "it would only have been a matter of time before some other incident would have brought about the same result." The report went on to say, however, that Reno ran her office "in such a way as to support the black community's perception of the office as racist," pointing to "an alliance" with police agencies that protected bad cops in cases like the wrong-house raid on the LaFleurs.

Reno rebutted that the committee's investigation had been too narrow and hadn't delved deeply enough into the challenges facing her office, including its caseload.

Two years after the riots, a report by the U.S. Commission on Civil Rights went further in probing the root causes of Miami's unrest. It cited poverty, unemployment, poor housing, and declining public schools—all of which blacks suffered in disproportionate numbers—along with a widely held belief that the criminal-justice system was biased. In criticizing Reno's office, the report noted that three times as many blacks were being prosecuted in Dade's juvenile courts as any other racial or ethnic group. Reno said the report offered few constructive suggestions for change. "It will only exacerbate community tensions," she said.

Meanwhile, some riot-related prosecutions dragged on, increasing hard feelings and suspicion in the black community. The case of Nathaniel Lane got the most attention.

Lane, a teenager charged with killing a white motorist named Bennie Higdon by smashing him in the face with a chunk of concrete, was brought to trial three times by Reno's prosecutors. His lawyers claimed mistaken identity. All three times, the juries deadlocked. Reno finally dropped the case.

Governor Graham believed the crisis of the riots made Reno

stronger. "The fact that she was under attack was not only distressing to Janet because she felt she had acted appropriately, it was the first time in her career she had been subject to this sort of exposure," he said. "In terms of her own growth and maturity, it was a good experience. She certainly withstood the challenge in the longer assessment of history."

In a letter Reno wrote to her college roommate Bettina Dudley in 1982—one of just four letters from Reno that Dudley has received in more than three decades of friendship—Reno marveled at her political rehabilitation. Simply for telling the truth, she wrote, "I am something of a folk hero and everyone's congratulating me. . . . I will never understand the public."

Five years after the riots, Reno's redemption seemed complete when she was greeted with cheers and applause as she marched in the annual Martin Luther King, Jr., parade through Liberty City. Unlike other politicians who would ride in cars and wave, Reno hiked the route with her mother and shook hands with people along the sidewalks. It became an annual tradition.

Thirteen years after the 1980 riots, Reno joined the thirtieth anniversary observance of King's 1963 March on Washington. Walking at her side that day was Jesse Jackson.

In an office as embattled as hers, Reno understood the importance of supporting her team, socially and professionally. She hosted Halloween parties at her house for the staff and their families. They also gathered at the beach for parties and volleyball games. She played first base on the women's softball team.

"We had a real feeling of cohesiveness," recalled one prosecutor. "Janet conveyed the sense that we had a mission in the community, that we were here for a higher good."

Young, idealistic attorneys were dazzled by her commitment to fairness. At one staff meeting, she singled out for praise a prosecutor who had been assigned a case, investigated it thoroughly, decided the defendant had been wrongly charged—and had dropped the charges. That was Reno's idea of justice.

She depended on her staff, and they could depend on her. One newly hired attorney, fresh from law school, had been in town just a few months when she was severely injured in a car crash. Problems with state medical insurance were delaying the surgery she needed, and her frantic boyfriend called Reno at three in the morning. Reno got out of bed and went to the hospital. The young woman was promptly scheduled for surgery.

With neither diplomats nor armies at her disposal, Reno found herself battling a foreign tyrant, Fidel Castro.

In April 1980 Castro threw open the harbor at the fishing port of Mariel to allow boats to come and go. For years he had been irritated with American immigration policy, which treated Cubans differently from other foreigners. Any Cuban who made it to American soil could expect asylum without having to prove that he or she was personally endangered because of political activities back home. The policy had proved an irresistible lure to hundreds of thousands of Cubans eager to exchange a harsh life under a communist dictator for America's beckoning shores.

With the opening of Mariel, Cuban-Americans jumped into boats and headed south to pick up relatives and friends left in Cuba, pausing in Key West to top off their fuel tanks for the trip across the Florida Straits. When they arrived in Mariel, Castro's soldiers filled the boats with the occupants of Cuba's jails and hospital wards for the criminally insane. "Castro was snookering us," Reno said.

Only an order from Washington could have stopped the flow, but President Carter decided to hold off for reasons never explained. Dade County bore the brunt of his folly. In less than five months, more than 120,000 Cubans entered Miami. They were housed temporarily at the Orange Bowl and in tent cities. Most of them quickly found relatives, friends, or church groups to act as sponsors and help them settle in. About a thousand convicted felons were arrested immediately by immigration agents. But as many as 10 percent of the arrivals were left to fend for themselves, and the county's crime rate—for offenses both petty and profound—began to spiral upward.

Many of the so-called Marielitos found their way into the drug networks that imported, processed, and distributed cocaine from Latin America. Reno's office, already overworked, was on the verge of being overwhelmed. Her 130 prosecutors handled more than twenty-five thousand felony cases in 1980–81, up from fifteen thousand in 1977–78. The homicide rate grew so rapidly that the county medical examiner rented a refrigerated trailer from Burger King to store the backlog of corpses.

Given the crisis in law enforcement, it was hardly surprising that the filing deadline for the 1980 election passed and no challengers appeared for Reno's job. "My mother said it was because no one wanted the job," Reno said wryly.

The woman who had been the county's most despised elected official just six months earlier won her first full, four-year term without opposition.

It was a hot July afternoon in 1979, the kind that drives Floridians into the chilled air of malls like Dadeland, the region's largest. No one noticed the arrival of an armored Ford van, outfitted with gun ports and one-way glass, until machine-gun slugs sprayed the parking lot. Shoppers dived for cover, but two men, members of a Colombian narcotics ring targeted for murder by a rival ring, were gunned down in a mall liquor store. In that bloody shoot-out, Miami's cocaine cowboys exploded into public consciousness.

Reno and other state and local officials blamed the federal government for not halting the flow of illegal drugs, especially cocaine, into Florida.

As the violence escalated, Reno spoke out. "The security of South Florida must be protected," she declared. "That security has been impaired by drug traffickers and by illegal aliens. The United States of America has the resources to make our borders secure."

Incredibly, she found herself battling federal agents, who often seemed as concerned with claiming credit for a bust as with catching the bad guys. One contentious case, dubbed the "Video Canary," took an irate Reno to Washington for her only visit to Justice Department headquarters before being nominated as attorney general.

For six months in 1978, investigators from Reno's office and other agencies had worked undercover with an informant, Ron Braswell, to track drug smugglers. The burly Braswell entertained lavishly at his expensive house; though his claim to be a former pro football player was a lie, his connections to the drug world were real. With his cooperation, two cameras hidden in Braswell's office recorded more than nine hundred minutes of incriminating dialogue. Wiretaps picked up more than thirty-two thousand telephone conversations. Several conversations contained information about murders, including the killing of a man named Juan Rodriguez, whose body was found floating in a sleeping bag in Biscayne Bay.

To help gather evidence, police and investigators from Reno's office, led by Martin Dardis, went undercover in several drug deals. Dardis was the snowy-haired, pot-bellied chief investigator Reno had inherited from Gerstein. For this case, he posed as a crooked cop known as "Big Al, the Dopers' Pal," who controlled a remote airstrip near the Homestead Air Force Base where planes could land and unload their illegal cargos.

But local agents from the U.S. Drug Enforcement Administration (DEA) objected to the undercover roles of state investigators, claiming it was more important to stop the shipments before they hit the streets than to pursue the limits of the ring. The operation deadlocked, and a frustrated Reno flew to Washington to straighten things out with Attorney General Griffin Bell, Customs Commissioner Robert E. Chasen, and DEA administrator Peter Bensinger. She went home with their approval.

DEA officials in Miami, however, continued to interfere with day-to-day operations, demanding more control. Regional administrator Frederick A. Rodey once threatened to arrest Dardis and another investigator if they helped unload a smuggler's plane. Reno, in turn, threatened to arrest Rodey for obstruction of justice.

The Video Canary stopped singing in January 1979, when Dardis and Riley had their cover blown. Reno mistakenly had authorized a search warrant that identified the two as her investigators. After the warrant was served at a drug ring warehouse, she realized that she had made a potentially fatal error. When she told Dardis of the screwup, he and another investigator had to pull out in the middle of a drug deal and flee for their lives.

Reno offered to get federal protection for the investigators and their families. "Janet, I don't want any government agency guarding my family," Dardis testily replied. "I don't trust them."

Five months later, a task force of officers fanned out across six states with 120 arrest warrants. Bonds for the suspects totaled more than $17.6 million. At least 62 dealers were caught, tried, and convicted.

The day the case went public, Rodey claimed all conflicts had been "adequately resolved and smoothed over." Reno wasn't ready to forgive and forget. "Without a change in the players," she said, "it's going to be virtually impossible for the state and DEA to cooperate effectively."

Fed up and embarrassed on Reno's behalf, civic leaders began to lobby Washington for help. The effort was organized by Miami Citizens Against Crime, a group founded by Alvah Chapman, then chairman and chief executive officer of Knight-Ridder, Inc., the communications conglomerate that owns the *Miami Herald.*

The Reagan administration was under pressure to step up the battle against drugs. Vice President George Bush, who had family connections to Florida and saw a chance to further his own political ambitions, spearheaded the creation of the South Florida Task Force, a multiagency effort to target major drug smugglers. Resources increased and cooperation improved, and by the time she left Miami, Reno had a good relationship with new DEA personnel.

"She's the hardest-working government official I have ever met," said Tom Cash, who had been the DEA's special agent in charge in Miami for five years when Reno went to Washington. "She's a person who looks for solutions. She's not one of those who continues to describe the problems."

But Reno often cited the conflicts in the Video Canary case as an example of how the feds could stifle creative work by state and local officials.

Dardis, who had cracked the Miami connection to Watergate under Gerstein and was portrayed in the book and film *All the President's Men,* retired from the state attorney's office in early 1980, seven months after the Video Canary case became public. He blamed Reno in part for the paperwork snafu that had put his life at risk. Dardis became an outspoken Reno critic, saying she soft-pedaled public-corruption cases, and endorsed her opponent in the next election.

Dardis was replaced as chief investigator by Ray Havens, who had worked his way up to lieutenant in the organized crime bureau of the Metro-Dade police department. Havens later moved to Washington to be a special assistant to Reno at the Justice Department.

There was turnover in other key positions at the state attorney's office. William Richey, one of the two lawyers who left private practice to become a chief assistant, quit in May 1981, citing the stress of the state attorney's office.

"The nature of this job is very demanding," Richey said when he resigned. "These are critical, unsettled times. It will be nice to return to private practice without having to think that each day will bring a new catastrophe."

Despite the sophisticated surveillance aircraft and other tools George Bush brought south, the good guys simply couldn't keep up with the bad.

A Dade County grand jury estimated that the vice president's task force had helped boost from 15 percent to 25 percent the proportion of cocaine shipments intercepted before the drug reached South Florida's streets. But experts said 75 percent would have to be seized before it made a difference. Indeed, the price of seized cocaine dropped and the purity increased; if interdiction were effective, it should have been the other way around.

Still, the number of arrests overwhelmed the prosecutors, judges, and courtrooms. Caseloads grew so great that Reno told federal authorities her office would no longer prosecute drug cases made by federal agents. The U.S. Attorney in Miami was so busy with big busts that he had been referring to the state any case involving less than a kilo of cocaine or a thousand pounds of marijuana.

Truth be told, some Miamians didn't mind the drug activity. When an economic slump hit other parts of the state, Miami seemed recession-proof. Civic boosters credited Latin commerce and overseas investment in the new office skyscrapers and condominium towers. But evidence was undeniable that much of the cash was coming from the drug trade.

The Federal Reserve said South Florida put more used currency into the banking system than any other urban area in the country. And when a *Miami Herald* reporter borrowed twenty-dollar bills from eleven civic leaders and had them tested for cocaine, traces of the drug showed up on ten of them—including bills from the wallets of Reno, Catholic archbishop Edward McCarthy, and Jeb Bush, the vice president's son, who was then the chairman of the Dade County Republican Party. To pick up a trace of cocaine, a bill had only to brush up against a tainted one in a cash register's drawer, experts said, but the story was a shocker.

"If you don't use [cocaine], if you don't know anyone who uses it, if you don't see it around, it's hard to focus on the problem," Jeb Bush said. "This brings it home better than just a statistic from some medical report."

The lure of drug-related cash contributed to widespread corruption. Even Reno's office was not immune. In the summer of 1981, three of her assistant prosecutors and three secretaries were caught dealing cocaine out of a rest room in the basement of the Metro Justice Building. They were convicted. That same year, *Time* magazine played up Miami's travails in a cover story headlined "Paradise Lost?"

Reno went to Tallahassee to lobby the legislature for increased funds for her office and came home with a 35 percent budget increase for 1982, an unprecedented jump in resources. She was able to expand to 165 lawyers. (The state's other 19 prosecutors elected her president of their association from 1984 to 1986 to capitalize on her lobbying clout.)

The zeal to strike back at smugglers and dealers sometimes created additional problems for Reno. In some cases, inexperienced prosecutors made mistakes, and overworked police cut corners.

One major case against a drug-trafficking ring took more than a year to develop. With advice from Reno's office, Miami police detectives got approval for wiretaps that recorded more than a thousand hours of conversations about drug deals. One bug was hidden in a clock, hence the code name "Operation Tick Talks."

After indicting fifty-three people, Reno's office acknowledged that some evidence was shaky and dropped charges against twenty-five. Then one defendant, Rafael Villaverde, a well-known anti-Castro activist, disappeared in April 1982. Friends claimed he had vanished in a boating accident; his body was never recovered.

Operation Tick Talks collapsed completely in September 1982. Circuit Judge Gerald Kogan agreed with defense attorneys that the wiretap evidence had been collected improperly, and it was thrown out. Kogan said the cops had been too hasty and did not exhaust other investigative methods before getting wiretaps. Nor had they told the judge who authorized the taps that their key informant had a criminal record, and thus his motives for cooperating were suspect. Reno's office dropped the case.

The federal government also frustrated Reno in a case that seemed the quintessential candidate for a made-for-television movie. It drew headlines coast to coast.

A Saudi Arabian prince, Turki bin Abdul Aziz, took a fancy to South Florida during a visit in 1980 and made it one of his homes. Rumor had it that the prince, a former deputy defense minister for Saudi Arabia, was fifth in line to the Saudi throne.

Prince Turki certainly had the wealth of a king. He bought a $3.2 million home on Indian Creek Island on which he began extensive renovations, and he ingratiated himself with the community by making lavish gifts to South Florida charities.

But word had reached the police department that servants were being kept as virtual slaves by the prince's retinue. On February

26, 1982, police raided his suite at the exclusive Cricket Club. During their search, the prince's wife, mother-in-law, and employees scuffled with police officers.

Reno's office began an investigation but was brought up short when the U.S. State Department granted a request by the Saudi embassy for diplomatic immunity for the prince and his family. Reno argued that the prince held no official position with the Saudi government. "All evidence indicates the State Department conferred diplomatic immunity on Prince Turki solely to prevent him from being charged by this office and not because he was on any special diplomatic mission."

But the State Department dug in. The incident dissolved when both the police officers and the royal family and bodyguards filed civil suits and countersuits claiming injury. The prince left the country.

Later, Reno was delighted to hear that Saudi officials were complaining about a "Judge Reno" who had driven out a member of the royal family. "The Saudis were not as upset by the fact that he had been forced out as by the fact that a woman had done it," she explained.

Perhaps it was the tantalizing opportunity to put words in the mouths of her oft-outspoken friends, but Reno decided in her off hours to revive the lost art of play-reading.

Her first quasi-theatrical effort was *Saint Joan* by George Bernard Shaw. She bought copies of the play, then assigned roles to her pals and sent them their scripts.

After suitable preparations, they appeared for a potluck dinner at Jane and Janet's home. Afterwards, the group sat around the big table on the porch, reading Shaw's brilliant lines about history's memorable martyr, a plain-spoken young woman whose passionate convictions and defiance of the old order opened the door to new ideas.

One time, the Renos invited friends over for more than entertainment. The Reno house needed a new roof. Rather than hire a roofer, Jane and Janet decided to replace the tar paper and shingles with the help of family and friends. So they hosted a weekend-long party, much like an old-fashioned barn raising. Several dozen people showed up, and everyone was assigned a chore.

Dale Webb, Reno's friend who later dated a top assistant state attorney, worked with Jane to help fix lunches and dinners. But she recalls Janet up on the roof, sweating and hammering and calling encouragement to her coworkers.

The hammering aggravated a touch of arthritis in Janet's right thumb, which has left her with a bump on her knuckle.

While Reno was reading Shaw, the rest of the nation was watching "Miami Vice," the NBC television show that redefined Miami for the world. Debuting at nine on the night of September 16, 1984, and continuing for five seasons, "Vice" filled the screen with hard-driving electronic music and flashy, fleshy scenes of the suddenly exotic world of Miami.

"No earth tones," producer Michael Mann had decreed, so the show captured the cool pastels of art deco on Miami Beach and the hot neon of the city. For glamorous night shots, the crew hosed down the streets to reflect the lights. Miami saw how good it could look.

In its 107 episodes, "Vice" depicted drug-fueled violence and terrorism, portrayed extravagant wealth next to third-world poverty, and reinforced Miami's image as the crime capital of the United States. Yet it was all so . . . so glamorous. Tourists flocked to the city.

Reno never watched the show. For her, Miami's vice was all too real.

Not long after Reno went to work in Washington, actor Don Johnson, who became famous as detective Sonny Crockett on "Miami Vice," visited the Justice Department while he was filming a movie in the capital city. A mutual friend arranged for them to meet.

Reno took him to lunch in the cafeteria. They talked about children.

"She's a Pied Piper with children," old friend Marcia Kanner said of Reno. "They loved her and wanted to please her because she made them feel like they could do things, that they were competent. That's the way Jane raised her."

Katherine Fernandez Rundle would bring her young twin sons when she and Reno hiked and canoed through the Everglades. On one trip, Reno walked through the waving grass, holding each boy by the hand, reciting lines from Marjory Stoneman Douglas's landmark 1947 book, *The Everglades, River of Grass.*

Douglas, one of the first women to work as a reporter at the *Miami Herald,* was an inspiration to Jane when she began her career as a journalist. Douglas's book and her environmental activism inspired the movement to preserve the fragile ecosystem of the Glades. In November 1993, Reno sat in the front row of the White House East Room as President Clinton presented the Presidential Medal of Freedom to Douglas, then a frail but still spunky 103 years old.

Despite the boost in Reno's personal popularity, four years after the Liberty City riots, in 1984, racial harmony had failed to materialize in Miami. Another police officer was acquitted in the death of another black man, and mobs again took to the streets. The officer, Luis Alvarez, shot Nevell Johnson, Jr., in an Overtown video arcade.

According to Alvarez, he was patrolling the neighborhood and stepped into the arcade looking for suspicious activity. When he spoke to Johnson, the man reached toward the small of his back. Alvarez thought Johnson was reaching for a gun and fired his revolver. But no gun was found, and witnesses said Alvarez had provoked a confrontation for no apparent reason. After the trial, Reno's handling of the prosecution again drew scrutiny and criticism in the black community.

This time, when Reno came up for reelection, opponents filed against her. She responded with a grassroots campaign. She hired her cousin, Sally Wood Winslow, a professional artist, as her campaign coordinator and paid her three hundred dollars a week.

Although Winslow, a resident of the Florida Keys, was a veteran of only a single local race—which her candidate lost by one vote—she said she could provide "loyal, trustworthy help. And I had this weird perspective: I adored her and thought she could do no wrong."

Winslow's chief job was to keep track of Jane and hundreds of other volunteers who passed out leaflets, posted signs, attended rallies, and did anything else they could think to do. A campaign office had been rented on Bird Road in South Miami, but Winslow worked mostly from the porch of the Reno house.

Jane, then seventy-one, declared that she was fed up with politics. "At one time I thought I'd rather my daughters had gone into disco dancing instead of politics. Politics takes so much time and it pays less money." Maggy had also entered politics, as a commissioner in Martin County, north of Miami.

Reno seemed unperturbed by the challengers. When defense lawyer Jeffrey S. Weiner, a longtime critic, called Reno "more concerned with politics and trying to read the media than with dispensing true justice," Reno responded curtly: "I don't think politics belongs in my job. I'm not out to please people. I'm out to do what's right based on the facts and the law."

But friends appreciated how tough the campaign could be and stepped forward to help. Margaret Kempel, a former nun who had gotten hooked on politics, helped with strategy. John and Sara Smith, friends from Reno's private practice days at Steel Hector, made phone calls. Frances Webb, a former *Herald* art critic, brought her teenagers to help stuff envelopes.

Reno captured 64 percent of the vote in the Democratic primary, but she had cause for concern. Many black community leaders still saw her as the symbol of a flawed criminal-justice system and attacked her on black radio stations. Her primary challenger, a political novice named R. Jerome Sanford, got 71 percent of the black vote. In the November general election she faced an opponent who was better known and better financed.

Former Miami city attorney Jose Garcia-Pedrosa was a prominent member of the Cuban exile community. He campaigned as an experienced administrator who could more efficiently manage the state attorney's office and attract better talent. Though most of his support came from Republicans, he decided he could draw support from both parties by running as an independent.

The *Miami Herald,* Reno's father's newspaper, refused to endorse her for reelection. In a stinging editorial published October 25, the *Herald* described Reno as "the personification of a troubled and ofttimes overwhelmed criminal-justice system . . . a lightning rod for much of this community's free-lance hatred and frustration."

Though it dismissed suggestions that she was racist or slavishly devoted to popular sentiment, the *Herald* said Reno should be held responsible for the operations "of her critically important office. It is by that standard, alas, that her performance as state attorney must be found wanting."

Even after she had nearly doubled the number of staff attorneys (from 91 to 175), the editorial noted, more than five hundred cases had been thrown out in the previous two years because inexperienced prosecutors were not ready to go to trial within the state's six-month "speedy trial" rule.

The editorial concluded, "For her years of unstinting integrity and devotion to duty, Ms. Reno deserves the appreciation of all Dade Countians. But as the beleaguered state attorney's office moves to confront unprecedented challenges, it requires the superior leadership skills and administration talent evinced by Mr. Garcia-Pedrosa."

Reno was hurt and angry and even more determined to win.

In its news pages, the *Herald* repeatedly analyzed how Garcia-Pedrosa could pull off an upset by drawing near-unanimous support from Hispanic voters and putting together an alliance of Anglos and blacks dissatisfied with Reno. In the final weeks, Garcia-Pedrosa spent a hundred thousand dollars more than Reno for advertising on local radio stations and for other promotions.

Seymour Gelber, an old friend from Gerstein's office who went on to become a judge and then mayor of Miami Beach, said Reno wouldn't give up without a fight. "Janet is a very tough lady who wants to leave the job with her head held high and her flags unfurled. She doesn't want to leave it in a situation where there will be a community sigh of relief."

Reno went out again and again into the neighborhoods to talk directly to people. The weekend before the election, she spent Friday evening introducing herself to shoppers in Little Havana. On Saturday, she strolled through Liberty City with a band. When a group on one corner started chanting "Reno must go!" she veered across the street and shook each person's hand. On Sunday, she toured Overtown.

When the votes were counted that Tuesday, Reno won with a nearly 2-to-1 margin. She had taken 40 percent of the Hispanic vote from Garcia-Pedrosa to back up the broader support she received among blacks (74 percent) and Anglos (72 percent). Commentators said her victory helped redefine political campaigns in Dade County, showing that racial and ethnic appeals could backfire.

"The melting pot of America," a joyous Reno called it. "This office, which had been the focal point of so much division, is now the focal point of a community coming together."

Garcia-Pedrosa said he should have run as a Republican, rather than as an independent, to capitalize on Ronald Reagan's coattails.

Ultimately, Reno salvaged the race and her reputation through old-fashioned grassroots campaigning. Behind by all the conventional benchmarks—money, endorsements, lingering resentment in the black community—she refused to cave in. She campaigned personally and tirelessly, shaking as many hands in as many neighborhoods as she could reach. And riding over the hill to her aid came a cavalry of Reno friends and relations, fired up by Sally Winslow.

The victory party at the Reno house was so boisterous, Jane claimed that it killed a patch of grass in the yard.

It was hardly like Jane to complain about a party. As eccentric and outspoken as her oldest daughter was straitlaced and tight-lipped, Jane was a popular interview for reporters. A 1979 profile dubbed her "Calamity Jane," and the name stuck. "I do a lot of forgetting, but I still believe in mischief," she said in 1982.

During gatherings at the house, she would hold forth from her chair on the porch, telling stories about the old days and scolding people for their rigid opinions and intolerances. "Oh, mother . . . ," Janet would say patiently.

As her remaining teeth went bad, Jane couldn't wear her bridge-work and refused to visit a dentist. She did, however, have cataract surgery on one eye so that she could continue playing cards and other games.

She loved beer and sour-mash whiskey and often started im-bibing before lunch. Several times in the 1980s, she got picked up for driving under the influence. Once Janet got a call from the Florida Keys, where her mother had been arrested and needed to be picked up. When the Dade County state attorney arrived in the neighboring jurisdiction, her mother was still railing at the state trooper who had arrested her, calling him "a pipsqueak."

Janet posted her bond, but she asked Maggy to accompany their mother to the trial. Both insisted that their mother serve the required sentence.

Drug-related violence and deaths skyrocketed again in 1985, when Miami's cocaine dealers became the first to produce "crack" in large quantities. Crack, a crystallized form of cocaine that could be smoked for a quick rush, was considered far more addictive than the powder. It was also easy to produce and cheaper.

Reno hadn't fully appreciated the damage caused by the drug until she visited the maternity ward at Jackson Memorial Hospital, where she herself had been born. There doctors showed her new-borns whose mothers were crack addicts. She wept as the babies screeched, bawled, and shook uncontrollably, wracked with pain from withdrawal.

Cash from the cocaine trade seemed pervasively corrupting. When members of a ring of crooked cops who preyed on drug smugglers tried to rob a boat on the Miami River, three smugglers jumped overboard and drowned. Reno's office worked with federal prosecutors to break up the ring. After a mistrial in 1987, Reno took three of the "River Cops" to trial again and convicted them in 1988. Another eleven pleaded guilty.

When it came to longtime employees who worked hard for her, Reno could be loyal to a fault. One of Reno's top prosecutors, John Hogan, got in trouble in 1987 for being amazingly naive—or stupid.

Like several prominent Miami figures, Hogan got an incredible deal on a couple of suits from Emeterio Marino Pijiera, who operated a discount clothing store in a duplex in a run-down residential neighborhood. Just one hitch: The suits turned out to be stolen. That explained the store tags (Bloomingdale's, Neiman-Marcus, Burdine's, Jacobson's) and the heavy discounts. Hogan paid $125 each for suits valued at $275 retail.

Pijiera was busted for selling hot suits in February, an affair that naturally came to be known as the "Suit Case." Hogan didn't come forward to admit that he had been a customer; one month earlier, he had been appointed statewide prosecutor by State Attorney General Bob Butterworth, a seventy-thousand-dollar-a-year position for which Reno had recommended him.

To appease his conscience, Hogan sent a check for the wholesale price to the Chicago store whose labels were in the suits. In May, he finally admitted being a customer. Reno withdrew from Suit Case at that point, and the governor named the state attorney from the Keys to continue the investigation. It led to only one indictment of a customer, Dade County Manager Sergio Pereira, who had bought seven suits. He was suspended from his job.

But the publicity damaged Hogan's credibility, and he resigned as statewide prosecutor in October. Reno proved her loyalty when she excused his lapse in judgment and rehired him in December 1988. Hogan returned to his former position as chief of the Felony Division, and his salary jumped back up to eighty-seven thousand dollars.

A judge dismissed the charges against the county manager, and Pijiera was given two years of house arrest.

When Reno went to Washington, she brought Hogan along as a special assistant attorney general for high-priority cases. He didn't have to be confirmed, so no one questioned his past—or his wardrobe.

Reno's ugliest race for reelection occurred in 1988. Her challenger was a Coral Gables lawyer named John B. "Jack" Thompson, who was in the vanguard of the growing religious right movement in Florida.

Thompson's campaign speeches were moralistic sermons in which he accused Reno of having skewed priorities in her prosecutions. He claimed she was going easy on pornographers, especially those who peddled child pornography. And he suggested it was because she was a lesbian.

At one debate, Thompson handed Reno a questionnaire that asked her to check a box indicating her sexual preference: homosexual, heterosexual, or bisexual. Reno crumpled the paper and refused to respond, and it never became an issue. This time, the *Herald* endorsed her, stating editorially that "Dade voters would be foolish to trade her experience and proven dedication to the community for her little-known opponent's raw ambition and bad temper." Reno won the election in a landslide. But Thompson wouldn't relent. He became a popular fixture on the South Florida talk radio circuit, where he found a forum for his criticism of Reno and her office.

More than a year later, as the *Herald* was preparing a profile of Thompson, Reno was asked to comment on his old allegation. Her response put Thompson in his place: "He has nothing to worry about. I am attracted to strong, brave, rational, and intelligent men."

Thompson, though, would be back.

In January 1989, as Miami hosted the Super Bowl, three days of civil disturbances in Liberty City marred the celebration and tarnished the city's image yet again.

Once again, a policeman had killed a speeding black motorcyclist. City of Miami Officer William Lozano, a Hispanic, stepped into the street and shot Clement Lloyd. When Lloyd's motorcycle went out of control and crashed, passenger Allan Blanchard also died. Lozano said he felt he was in danger; Reno charged him with needlessly shooting Lloyd.

With Hogan leading the prosecution and Lozano's partner testifying against him, Lozano was convicted on two manslaughter charges. But an appeals court ordered a new trial, saying the jury was likely influenced by the unrest that followed the shooting. The second trial was moved to Tallahassee, and Lozano was acquitted in May 1993, after Reno had left Miami.

Another high-stakes case broke during 1992. In "Operation Court Broom," lawyer Raymond Takiff helped gather evidence against four Dade judges suspected of taking bribes to fix cases. One judge was accused of turning over to Takiff the name of a confidential witness, knowing that Takiff planned to pass the name along to drug dealers who wanted to murder the man.

Reno handed the case over to federal prosecutors, but she sent lawyers from her office along to help. They were "cross-designated" as temporary assistant U.S. attorneys. It was the latest in several public-corruption cases in which she worked with the U.S. Attorney's Office.

Some detractors said Reno either was admitting that her office wasn't up to winning such complex cases or was trying to dodge the political fallout from taking on popular local officials.

Reno insisted it was neither. Rather, she complained that Florida's rules for pretrial discovery—the right of the defense to know what makes up the prosecution's case, including lists of all evidence and witnesses—made winning such complex cases more difficult. She also noted that the U.S. Attorney had the power to call in the Internal Revenue Service to track payoffs through bank accounts, which could lead to additional charges of income tax evasion.

"I think it's an example of what state and federal officials can do, working together, without everybody being concerned about turf and taking credit for something," she said.

Riding high on the publicity of Court Broom, Reno was unopposed when she came up for reelection in 1992 and was returned to office for the fifth time. She was long gone when two of the judges were convicted but two won acquittals.

During Reno's fifteen years as state attorney, her office won death sentences 103 times—more than any other prosecutor in Florida. So it shocked many criminal-law experts when Reno said on the day of her nomination as U.S. Attorney General that she personally opposed capital punishment.

"If she was opposed to the death penalty, I never knew it," said Andrea Hillyer, the lawyer who handled capital punishment cases for Bob Martinez, the conservative Republican who served as Florida's governor from 1987 to 1991.

Reubin Askew, who had appointed Reno as state attorney, refused on moral grounds to sign death warrants and was reelected. But in the far more violent 1980s, Reno couldn't refuse to press for the death penalty and survive politically; polls showed that more than 80 percent of the residents of Dade County and the rest of Florida favored capital punishment.

Seemingly untroubled by any moral dilemma, Reno said simply that she took an oath to uphold the law, and the law required her to seek the death penalty when the circumstances of the case required it. But she used her political capital to argue against it in private, even with governors who favored it.

"I don't recall anyone as plainspoken as Janet on anything," said Samuel "Buddy" Shorstein, an accountant from Jacksonville who served as Bob Graham's chief of staff. "Normally, people are somewhat awed when they walk into the governor's office. Not Janet. She spoke the same way to anyone, whether the governor of Florida or one of her assistants or somebody on the street." And she told Graham "right to his face that the death penalty didn't serve the purposes of deterrence that he and everybody else claimed," Shorstein said.

After she was confirmed, Reno told an audience of Young Democrats in Washington that "all of punishment is arbitrary. When a father spanks two brothers, and one complains that the father spanked him harder than the other one, the father can make up for it with love and affection. You can solve the inequities in sentencing through probation, pardon, mitigation, parole, clemency. But once that death penalty is carried out, you can't."

Reno concluded: "I think that the only justification for the death penalty is vengeance. While my mother lived, if I had walked on to my front porch and found that somebody was still there and they had murdered her, I would tear that person apart from limb to limb with all the vigor that I could muster, and that would be vengeance as a personal sentiment that I think people could have some understanding of.

"But I don't think that a civilized society can engage in vengeance."

That lesson was driven home for Reno in 1989, when Governor Martinez assigned her to investigate the case of fruit picker James Joseph Richardson, who had spent twenty-one years in prison after being convicted of poisoning his seven children in 1967 in Arcadia.

If the U.S. Supreme Court had not held the death penalty as applied unconstitutional in 1972, Richardson likely would have ended up in "Ol' Sparky," the Raiford State Prison electric chair. His death sentence was converted to life in prison. But the subsequent confession of a woman who baby-sat for the children and the discovery of evidence that prosecutors had withheld in his original trial convinced Reno that Richardson was innocent. At a dramatic hearing, she recommended that he be freed, and the judge agreed.

"For as long as I live, I will remember looking at that man the entire day in that old southern courtroom—looking at a man who had been in prison for the last twenty-one years for a crime I did not believe he had committed," Reno said.

"Then as I left the courthouse and turned and looked over my shoulder and watched him walk out of the courthouse a free man, I understood more clearly than ever how, no matter what we do as prosecutors, we've got to remember that one of our first objectives has got to be to make sure that innocent people don't get prosecuted. And the second, equally important, objective has got to be to make sure that we convict people based on principles of due process and fair play."

As Reno acquiesced to society's demand for the death penalty, she also aggressively sought ways to salvage lives.

CHAPTER 5

Part Crime Fighter, Part Social Worker

With a fleeting smile, a wry quip, Reno would occasionally let the public glimpse another side of Miami's top cop. As the daughter of a tough old gator wrestler, sentimental displays were not for her, although she invariably got teary at citizenship ceremonies for immigrants.

Jane had taught her eldest daughter to be strong, but she had also shown her, by example, how to use her heart. As Reno's assurance grew with her tenure and political success, she revealed her concern for those who needed a hand along life's bumpy path.

Reno developed or supported trailblazing programs to attack child abuse, drug abuse, and domestic violence. She unleashed prosecutors to take on slum landlords. She created a victim's advocacy program. She increasingly spoke out on health care and education, calling them crime-prevention tools.

She also created the Drug Court, a program designed to give first offenders another chance. "For a tough, law-and-order prosecutor to say, 'Let's take a chance and develop a program to treat felony offenders' was—at the time—unheard of, and it's still pretty rare right now," said John Goldkamp, a criminal-justice expert from Temple University who studied the Drug Court.

None of Reno's initiatives could be laid to the fact that she is a woman, she insisted. When she was invited to write about her role as a prosecutor for a book on female lawyers in 1984, Reno buried references to her gender at the end of her seventeen pages.

"What effect has my being a woman had?" she asked rhetorically. "None, I would say.

"About five months after I took office, a newscaster for a local television station said that when I was sworn in, he felt so bad for me because he did not think a woman could do the job. Five months later, he said he had changed his mind. I think I am respected, abused, liked, and hated in my role as a prosecutor, as a person, not as a woman.

"At the same time, I have been personally treated with gentle courtesy by most men, including police officers, black leaders, and Hispanic merchants who do not seem troubled at all by the fact that they are dealing with a woman."

Katherine Fernandez Rundle, who became one of Reno's closest friends as well as her top assistant, said gender "may have something to do with the way people look at her, but she is usually able to transcend that. I've watched her in meetings with people who have never met her before. They may start out being especially polite. She's so focused, so direct that after about thirty minutes, you don't really attach a gender to her."

Still, Rundle said, Reno "developed a softness as time went on. She was always very strong and had a tough will. There was real character and determination there. But she began to be more open and caring with people here [in the office], and even in her speeches she showed a softer side."

"Frankly," said Dan Kavanaugh, "Janet was not a very polished politician when she started. But she had an enormous confidence in herself and her ability to handle a difficult situation."

Of that there was never any doubt. One can only imagine the surprise of a misguided purse snatcher in Brooklyn who grabbed Reno's bag as she and Maggy walked late one night from a subway to brother Bob's apartment. When two women well over six feet tall and in high heels raced after him and yelled "Stop, you son of a bitch," the man dropped the purse—and kept running.

When it came to running her office, Reno wasn't afraid to tackle difficult situations, but she also learned to be more politically adept over time, to forgo a futile chase when the odds were bad. Part of the lesson was backing off when she realized she had made a bad call, as when, at the beginning of her term, she called for an end to all plea bargaining in violent crimes. By 1981, she had retreated, saying only that plea bargains shouldn't be used simply to reduce caseloads.

She called on defense lawyers to join prosecutors in a public-awareness campaign about plea bargaining. "We must explain that if a judge has five hundred cases on his calendar in a year, he can, at the most, dispose of ninety cases by trial. In order to dispose of his other cases, he must persuade the defendant to plead guilty. He can only do that by creating a risk for the defendant if he goes to trial. He does that by giving the defendant a stiffer sentence if he goes to trial than if he pleads guilty."

In other words, plea bargaining was a necessary evil that had to be sold to a skeptical public already fed up with crime. But Reno also required consultations with crime victims and the police officers involved in a major case before a plea to a lesser charge could be accepted.

High-profile criminal cases were making Reno's office famous, but the cases of which Reno was proudest didn't always end up on the six o'clock news. These cases, involving the use of creative legal approaches, often had a more direct impact on people's lives. One such effort, growing out of her strong conviction that the cycle of crime had to be broken early, helped improve conditions in low-income housing in Dade County.

Starting in 1979, Reno dispatched Katherine Fernandez Rundle to civil court to file lawsuits against owners of run-down apartment houses in Culmer and other poor neighborhoods. The ramshackle buildings, many of them wood-framed structures two or three stories tall, were infested with rats and roaches. Roofs leaked. Wiring was frayed. Raw sewage spilled from cracked drainpipes.

Reno aimed for real change, not merely a coat of paint. Instead of seeking one-shot misdemeanor convictions for violations of housing codes, which carried maximum penalties of a five-hundred-dollar fine and up to a year in jail, her prosecutors sought court orders that declared the properties public nuisances and mandated repairs. That allowed housing inspectors and judges to supervise the renovations for however long it took to make them—and sometimes it stretched into years. If the property was sold, the new owner inherited the court order and the responsibility for the repairs.

Reno was the first Florida prosecutor to take the renovation route, and it proved so successful that Rundle even went after the largest owner of low-rent housing in greater Miami: the Dade County Housing Department.

Rundle showed in court that the county's twelve thousand public-housing units had never had a comprehensive inspection and that the conditions at many of the buildings, like those at many privately owned apartment houses, were endangering the tenants.

Three court orders resulted in a reorganization of the housing agency, an audit of conditions, and a plan for long-term corrections. In less than ten years, the county raised more than $150 million for repairs from local and federal sources.

Reno also went to court to challenge the city of Miami Beach's plan to use $380 million in tax-backed bonds to redevelop 250 acres at the southern end of the city.

Bond validations normally take one quick rubber-stamp hearing before a circuit judge. Over sixteen months in 1979 and 1980, Reno pushed this one to the state supreme court, contending that the city's sweeping plan would displace thousands of longtime residents in favor of developers of new hotels and condominiums. Among those forced out would be the elderly Jewish snowbirds from New York. They were a fixture on Miami Beach—sitting on the porches of the modest hotels that lined Ocean Drive and Collins Avenue.

The development plan called for razing almost every building south of Sixth Street and constructing nine luxury hotels, condominiums, a marina, shopping malls, and a park within a network of canals. At the very least, Reno argued, there should be a public referendum before the bonds were issued. She eventually lost by a 5-2 vote of the state supreme court, but the plan was altered to allow many of the older buildings to stay.

Reno's intervention helped pave the way, a short time later, for the historic preservation movement that revived the old art deco district. With its unique decorative motif—complete with pink flamingos—restored to its original idiosynchratic state, the district became the centerpiece of the South Beach area rebirth in the late 1980s as a hot spot for fashion models, photographers, and young vacationers.

Reno began two programs that won her wide acclaim from advocacy groups for women and children. One cracked down on domestic violence, prosecuting spouse abuse and child abuse even when the victim didn't want to file charges. The other got the state attorney's office involved in collecting overdue child support from "deadbeat dads."

Both programs were so successful that they were copied statewide. It was hard not to notice them, especially with Reno's office always willing to let the chips fall where they might—even at the garage door of Jose Canseco. The Cuban-American baseball slugger was prosecuted in February 1992 when, following an argument, he raced his Porsche after his wife's BMW and rammed her. He made a plea agreement and was ordered to undergo twenty-six hours of counseling.

Reno had demonstrated her concern about domestic violence soon after becoming state attorney in Florida. At the invitation of the medical examiner Dr. Joseph Davis, Reno had sent a college intern to the morgue to analyze reports listing the cause of death of every murder victim in Dade County for the last twenty-five years. From the analysis she learned that 40 percent of the homicides at the time involved husband-wife, boyfriend-girlfriend, or ex-spouse violence.

She also believed domestic violence perpetuated itself: "The child who watches his father beat his mother comes to accept violence as a way of life."

The program not only offered aggressive prosecutions but also provided assistance to victims needing medical care, financial aid, and temporary housing. Reno herself served on the board of directors of a local shelter for battered women.

Children became crime victims when support payments weren't made, Reno reasoned, because single mothers often had trouble affording food, rent, clothing, and other necessities. She set up a one-stop processing center that allowed blood to be drawn for paternity testing at the same place that requests for court orders could be filed and payments processed.

Once the Child Support Enforcement Division was fully operating, collections of overdue payments in Dade County doubled, increasing from just under $17 million in 1986 to $33.6 million in 1992. That success won Reno the honor of being the only prosecutor in America with a rap song written about her. In 1988, new words were written to the tune of "Yankee Doodle." The song was performed by Anquette, a young female rapper. Reno once said she didn't understand the song and didn't like it much, but she confessed to friends that it secretly delighted her that she had been recognized by rappers, of all people. She didn't buy the recording, but a relative did and presented it to her.

Reno recalled, "When I would walk through a high school after that, young men would start humming, 'Janet Reno comes to town, collecting all the money,' and then they would say, 'I paid! I paid!' "

Reno herself paid child support payments for the children of her youngest brother, Mark, when he was between jobs and broke. He later earned his license as a tugboat and ship captain and worked in the oil business in Nigeria.

Reno remains close to her brother Mark's children, including Karin Hunter Reno. Karin, a willowy blond, at the age of fifteen signed a lucrative contract with a New York modeling agency and traveled all over the world for fashion shows and photo shoots for such magazines as *Mademoiselle, Elle, Cosmopolitan,* and *French Vogue.*

Reno simply would not tolerate rudeness to a crime victim or a victim's survivors. When she took office, she said, "I thought I was a sensitive person. I thought I understood what victimization was all about." But a female victim set her straight.

"I don't remember the name of the person, I don't remember the case—but I remember a face in torment, telling me how insensitive I was and I didn't understand what she was going through."

In a 1986 speech to the Institute of Human Relations of the American Jewish Committee, Reno said public confidence in the criminal-justice system was eroding because "our victims and witnesses continue to be the forgotten persons in the system."

She declared, "The law is not working and it is a hollow instrument when it sees to it that the man who abuses a child receives medical treatment in prison while it stands idly by and provides no treatment for the child he abused."

She created, and continued to expand throughout her tenure, a victim's advocacy program that employed more than two dozen people by the end of 1992. Reno wanted to have trained counselors available, at perhaps the most trying point in someone's life, to patiently explain the law, keep track of case schedules, coordinate witness appearances, and offer comfort during the trial. If a victim or a family member requested it, Reno always took the time to meet with them and explain the prosecution strategy, and she expected her assistants to do the same.

And Reno practiced the sensitivity she preached. In the mid-1980s, Reno and Jane were bothered at home by a woman who showed up inside their house—uninvited. The first couple of times, she left quietly. The third time, the police were called. But Reno, learning that the forty-six-year-old woman had a history of mental illness, got the woman sent to a program offering psychiatric treatment. The woman stopped bothering Reno and recovered.

One of the victims' advocates Reno hired was her cousin Lisa Reno, who had married South Dade insurance executive John Hardeman, Jr. Lisa and John learned firsthand how difficult it could be to deal with the criminal-justice system. Lisa's stepson, John Hardeman III, and his wife Gail were murdered on January 4, 1981, during a hunting trip near West Palm Beach.

A seventeen-year-old boy whose family was camping nearby had tried to steal Hardeman's new shotgun and killed Hardeman when he fought back. Gail was shot when she happened on the horrifying scene. The youth's brother helped him hide the bodies; after a week, they cracked and led police to the location.

The night the bodies were found, Reno went to her cousin's house and did the best thing she could think to do to console them. "She brought out the death-penalty information and explained aggravating and mitigating circumstances" that could be considered in sentencing, Lisa Hardeman said. "She did my job," referring to her later role as an advocate.

It took five years and nine months for the killer, Cleo D. LeCroy, to be sent to death row. The trial was repeatedly delayed by complicated appeals, which Reno helped explain to the Hardemans.

When it was finally over, when Lisa Hardeman had learned the system the hard way, Reno offered her a job. To make sure she couldn't be criticized for nepotism, Reno had Lisa hired by Dade County, not the state of Florida, so she had no control over her salary. Few people knew Lisa was Reno's cousin, and she quickly established herself as a caring advocate.

Reno insisted that Hardeman and the other advocates offer sensitivity training to prosecutors and judges. "At first the prosecutors said to me, 'But wait a minute, she's going to be looking over our shoulders.' And I said, 'Don't let her look over your shoulder, bring her into the circle.'

"That lady is the prosecutor's right hand and left hand now," Reno said.

Ten days after the 1984 election, Reno's friend Frances Webb died of liver disease. She was forty-nine. Her obituary said the memorial service would be held at Reno's home, but that only hinted at the close relationship between the Webbs and the Renos.

Webb and her husband, Al, an artist and illustrator, had been friends of the Reno family since Fran worked at the *Herald* in the 1960s. After Al died in 1981, Frances and her four children became part of the extended family that orbited around the Reno ranch.

When she knew she was dying, Fran asked Reno—her most responsible friend—to be guardian for her fifteen-year-old twins, Daphne and Daniel. Webb's older children, Allan and Ann, had outgrown the need of a guardian.

Reno took control of the twins' finances and oversaw their schooling. But she didn't live with them. They decided they wanted to stay in their family home, and Mark Reno volunteered to stay with them. That arrangement lasted six months. Then, Sally Winslow moved in. Janet remained their legal guardian and would talk to them or drop by almost daily, but Winslow was their full-time parent.

Reno never spoke publicly about the arrangement until she got to Washington. By then, the twins had established independent lives. Daniel worked for a commercial bakery in New York, and Daphne was developing a career as a theatrical stage manager in Miami. She thrilled Reno by showing up at her confirmation hearing.

After she became attorney general, Reno would invoke the twins, though not by name, when she talked about the importance of parenting.

"I think raising children is the most difficult thing I know to do. It takes hard work, love, intelligence, and a lot of luck," Reno said in speeches. "And you may say, 'Well, Ms. Reno, what do you know about raising children? You have never been married.'

"Eight years ago, a friend died, leaving me as legal guardian over fifteen-year-old twins, a boy and a girl, and the girl was in love. And I have learned an awful lot about raising children.

"I will also tell you that it is one of the most rewarding things you can do, because when I put the young lady on the plane to go to college, and then three years later when she graduated cum laude, she threw her arms around my neck on both occasions and said, 'Thank you, I could not have done it without you.' That is as rewarding as any professional fulfillment."

Reno's interest in parenting wasn't just a family affair. Without any public relations fanfare, Reno quietly served as a mentor for students in public schools in Dade County. In fact, White House auditors who were reviewing her personal finances raised their eyebrows over some unexplained personal checks Reno had written. Reno explained that she occasionally helped needy students with emergency expenses.

For four years, she helped a young black woman through high school in Miami. When the woman enrolled at Washington's Howard University in the fall of 1993, Reno continued to stay in touch with her—and refused to publicly identify her. "It makes me so proud to see what she can do," Reno said.

Reno's concern about child abuse became a top priority when her office had to handle a series of prosecutions against adults who sexually abused children left in their care.

The first case, in 1984, involved a South Miami police officer who would occasionally watch children for whom his wife babysat. Harold Grant Snowden was convicted of the sexual battery of a five-year-old girl and her infant brother.

Days later, Reno charged a couple with sexually abusing children at the baby-sitting service they operated in Country Walk, an upscale Miami suburb. It was one of the first cases of abuse in an "institutional" setting and led to a book and a television movie.

Reno's office pioneered several techniques in handling such cases, including videotaped and closed-circuit testimony by the children and special counseling to protect them from further emotional trauma. Defense lawyers and some psychologists complained about the tactics, contending that the children's testimony had been coached. But Frank Fuster Escalona was sentenced to six life terms, in part because his wife Ileana—who said she also had been abused by Fuster—testified against him. She served four years and was deported to her native Honduras when released.

The Country Walk case brought Reno to the attention of Marian Wright Edelman, founder of the Children's Defense Fund, and other national advocates. Edelman would later prove to be a persuasive advocate for Reno's nomination as U.S. Attorney General with the former chair of CDF's board of directors, Hillary Rodham Clinton.

After the Fuster case, Reno opened a special full-time center to help children who were victims of crime. It assisted the prosecutors when children had to serve as witnesses, helped children deal with the loss of a parent or other loved one, and even arranged for lawyers to represent the children when necessary.

In 1986, with her credentials clearly established throughout Florida, Reno was named to head a statewide task force on the crack cocaine problem. In mid-October, the hard-charging panel called for an emergency session of the legislature to consider its recommendations. Among them: appointment of a state "drug czar," enactment of stiffer penalties for cocaine possession, construction of more prison cells, and development of better drug-treatment and antidrug education programs.

But the task force ignored the state's budget woes and get-tough mood when it also recommended that health insurers be required to provide coverage for substance-abuse treatment. Reno convinced the group to stop short of calling for mandatory sentences for possession of tiny amounts of cocaine, which many police and prosecutors said would have allowed them to target street-corner crack dealers. Because the state prison system was already so overcrowded—army surplus tents were being pitched on some prison grounds—Reno reasoned that mandatory sentences would have been "meaningless." Without additional permanent prison cells, she said, "The whole discussion of penalties is really absurd."

The task force's whole package proved politically infeasible. Although Governor Graham agreed to fund some of the proposals, at a price tag of nearly $73 million, including rapid construction of some prison cells, he was departing for the U.S. Senate. Incoming Republican Governor Bob Martinez, a former mayor of Tampa, and the new legislative leadership wanted more time to study the situation.

The following spring, money was appropriated for additional prison beds, but the delay meant the state was even farther behind in its game of catch-up, and Reno and others on the front lines suffered the consequences. Criminals were serving a third or less of their sentences before being paroled because of the shortage of prison space.

One of those released was Charles H. Street. Convicted in 1980 for attempted murder, he served only about a third of his sentence before his parole in mid-November 1988. But before leaving prison, Street vowed to kill the next cop who tried to arrest him.

Nine days after his release, Street had spent the little money he had on cocaine and was stranded in Miami. Trying to get a ride north to West Palm Beach, he began waving a three-foot pipe at motorists at a major intersection. When two police officers tried to subdue him, he managed to grab one officer's revolver. He used it to kill the officer and wound the second, then picked up the wounded man's weapon to finish the job.

Witnesses said Street announced, "Now I've got my ride," as he got in the police car and drove off. Later that night, after a chase, he was captured. Reno's prosecutors got convictions for the murders of both cops; Street got the death sentence.

The outcry that followed the Street case convinced the state Department of Corrections and the Parole Commission to tighten its rules on the early release of violent felons.

Holding one of the toughest criminal-justice jobs in America, Reno saw her prestige growing in the national legal community—and the work on her plate piling up higher and higher.

In 1986, the same year she chaired Florida's cocaine task force, Reno was tapped by former Watergate prosecutor Sam Dash to serve on the American Bar Association's Special Committee on Criminal Justice in a Free Society. The blue-ribbon panel had been convened in response to complaints from Ronald Reagan's law-and-order attorney general, Edwin Meese, and other conservatives that accused criminals were getting too much protection from the courts. Meese argued that police and prosecutors were being hamstrung by search-and-seizure limitations and by the need to read suspects their rights—the so-called Miranda warning.

Dash, the panel's chairman, said he wanted the committee to represent a wide range of views, and he invited Reno because she had a reputation as "a reliably tough prosecutor who clearly wanted to enforce the law." He also invited the California attorney general, a federal appellate judge, the police chief of Washington, D.C., and several law school professors.

After surveying eight hundred lawyers, judges, prosecutors, and police administrators across the country, the committee issued its report in November 1988. In a rebuke to Meese and his brethren, the committee concluded that court-imposed protections had done no harm and had in fact resulted in better police work and fairer prosecutions. The committee found, for example, that prosecutors dropped fewer than 3 percent of all adult felony arrests because of illegal searches.

Dash said that Reno's attitude surprised him: "I didn't expect to hear such a tough district attorney saying some of the things she said. She proved highly sensitive to the rights of defendants. She was very much concerned with the adequacy of counsel for the indigent. And she was terribly worried about children and juveniles."

Dash, too, became an advocate for Reno when the White House was checking her references in 1993.

Reno later accepted invitations to serve on the board of the American Judicature Society and to sit on a second ABA panel, this one chaired by her old friend and former law partner Sandy D'Alemberte, who served as the ABA's president in 1991–92.

This panel examined allegations of bias in the criminal-justice system and issued a lengthy report, "Achieving Justice in a Diverse America," in July 1992. Its recommendations were sweeping, including calls for more minorities and women at all levels of the criminal-justice system, from police on the streets to judges; expanded jury pools to include more minorities; and better hiring and promotion practices at law firms to increase diversity in private practice.

After the Los Angeles riots in 1992, a spin-off ABA task force studied the unmet legal needs of children and youth, especially those in minority communities. That task force was led by retired federal appeals Judge A. Leon Higginbotham, Jr., of Philadelphia, whose name surfaced briefly as a possible nominee to the Supreme Court.

Higginbotham's panel presented its report to Attorney General Reno in August 1993. It didn't stop at the unmet legal needs of children but called on lawyers to get involved in a vast range of reforms, from overhauling welfare to improving public education to creating more after-school activities for kids at risk.

Reno was delighted. The report's recommendations dovetailed perfectly with her emerging agenda for children. "We must reweave the fabric of society around children," she said, and lawyers should lead the way. "Most of us understand that problems are not solved in courtrooms."

Higginbotham predicted that, by focusing on those issues for the first time, Reno would become "one of the greatest attorneys general ever to occupy that office."

Reno actually had been focusing on children's issues for nearly a decade. She had begun rather tentatively, first addressing the need for welfare reform. That fell within her purview because the state attorney's office prosecuted welfare fraud.

In a 1986 speech to a local chapter of the American Jewish Congress, she decried the "development of an underclass composed primarily of single mothers living in poverty with their children."

The system prevented women from trying to work their way up by taking even part-time, minimum-wage jobs, Reno complained, because they would lose their Medicaid benefits. Mothers had to choose between working and having health-care coverage for their kids, she said.

"We are in the third and fourth generation of children being raised in that atmosphere," she continued. "These people see no light at the end of the tunnel. They have no hope or self-respect. They have no sense of dignity. Our welfare system is going to have to be renewed to give people a sense of hope, to get them off this bureaucratic treadmill and to give them an opportunity for self-respect."

Among other things, she came out strongly for transitional assistance during a woman's return to work, including providing health care and child care.

By 1990, Reno was speaking out more aggressively on children's issues. "Florida has been penny-wise and pound-foolish by waiting until a human crisis occurs and then spending thousands of dollars to try to cure it," she wrote in the report for yet another task force, this time a governor's task force on social services, which she chaired in 1990. "By then, it's too late, and the dollars do not begin to deal with the problems created by such neglect."

Reno the prosecutor/social worker evolved into Reno the radical social engineer, advocating nothing less than curtailing the work day to conform to school hours.

"We could eliminate the need for child care in many instances," she wrote in the *Florida Bar Journal* in March 1990. "Working parents will be less rushed and more attentive than they are now in the brief morning and evening hours they are with their children, hurrying them to school, or rushing to fix dinner.

"The nine-to-five work day was established in another century of gas lamps and no computers. We can accomplish far more today working from nine to two than we could accomplish in nine to five a century ago."

Suffice it to say, employers didn't leap to embrace the idea. Nor did Reno shorten her own employees' work days. She had to conform to court schedules, she said. But she did give workers time off to attend school conferences, chaperone trips, and the like. Workers without children were allowed time off to tutor at public schools.

In her search for ways to stop criminals before she had to deal with them in court, and to stem the growing tide of injuries and deaths from handguns, Reno began calling for gun control in the mid-1980s. To the irritation of the National Rifle Association's

Florida chapter, she advocated a waiting period for handgun purchases, gun registration, and gun owner licensing. The license would require a gun-safety course and a proficiency test—just like a driver's license, Reno often noted.

But Florida legislators, cowed by the NRA, wouldn't act. This was one chase Reno was not about to quit. In July 1988, she joined forces with state Representative Ron Silver, a liberal lawyer from North Dade, to launch the "Cool It, Florida!" campaign. Its goal: collect enough signatures to give voters across the state a chance to do what their chicken-hearted legislators wouldn't, impose a mandatory seven-day waiting period between the purchase and the delivery of a gun.

Proponents of the waiting period believed the week's delay would give angry gun buyers time to cool off before using the weapon in a crime of passion, such as a domestic argument. And it would give police time to check the background of a buyer for a criminal record or a history of mental illness.

The symbolic leaders of the campaign were friends and relatives of Floridians claimed by handgun violence, including Toni Rakow, the widow of a Miami Beach cop. A fleeing drug suspect had shot Scott Rakow in the head, and Reno's office sent his killer, Freddy Andrade, to prison for life.

"Cool It, Florida!" won a place on the 1990 ballot by collecting more than 343,000 voters' signatures in just over a year. That November, voters slam-dunked the resulting referendum by a vote of 2,824,582 to 530,377.

The voters were right about the waiting period. In less than three years, computer checks conducted by the Florida Department of Law Enforcement prevented some twenty-seven thousand people with criminal records from buying guns through licensed dealers. Moreover, there were outstanding warrants on nearly seven hundred of those would-be gun buyers, and many were picked up by police when they returned to the gun store to pick up their purchase.

For more than a decade, Reno had searched for a way to dent the county's steadily growing epidemic of drug abuse. In October 1988, a couple of judges and Dade County public defenders began selling Reno on an ambitious experiment to intervene with drug abusers before they had thrown their lives away. With this program, they could reach out to those arrested for the first time on a drug charge, usually possession, who had no history of violence. Reno embraced the idea and began promoting it to resistant judges and cops.

At the time, Miami was under siege. It was not unheard of for police roundups to deposit two hundred new drug violators in jail in one night. The tsunami of cases flooding the courts forced judges to accept quick guilty pleas from first-time offenders and sentence them to time served, often just a day or two in the county lockup. The person was released having received neither real punishment nor treatment.

Reno's selling job worked, and in June 1989, the Drug Court was created. It allowed specially assigned Judge Stanley Goldstein, a streetwise, wise-cracking former cop and prosecutor, to refer a first-time offender to a treatment program that now includes acupuncture therapy, counseling, and job training, all while undergoing random drug testing.

If the offender successfully completes the program, the state attorney's office does not prosecute, and the charge is dropped. If he or she stumbles, Goldstein can throw the offender in jail. Reno calls it her "carrot and stick approach." It solidified her image as part sympathetic social worker, part stern prosecutor.

Goldstein doesn't mince words. To an addict who had failed to show up for a previous court appearance, he said, "Why don't I just send you to prison and you can stay there until you get out, and then you can commit suicide. Wouldn't that be easier?" But the man asked for another chance. "Don't screw up, babe," the judge warned. "Don't mess with me. If you don't give a rap, then I don't give a rap."

When the program began, it was designed for "virgins and Boy Scouts," as Tim Murray, director of Dade County's Office of Substance Abuse Control, put it in an interview with the *Miami Herald*. Now, however, the $1.3-million-a-year program accepts offenders with multiple drug possession arrests and even defendants charged with burglary and other nonviolent felonies, if drug abuse is involved.

The long-term success of the program remains to be seen, but initial results are very promising. Thus far, more than thirty-two hundred offenders have graduated. Only 9 percent of first-time offenders were rearrested within a year of graduation; however, the success rate falls to about 60 percent when all who participate are counted, including hardened addicts. The program certainly makes fiscal sense: six hundred dollars a year per offender, compared with seventeen thousand dollars to jail a drug offender for the same period.

One who made it was a twenty-eight-year-old father of two. In February 1992, Miami police caught him with cocaine and marijuana as he was leaving a drug den known as "The Hole." But after a year in the program, some two hundred drug tests, and work with a drug counselor, he found steady work detailing cars and graduated. "At first I thought it was all a big waste of time," he said. But after a few months, he decided the judge was "a good guy."

The Drug Court's early success convinced Reno to insist that a new thousand-bed county jail facility should be designed as a drug-treatment facility for repeat offenders. She argued that such approaches not only give the offenders second chances but also help ease prison overcrowding.

Reno's support of the Drug Court delighted Dade County's public defenders, who represented most of those referred to the program. They had had serious concerns at the beginning about the prosecutor's commitment, particularly to sealing and expunging records of those who completed the program.

"From what I had encountered in the courtroom, the way her folks had been trained, I expected real rigidity on Ms. Reno's part," said Hugh Rodham, a senior public defender who was assigned to develop the court. "Much to my surprise, she believed it was a good idea, and she helped us take this raw idea and shape it and smooth the edges and develop its selling points.

"I really felt that this was someone who advocates for the people."

Such praise proved of immense importance to Reno. Hugh

Rodham is Hillary Rodham Clinton's brother. His talk of Reno's innovative spirit led Hillary to meet Reno as part of a Miami stopover during the 1992 campaign. A year earlier, the governor of Arkansas had tagged along with his brother-in-law to take a look at the Drug Court.

Hugh Rodham mentioned Reno to Clinton just hours after the election that November. It was during a family dinner in the governor's mansion in Little Rock, Arkansas.

"I suggested she might make a fine attorney general," Rodham said. "I guess he filed it away back in that phenomenal memory of his."

Reno also became an advocate of an old-fashioned brand of law enforcement that now has a fancy new name: community policing. In essence it's cops-walking-the-beat police work, with a little social work thrown in. From her earliest days in juvenile court, Reno had wondered why social service agencies didn't do more to follow up when, say, a child was first reported truant from school.

In April 1992, she helped create a Neighborhood Resource Team consisting of a police officer, a social worker, a public-health nurse, and a housing adviser. They were sent to check out reports of drug dealing and gang violence in a low-income neighborhood in the West Perrine section of South Dade.

The team went door to door, meeting and interviewing residents about their problems and needs. It helped the neighborhood get medical attention, day care, job training, and much more. Tenecia Tripp got guidance in securing a community college grant. And when the twenty-year-old couldn't afford books, the team found an anonymous donor to pay the tab. The team's nurse helped Tripp's mother find doctors to treat her back and dental problems. Reno was delighted that the team members organized fishing trips and other outings for neighborhood kids.

Though the first team's work was interrupted by Hurricane Andrew, a second team has been established for Goulds, another poor neighborhood. But it wasn't easy getting started.

"We had meeting after meeting, but we couldn't seem to get a commitment," recalled Metro-Dade police Major Frank Boni. "Finally, Ms. Reno looked at me and said, 'Frank, I don't see why we can't do this right now.' If you know Ms. Reno, you know that my answer was, 'Well, Ms. Reno, we can do it. We'll do it right this minute.'"

Throughout her tenure as state attorney, Reno had to contend with Miami's aggressive media. She tried to return calls from journalists promptly, but she irritated reporters regularly with her rigid refusal to comment on any pending case.

Unlike many prosecutors who liked to sniff out information and test theories with leaks to the press, Reno refused to play the game and tried to keep her assistants from leaking. When a case was closed or a trial concluded, though, Reno felt she had an obligation to explain her actions to those who asked. And, with certain exceptions, she had to open her files under Florida's Sunshine Law, which mandated accessible government records.

Reno later found that worked to her benefit, as she told a group of lawyers who deal with national security matters. "I frankly thought that when my name was first mentioned in February for attorney general that I would never, ever be considered because nobody would want to vet fifteen years as prosecutor in Dade County. . . . There would be too many problems and too many minefields in that fifteen years for anybody to want to examine."

But as she was quizzed about cases by the White House screening team, "I was amazed to look back and watch how my office responded. As questions arose, there was a memorandum. As another question arose, there was a case filing. In another question, there was a close-out document explaining why we had done something, why we had not charged, what our sentence recommendations were, and how we had handled a particular matter.

"We were able to do this because we had participated in open government, and we had explained ourselves to the people in an appropriate way."

She brought Florida's government-in-the-sunshine approach to Washington, launching a long-overdue overhaul of the federal Freedom of Information Act within eight months of taking office.

For all her belief in openness, however, Reno could be short-tempered, even rude, when reporters asked what she believed were silly, uninformed questions, or focused on process and politics rather than policy. At the end of a question-and-answer session with a high school or college audience, she invariably told them, "Thank you for reaffirming my belief that students usually ask better questions than reporters."

Reno also was not shy about correcting reporters or columnists if she disagreed with an article's facts or conclusions. She would call and chew them out, often angrily. "She's capable of great, real rage," said Martha Musgrove, associate editor of the *Miami Herald's* editorial board. "The phone will melt in your hand. But she doesn't hold a grudge."

Nor does the *Herald*. In endorsing her for attorney general, the paper enthused: "If the president wants an attorney general who would restore to the Department of Justice the rectitude that it lost under attorneys general such as John Mitchell and Ed Meese, Janet Reno is his restorer. Among her several strong suits, none is stronger, more essential than her unquestioned character."

Reno's relationship with her mother changed as Jane aged. The roles of a lifetime reversed as Janet took care of Jane, with the help of friends who would often visit during the day while Janet was at work.

Feisty as she was, Jane made the transition fairly gracefully, so long as her children and grandchildren helped satisfy her love of adventure and her yearning to travel. Instead of cruising the state's waterways in a nineteen-foot motorboat, as she and Janet had done in 1977, Jane settled for a houseboat tour of North Florida's St. Johns River one year and a cruise of the Caribbean another.

Janet also took her to parties when Jane felt up to it, such as the annual St. Patrick's Day champagne bash hosted by Sister

Jeanne O'Laughlin, an old family friend and the president of Barry University.

During the summer of 1992, with Jane's health failing, Janet and Maggy decided on one last adventure. "She had cancer, and I knew she didn't have long to live, and she'd gotten so she couldn't get around," Janet said. "So my sister and I piled a wheelchair into a motor home and off we went."

They stopped in Sunnyside, Georgia, to see Jane's grandmother's house. They cruised up the Blue Ridge Parkway. And they stopped in Washington, D.C.

"She couldn't see very well by that time," Janet recalled, "and I said, 'Well, we'll go see the dinosaurs! Those will be big enough for you to see.'" So they visited the Smithsonian's Museum of Natural History. "Well, she loved the dinosaurs. Then, she'd always loved El Greco, so we roared her through the National Gallery because she could see the big El Grecos. Then we roared her down around the Capitol in the wheelchair.

"She had a wonderful visit and got home and a week later, Hurricane Andrew went through. And she was a model to me of how not to be upset in the middle of a hurricane.

"And the fact that I cared for her and made sure she was okay is as important to me as anything I've ever done professionally. . . . A commitment to family should be, and personally to me has been, as rewarding as anything that I've ever done."

Reno recalled her mother's reaction to that furious storm this way: "Hurricane Andrew hit South Dade on the early morning of August the twenty-fourth. About three in the morning, as the winds began to howl, my mother woke up. Old and frail and dying, she went and sat in her chair, folded her hands in her lap, and although trees were crashing around the house and the winds howled, she sat there totally unafraid. For she knew how she had built that house. She hadn't cut corners. She hadn't compromised her standards. She'd built it the right way.

"When I went out in the gray dawn, the scene resembled a World War I battlefield, but that house had lost one shingle and a couple of screens."

She looked at her mother and declared: "Old woman, you built one hell of a house."

By mid-December, the cancer in Jane's lungs made each breath more difficult. Maggy joined Janet at the house. One night, as each daughter took an arm and walked their mother to bed, they began singing "The Battle Hymn of the Republic." That night, Jane slipped into a coma, and two days later, on December 21, 1992, Jane Wood died in her bed in the house she had built.

Mark, who had been in Africa, was the last of her four children to reach home. Through his tears, the legendary Reno wit appeared. When he heard how Janet and Maggy had sung to Jane, he accused them of killing their mother with their off-key singing. "If I'd been here, I might have prevented it," Mark said.

The hundreds who attended the funeral laughed as stories of Jane's antics were retold. "Jane Wood Reno was no saint. I take some small comfort today in knowing that Mother will not insult anyone or embarrass the family," Janet said. "She was responsible for the most excruciating moments of my life. But as I look back over all the years, almost all of her outrageous foolishness was directed at puncturing the pomp and arrogance of this world."

She eulogized her mother's adventurous yet caring spirit with a nursery rhyme: "Wynken, Blynken and Nod one night sailed off in a wooden shoe/Sailed on a river of crystal light into a sea of dew ... "

Her love of adventure would send Jane in search of wonders like North Florida's mystically beautiful deepwater springs. Janet quoted her mother's writing about such springs:

"Funnel shaped, they shade from crystal water on the sandy shore, to sky blue, then to the deepest royal blue at the center. ... You can float over the shafts where the cool water wells and see specks of mica glinting on sandy floors of caves, forty, sixty, ninety feet below, as though you looked through air ... "

Her mother, Janet said, "could say 'I love you' better than anyone I know."

At Jane's request, four favorite pieces of poetry were read at the ceremony, lines from Shakespeare, Swinburne, and Spender. And a bit of her own:

Dying and fire, being two mysteries,
Let me adore them, now while I may.

Someday I shall be breathless and fireless,
My hands will look living, but I shall be gone;
Because of that day, this day is so lustrous.
Death will still be here when I am God.

Tested for fourteen years by the toughest job in Miami, Janet Reno had weathered a rocky ride in the popularity polls. Friends and supporters saw her as an innovator whose holistic vision of justice could play on a larger stage. With the death of her mother, Reno faced inevitable change.

PART THREE

Moving into the National Spotlight

CHAPTER 6

Nomination

Like millions of Americans, Janet Reno had been following the plot twists and turns in President Clinton's latest attempt to name an attorney general and complete his cabinet. But she was stunned late one night when a friend phoned with the latest development: Kimba M. Wood, the president's second selection, had been dropped from consideration.

It was close to midnight on Friday, February 5, 1993, when Katherine Fernandez Rundle called Reno to share the news. Earlier that evening, Reno had had dinner with Rundle and her husband Christopher, a lawyer who also worked in the state attorney's office. They discussed Wood's prospects as she faced the Senate confirmation process, debating whether her short stint as a Playboy Club bunny would become grist for the Judiciary Committee and whether she would face the third degree on her child-care arrangements, the issue that defeated Clinton's first choice, Zoë Baird.

Would a male nominee have faced the same scrutiny? Unlikely, the three agreed. Reno called the far-off drama "strange and rather sad."

Reno headed home while the Rundles went to the opera, their tickets a Christmas gift from Reno. When the Rundles got home, they saw on a television newscast that Wood had withdrawn, or, more accurately, been dumped. Rundle knew her boss rarely watched television, so she called with the news.

"You're kidding!" Reno exclaimed, then went to bed.

Less than seventy-two hours later, she would be in a Washington hotel room preparing for a job interview at the White House—and the intense scrutiny of the national spotlight.

Wood, a federal judge from Manhattan, had stepped into a quagmire involving nannies and taxes created by Clinton's first nominee, Connecticut corporate lawyer Zoë Baird. In 1990, Baird and her husband, Yale law school professor Paul Gewirtz, had hired a Peruvian couple to work as live-in nanny and driver, knowing they were illegal immigrants. Despite Baird's insistence that they had followed the advice of immigration experts to get the workers' papers in order, the public bristled at perceived impropriety by a well-to-do lawyer. During two painful, intense days of questioning, interrupted by Clinton's inauguration, Baird offered her contrition. But to Senate Judiciary Committee members, her expressions of remorse were drowned out by irate phone calls from constituents back home, where tolerance was scarce for rich lawyers and their excuses. With opposition building, Senator Joseph Biden, Delaware Democrat and chair of the Committee, advised Clinton to "take her down," which the White House did at 1:30 A.M. on Friday, January 22.

Wood's situation was more complex, because she broke no law when she hired her baby-sitter, an undocumented worker from Trinidad. In fact, Wood and her husband, Michael Kramer, chief political correspondent for *Time* magazine, had helped the sitter get a residency permit and had paid all taxes on time. So White House aides expected no serious problems and floated Wood's name as the likely second nominee.

But on Capitol Hill, senators feared attempting to explain to constituents the distinctions between Baird's case and Wood's. The furor over Baird was too fresh for Clinton to risk another controversy. Clinton himself felt Wood had been less than forthcoming about her situation. So Wood was jettisoned two weeks after Baird.

Clinton's top aides frantically returned to their lists of candidates. White House counsel Bernard Nussbaum, personnel chief Bruce Lindsey, and most other top White House officials spent the weekend phoning senators, House members, old law partners, academics, campaign contributors, anyone with a lead on a solid contender.

Names that had circulated after Baird's withdrawal appeared again in press reports, among them former Virginia Governor Gerald Baliles, Yale law school professor Drew S. Days III, District of Columbia Bar Association president Jamie S. Gorelick, U.S. District Judge Diana Murphy of Minneapolis, U.S. Court of Appeals Judge Patricia M. Wald of Washington, and U.S. District Judge Rya Zobel of Boston.

At Washington dinner parties that weekend, a female nominee seemed the odds-on favorite. Although Clinton officially denied it, many assumed he had set quotas for women and minorities in his cabinet. Having sent up one woman and floated a second, he didn't dare send a man in their place. And certainly, it would appeal to Clinton's sense of history to be the president who named the first female attorney general.

Reno's name wasn't in the papers that weekend, but inside the White House she had moved to the short list after an angry Senator Biden got word to the president to find an experienced prosecutor who would bring a law-and-order reputation to the Justice Department. And it wouldn't hurt if the nominee had a spotless reputation, Biden pointedly added.

Biden didn't know Reno well, although she had appeared as a witness before his committee in June 1988 on issues relating to violence and drug abuse. He had sought her perspective because of Miami's reputation as the nation's cocaine capital.

He remembered with amusement how she had challenged the title he used—"Drug Czar"—as he sought to create a national drug policy coordinator. To Reno's populist ear, "czar" sounded decidedly undemocratic.

"Americans don't like the word 'czar.' Abolish 'czar' from your vocabulary," Reno had instructed Biden.

"The press dubbed it 'czar,' " Biden replied defensively.

"And you repeated it. You shouldn't," Reno shot back.

"That's true. You're right," the senator said, adding with a smile, "Why don't you come work for me?"

Congress approved the Office of National Drug Control Policy in 1989; the unofficial title, notwithstanding Reno's disapproval, stuck.

When White House lawyer Ron Klain asked Biden's opinion of Reno, Biden agreed that it was time to look at the outspoken prosecutor from Miami. With that signal, Reno became a leading contender by Sunday evening.

Reno already had been pushed hard by members of Clinton's Florida camp, among them Democratic Senator Bob Graham and Lieutenant Governor Kenneth "Buddy" MacKay, a former congressman who had been Clinton campaign chairman in the Sunshine State.

Graham and MacKay had pitched Reno for a top job, even mentioning the attorney general spot, at a meeting with Clinton in early December, during a two-day visit to Washington by the president-elect. The Floridians had been invited to brief Clinton on the deteriorating situation in Haiti, and they used the occasion to hand-deliver their list of Florida candidates for appointments.

Reno's banner was also being carried by a coalition of feminist leaders, led by Harriett Woods of the National Women's Political Caucus, who listed her among qualified women who should be considered for top-level jobs in the new administration.

The Clintons heard personal recommendations from Marian Wright Edelman of the Children's Defense Fund, who knew Reno's work as a pioneer in child sex-abuse investigations, and Hillary's brother, Hugh Rodham, who as a public defender in Dade County had considerable contact with Reno and had already mentioned Janet to his brother-in-law.

"They said they wanted the straight poop from somebody who had been in an adversarial relationship with her. Well, I could not have given her higher marks," Rodham said.

In one of his trademark late-night calls, Clinton phoned Senator Graham at his Miami Lakes home at 11:40 P.M. Sunday, February 7, to chat about Reno. Clinton and Graham had developed a friendly relationship during their overlapping tenures as southern governors. When Clinton was looking for a vice presidential running mate, he had given Graham serious consideration.

"You're working too hard. It's late," Graham told Clinton.

"I'm working on finding an attorney general. Tell me about Janet Reno," the president said.

Graham reiterated his earlier recommendation. He had known Reno since Harvard Law School, where Graham was a year ahead of her. He'd heard about the young woman from Miami and searched out Reno, introducing himself to her in the law library one evening. Reno recalled that Graham was serious at their first meeting "but with a twinkle in his eye."

"I thought she might be able to vote for me someday," Graham said, laughing.

Thirty years later, it was Graham who was endorsing Reno for the nation's top legal job. During his fourteen-minute chat, the president focused on two issues: Reno's reputation and her experience. "He obviously knew a lot about her, based on the questions that he asked," Graham said.

Graham told Clinton that Reno would be "an excellent selection. She has run one of the largest, most difficult prosecutorial offices in the country for fifteen years . . . with great distinction, community support, and no questions about her ethical standards and professionalism."

Clinton asked whether Graham knew of any skeletons in Reno's closet. Graham said she was "beyond reproach."

"Would it be better if she had some federal experience?" Clinton asked. "Probably," Graham said, but he added that since her job required her to work with the DEA, FBI, U.S. Customs Service, and other agencies in the vice president's task force, as well as the U.S. Attorney's Office, she had extensive knowledge of federal law enforcement.

Clinton said that he would "probably be asking Janet to come to Washington."

As soon as their conversation ended, Graham checked his pocket notebook for the phone number of Reno's sister Maggy in Stuart. When he had spoken to Reno on Friday about other matters, she had told him she planned to spend the weekend at Maggy's house, where she would sprawl on the floor to play with her grand-niece Kymberly.

Graham called Reno at 11:55 P.M. to deliver the news: She could expect an invitation to the White House the next day. Reno was "very happy and appreciative. And anxious to get that telephone call," Graham said.

"Never did I dream that this would happen," Reno told her sister and brother-in-law. She could barely sleep.

When Reno got to the office the next morning, her staff noted her particularly good humor. She kept her news under wraps for a while—it was far too early to raise hopes—but finally, she asked Rundle and a few other close aides, "What would you think if I became attorney general?"

Graham's news hadn't been a complete bolt from the blue. Just two days after her mother died, Reno had gotten a call from a member of the Clinton transition team asking if she would be interested in an appointment at the Justice Department. The office of attorney general was not mentioned.

When that call came, Janet was home taking a nap. "Oh, shit," she said groggily, when Maggy awakened her to ask if she wanted to take the call. A pause. "Mother would like that, wouldn't she?"

Reno expressed interest. Later that day, December 23, Clinton announced Baird as his nominee. Weeks passed, and Reno heard nothing more. She didn't discuss it, but Rundle and other friends sensed Reno was "disappointed."

Any disappointment was forgotten when White House counsel Bernard Nussbaum called late Monday morning to invite Reno to Washington. Nussbaum told her to bring background information, so she grabbed copies of her most recent tax returns. Reno booked her own late-afternoon flight to National Airport (a coach-class ticket, charged to her personal credit card) and debated what else to take with her. In her excitement, she hadn't asked how long she should expect to stay, and she later said she almost ran out of clean clothes.

She called Maggy and brother Bob to alert them that the FBI likely would be visiting. And then she phoned a half-dozen or so friends to ask if she could give their names as references—"so long as it wouldn't be too much trouble."

One of those she called was Gene Miller, a *Miami Herald* editor and an old friend of the family. She sounded excited, he recalled, but not overwhelmed. He made her laugh: "If they want someone to vouch that you haven't had a maid clean your house in at least twenty years, I'm your man."

While Reno made her preparations, the White House screening process kicked into high gear. The first round of quick inquiries strengthened her chances. Fellow prosecutors, lawyers, and political sources in South Florida praised her intelligence, her high ethical standards, and her tough-love approach. At the end of the day, one White House aide referred to Reno as "the first among equals."

News about Reno's trip leaked out of her Miami office late Monday. Sources on Capitol Hill confirmed that she had arrived in Washington, and the *Miami Herald* headlined a front page story on Tuesday, "Reno High on List for Attorney General."

Reno checked into the Washington Marriott on Twenty-second Street N.W., six blocks from the White House, where the Clinton staff had reserved a room for her.

On Tuesday morning, February 9, Reno was picked up in a government car and driven down Pennsylvania Avenue to the White House compound, which contains several buildings in addition to the White House itself. She was escorted into the Old Executive Office Building. It was her first visit to the White House.

Reno met with Lanny J. Davis, a lawyer with the well-connected Washington firm of Patton, Boggs & Blow and one of the campaign supporters recruited by the Clinton White House to screen candidates for top appointments.

Davis and Reno were joined by White House deputy counsel Vince Foster, the lawyer from Little Rock who had been Clinton's childhood friend and remained one of the president's closest confidants. Halfway through the interview, Foster excused himself. Reno worried that she might have blundered. But Foster had dashed out to call his boss, Bernie Nussbaum, with barely contained excitement. "I think we've got a live one," he said.

Foster was reassuring when he returned. Reno had cleared a major hurdle. She would next meet with assistants gathering still more background material on her.

The staff investigators—lawyers and accountants—asked "everything under the sun. They told me to give them my life history. I had written notes, and I just talked to them," Reno said. "They were very gracious inquisitors. Their job was to find out everything negative about me, and they told me that up front. I told them I understood."

They wanted her bank records. They wanted to know about her family, her education, her career, her politics, her elections, her philosophy, and her position on issues like the death penalty and abortion.

Reno's responses vaulted her over another hurdle and on Tuesday evening, she was told that her next meeting was with Clinton. She sat down to wait in the counsel's office suite. The minutes stretched to more than an hour and the always punctual Reno fidgeted as she waited for the inevitably tardy president.

When she was finally introduced to Clinton by Foster, the president soon put her at ease. They talked for ninety minutes in the Oval Office, formality and reserve giving way to enthusiasm and familiarity. He asked about her family, her work, her vision of justice.

She told how Jane built their homestead, and shared other stories about her family. Clinton warmed quickly to this straightforward, earnest woman, chuckling over some tales, moved by others.

They talked about issues; she warned him that she had enforced the death penalty but was personally opposed to it. Clinton stated emphatically that he wanted an attorney general who could provide independent legal advice, without regard to political considerations. He would expect recommendations on judicial candidates and other appointees without a litmus test on abortion or any other issue.

"I'm looking for excellence and diversity and judicial temperament," he told her. Reno pledged her best effort.

Reno found the president "one of the most intelligent, caring, warm, and informed people" she'd ever met. Said Clinton: "I admired her from the moment I met her."

After the meeting, Reno was asked to stay over at least one more day to respond to increasingly detailed questions from White House investigators. Reno's assistants in Miami faxed case summaries and grand jury reports and sent other background materials, including personal banking records, by air express. After unexpected revelations forced Clinton to abandon Baird and Wood, the investigators determined to leave no stone unturned in this probe. Reno found herself explaining her prosecution strategies in cop-shooting cases; how she decided which cases warranted the death penalty; her dealings with state and federal law-enforcement agencies; and her role in grand jury investigations on public-policy issues.

An overnight audit was performed of her personal finances. She found herself explaining such details as the $6,826.72 bequest she had just received from the estate of an old family friend, Margaret "Peggy" Ewell, the childless widow of a tile maker who had been one of her mother's tutors when building the house and, later, her brothers' scoutmaster. Reno used some of the bequest to pay for her Washington plane ticket and hotel expenses and to purchase some winter clothes, figuring that the Ewells would have enjoyed her sudden success.

Meanwhile, the national media had discovered Reno. Reporters were roiling the waters in Washington and Miami as they sought information about Reno and her chances of winning the nomination.

Dozens of reporters called the state attorney's office and Reno's family, friends, and former law partners. Out-of-town papers called the *Miami Herald,* seeking background and photographs. Washington and New York correspondents flew to Miami to look into her record.

In response to journalists' requests, aides to Senator Edward Kennedy, the Massachusetts Democrat who sits on the Judiciary Committee, asked Bob Graham's office for background. But Graham's office was being moved from the Dirksen Building to the Hart Building, and his files were inaccessible. Kennedy's aides had to turn to a Republican, Florida Senator Connie Mack, for information.

Under White House orders, Reno avoided the press. The Secret Service shuttled her back and forth to the White House in a nondescript sedan. When she set out Wednesday on a personal errand, she saw a television crew staking out the front of her hotel. Reno turned back and asked Sandy D'Alemberte to buy pantyhose for her.

Propitiously, D'Alemberte, the immediate past president of the American Bar Association, had stopped in Washington on Monday on his way home from an ABA meeting in Boston. He'd gotten Reno's message that she intended to use him as a reference. When he heard that Reno was due at the White House Tuesday, D'Alemberte decided to stay a day to wish Reno well and perhaps take her to dinner to help relieve the tension.

But as the excitement mounted, Reno asked D'Alemberte to stay on. He checked into the Marriott, and from his room and borrowed offices, he spent the week acting as Reno's press agent and lobbyist, providing background, steering questions to friendly sources, and arranging endorsements.

Among friends, D'Alemberte, who had been dean at Florida State University's law school, had made little secret of his ambition to snare himself a top Justice Department post in the new administration. He had his eye on the post of solicitor general, the lawyer who represents the government before the Supreme Court. In December and January, he interviewed with the Clinton transition team and agreed to a preliminary screening of his background.

But he put those hopes aside to campaign for Reno. He knew full well that two people from the same city and with ties to the same law firm would not be selected for sensitive jobs in the same department. "Janet so deserves this chance," D'Alemberte said. "She is one of the best people I've ever worked with . . . and she's the best-qualified person they've had on the list so far."

U.S. Representative Harry Johnston, a Democrat from West Palm Beach and longtime friend of D'Alemberte, had been pushing for his appointment. As a former president of the state senate, Johnston also had known Reno for years. She had been his Dade County campaign chairman when Johnston made an unsuccessful bid for governor in 1986.

Privately, Johnston thought D'Alemberte, with his national recognition through the ABA, had a better shot than Reno of winning a top Justice appointment. "Someone called me from Tallahassee over the weekend and told me I should jump on the bandwagon for Janet. But I didn't take it that seriously, and I said I was still supporting Sandy," Johnston said. "Then that first day Janet went to the White House, Sandy called and said, 'This could happen. Help her, by all means.' "

Reno was clearly moving closer to nomination on Wednesday, when White House investigators called her most outspoken political opponents.

Jose Garcia-Pedrosa, the former Miami city attorney whose unsuccessful 1984 campaign against Reno scrambled notions about ethnic politics in Dade County, said the researchers were "looking for land mines. They told me they wanted to get them before they read about them in tomorrow's *Washington Post*."

But Garcia-Pedrosa detonated no explosions. Although he had criticized Reno's record in the past, he said running the Justice Department "goes right to her strengths, her character, her integrity, and it stays away from her weaknesses." He considered those weaknesses to be in day-to-day administrative skills and case management, tasks that would fall to lower-level officials at the Justice Department.

Investigators also questioned Reno's 1988 challenger, Jack Thompson, the lawyer and antipornography crusader from Coral Gables. During that campaign, he had claimed that Reno was a lesbian who looked the other way when it came to pornography and failed to pursue smut with sufficient vigor. Thompson raised his allegations with the White House investigators but admitted he had no proof against Reno's denials. His charges were dubbed "a nonstarter" at the White House.

Thompson nonetheless cranked up his fax machine and peppered the media with his accusations. At Wednesday's daily White House press briefing, a reporter asked whether the question of sexual orientation was usually raised during the screening process for high-level appointments. Clinton spokesman George Stephanopoulos said, "I don't believe it is asked. . . . The president is against discrimination of all kinds."

The investigators pressed Reno's friends for any liabilities on her part, prodding fellow Democrats to help Clinton avoid embarrassment. When one friend delicately referred to Thompson and the messy 1988 race, the White House interviewer dismissed it: "We've been all through that stuff."

An elected official who has known Reno for nearly twenty years told a White House lawyer, "I know of no rumored woman lovers; I know of several rumored man lovers." The investigator didn't ask for any names.

Florida Attorney General Bob Butterworth, a former sheriff and judge in Broward County, just north of Miami, was pushed to identify "any minuses" but could name none. He had no doubt Reno was up to the job. "Look at what has happened in Dade County in the last fifteen years and the changes and problems she has had to confront. No state attorney or district attorney in the country has had to undergo what she has undergone."

Butterworth, who had occasionally seen Reno's ire when they tangled over a policy question, offered this bottom-line assessment:

"Janet Reno's not Mother Teresa, but she's probably the closest you'll get."

When his opinion was sought, Sam Dash, the former Watergate prosecutor who teaches law at Georgetown University, said Clinton "would get someone who's very sensitive to American prosecutors and what they want. But she cares about things that go way beyond just sending people away" to prison.

Because she was an innovator willing to look beyond lock-'em-up rhetoric to politically difficult solutions, Dash added, "It would take some courage to select her."

Reno began picking up endorsements from several national groups, ranging from the National District Attorneys Association, to which she belonged, to the National Organization for Women (NOW). She was not a NOW member, but NOW's national president, Patricia Ireland, was a lawyer from South Dade who had known Reno for years.

Ireland initially worried that Reno wouldn't be viewed on her merits but would be seen simply as the punchline to the Jay Lenoesque joke making the rounds in Washington: After Baird and Wood, the next nominee for attorney general would have to be a woman who is unmarried and childless and keeps a messy house.

"Her personal status has nothing to do with her record," Ireland said. "Janet is extraordinarily competent and extraordinarily bright. But as important is her experience and her ability to function in a political world. She has been able to manage that tumultuous office through many a crisis."

Ireland, who had quit her job as a stewardess to go to law school, said she and Reno worked and played together in the Women's Law League in the late 1960s and early 1970s. "Probably low on the White House list but high on mine is that she's a terrific softball player."

By late Wednesday, when his investigators had failed to turn up any red flags, Clinton began discussing Reno with Hillary and his top aides. He consulted chief of staff Mack McLarty, counsel Nussbaum, deputy counsel Foster, personnel chief Lindsey, and his old friend and golfing buddy Webster Hubbell, who had served as Clinton's eyes and ears at the Justice Department since the transition.

Hubbell didn't have to remind anyone of the urgency of getting an attorney general in place. The department was facing a series of problems, including the question of replacing FBI director William Sessions. In the waning days of the Bush administration, Sessions had been accused of embarrassing ethical lapses.

Clinton, a Yale-trained lawyer who had served as state attorney general in Arkansas, put reform of the Justice Department as a top personal priority. He was anxious to reverse the conservative political course set by William French Smith, Edwin Meese, Richard Thornburgh, and William Barr, the Reagan-Bush attorneys general.

The consensus: Reno would be a confirmable choice. She was bright, articulate, and direct, if a bit quirky. She had proven she could answer difficult questions. Politically, her record as a tough-minded prosecutor should please conservatives, while her commitment to fairness and her willingness to pursue innovative programs should satisfy moderates and liberals.

It came down to a question of whether the president himself was comfortable with someone from outside his personal Yale Law School–Renaissance Weekend–Democratic Leadership Council network. Clinton told his aides he was inclined to go with Reno but would sleep on it. The only message to reach Reno was a request to stay on another day. But that cheered her and her supporters. "I have a cause for optimism on this one," D'Alemberte said late Wednesday.

Early Thursday, February 11, Nussbaum called Reno at her hotel to say he and Foster would pick her up at two P.M., and that a press conference was being scheduled for four-thirty. To avoid any embarrassing leaks, the White House was staying mum. Nussbaum didn't make a job offer, but he suggested that Reno "write something out just in case," she said later.

Nor did Clinton ever officially pop the question. When she finally saw the president at the White House that afternoon, Reno said, "He didn't really say, 'Do you want it?' It was just, 'Well, are you ready to go?'"

She showed the remarks she had drafted to Nussbaum and others, and no one changed a word.

Late in the afternoon, for the benefit of the cameras, Clinton and Reno strode shoulder-to-shoulder from the Oval Office to the Rose Garden along the promenade that runs along the south side of the White House. Entering the Garden through a pair of French doors, Clinton and Reno approached a microphone stand on a small stage. Though a bright day, it was chilly, in the high forties, but neither Clinton nor Vice President Al Gore, who joined them on the platform, wore a topcoat. Nor did Reno, who didn't own one. She wore a blue-black plaid suit with three-quarter-length sleeves that accentuated her long arms.

It was the twenty-second day of the new administration. With his smug smile, Clinton looked like a struggling high schooler who has finally passed a difficult test. Wider smiles on the faces of Gore and senior White House staffers suggested immense relief.

Reno's smile was nervous as she glanced around the audience. Directly in front were several dozen reporters seated on folding chairs. Behind them were three decks of cameras behind ropes, flanked by more reporters to her left and White House staffers to her right. Reno twisted the cards on which she'd scribbled her lines.

Looking up, across the White House's south lawn, she caught her breath when she saw the Washington Monument, radiant in the brilliant sunshine. Her thoughts turned to how proud her parents would have been.

In announcing the final member of his cabinet, Clinton made his expectations clear. "No agency needs an injection of innovative spirit more than the Department of Justice. Americans demand and deserve freedom from crime in their homes, in their schools, and on the streets. Talking tough is easy. Actually getting results is much more difficult and much more rare."

After "years of political controversy and abuse, the Justice Department also needs an attorney general who will bring a sense of pride, integrity, and new energy to that agency," he said.

Reno was the one to do it, he declared. "She is a front-line crime fighter and a caring public servant. She has devoted her life to making her community safer, keeping children out of trouble, reducing domestic violence, and helping families.

"She has truly put people first."

Reno, who had been calming her nerves by taking deep breaths during Clinton's remarks, stepped quickly to the mike at Clinton's invitation. She brushed a shock of hair away from her eyes and prodded her eyeglasses back up her nose.

"I'm humbled by the honor that President Clinton has done me in nominating me as attorney general of the United States, and I'm going to do my very best to deserve his confidence," Reno said. Her nerves didn't show, although she chose to read the remarks she had written that morning "just in case" rather than speak extemporaneously, as was her custom.

In six simply worded paragraphs, she set out for Clinton and the nation a quintessentially Reno agenda that invoked integrity, children, the environment, civil rights, and protection against violent crime:

"I will work with the thousands of outstanding career lawyers in the Department of Justice to establish integrity, excellence, and professionalism as the hallmark of that department." She said she wanted "to form a true partnership between federal, state, and local law-enforcement agencies."

Of violent criminals, including drug traffickers, she said she would work for "strict and certain sentences that put them away and keep them away. At the same time, I want to work with all concerned to make sure that we have diversion programs for the nonviolent offenders that will enable them to get off to a fresh and to a new start."

She hoped "to end racial, ethnic, and gender discrimination and disharmony in America by enforcing the laws to ensure equal opportunity for all Americans, and by restoring civil rights enforcement as one of the top priorities of the department.

"I would like to use the law of this land to do everything I possibly can to protect America's children from abuse and violence, and to give each of them an opportunity to grow to be strong, healthy, and self-sufficient citizens of this country.

"I want to do what I can to make the law make sense to citizens and businesses alike. I want the laws to assist them in worthwhile endeavors, not to stand as bureaucratic obstacles.

"This is a beautiful country. Each of us has a favorite river, a mountain, just a patch of sky for some of us. I want to use the law to make sure that the waters, the land, and the skies of this nation are protected."

She closed with a touching reference to Miami: "I come from a thousand miles away. I have worked on the streets and in the neighborhoods of a city I love, a city that reflects the diversity, the dreams, and the problems of America. I have felt the impact of federal policies firsthand and watched how they touched, oftentimes adversely, the lives of the people. I want to use the knowledge gained in this experience to help President Clinton put the people first.

"Thank you, Mr. President."

So pleased was Clinton that he stayed at the mike to take twenty-two questions from the press. He deferred to Reno to let her answer about half.

He admitted that he had wanted a woman for the post, but insisted that he had "never felt hamstrung by any commitment" and had "seriously considered at least four men for this job. I really concluded, in the end, that Janet Reno would be best."

He said he had initially overlooked Reno because she was a state prosecutor, not a U.S. attorney. "But the more I dug into it, and the more I talked to people about it, the more I realized that you couldn't be the state's attorney in Dade County for fifteen years without having an enormous exposure to a wide range of issues that the Justice Department deals with."

Asked if he foresaw any issues "that might complicate the confirmation process," Clinton replied, "I don't. . . . I can tell you this: If you've been a prosecutor for fifteen years, this is like you've been a governor for twelve years. Not every call you make is right. Not every case you pursue is won. But I can tell you I have been literally amazed at the quality of recommendations that I have received for Janet Reno."

He also noted that he and Gore had carried Dade County over George Bush and Dan Quayle by just four percentage points, while she won her last election by forty points.

"If you know anything about Dade County, you know that is a truly astonishing accomplishment," he said.

In her first exposure to the Washington press corps, Reno fielded the questions in her usual manner: short, to-the-point responses. No speculation. "No comment" if she didn't know or wasn't ready to say.

She'd been coached to soft-pedal controversial issues by White House lawyers and image makers who sought to moderate her blunt-spoken ways in advance of the Senate confirmation hearings. But when asked her position on abortion, her answer was classic Reno: "I'm pro-choice." Nor did she mince words on the death penalty, stating her personal opposition, but adding that she would fully enforce laws that required capital punishment.

She said she had never hired an illegal immigrant and had paid all her taxes. "Certainly, in the vetting process in the last week, we've covered everything," she said with sufficient exasperation to draw a laugh from Clinton, Gore, and the White House staff.

Asked if she minded taking the job with "the perception of a pledge" from Clinton that it would go to a woman, Reno said simply: "I think this is one of the greatest challenges that any lawyer could have in America."

Clinton was delighted. Zoë Baird and Kimba Wood were behind him. His last cabinet member would soon be in place. He could move on. One reporter asked, "Mr. President, this has been a frustrating process for you in some ways. If you had it to do all over again, what would you do differently?"

Without a moment's hesitation, he said, "Oh, I would have called Janet Reno on November the fifth."

When the press conference ended, Clinton escorted Reno across the lawn toward the Oval Office. On the steps just outside, he introduced her to other cabinet members who had gathered for the announcement. The group broke into laughter when Donna Shalala, the secretary of Health and Human Services, who is more than a foot shorter than Reno, moved to a higher step before shaking hands.

In contrast to earlier nominations in which Mrs. Clinton was deeply involved, Hillary spoke to Reno only after her selection was announced. In the Oval Office, and out of view of the press, Mrs. Clinton welcomed Reno and said she was "delighted" with the nomination.

Some congressional reaction was quick. An ebullient Senator Graham called the process "a circuitous route to find clearly the best person for the job."

Biden and other members of the Judiciary Committee welcomed the nomination and promised to begin confirmation hearings as soon as they received background materials from the White House.

A staff aide to a senior Judiciary Committee Democrat was matter-of-fact. He said Reno had "put in a great performance" but committed a faux pas.

Nowhere in her prepared remarks, in which she promised to

work with other federal agencies, Justice Department career employees, and state and local law-enforcement officials, did she refer to Congress.

"That kind of thing gets noticed up here," he sniffed. "But she'll learn."

CHAPTER 7

Confirmation

Noisy, crowded, boisterous—it was a typical Reno party. More than fifty family members and close friends gathered on Sunday, March 7, in the furnished apartment Reno had just rented in downtown Washington. They were in the mood to celebrate. Only the youngest Reno sibling, Mark, was not there, as he was now a commercial ship captain and at sea.

Pots of soup and chili bubbled on the stove. Drinks and toasts gave way to reminiscences and family stories. In the coming week, everyone was confident, Janet Reno would make history.

After the festivities, Janny, Maggy, and Bobby wanted to clear their heads with some fresh air, so they set out on a late-night stroll to soak up the history that is unique to the nation's capital. Their three-mile circuit took them past the Washington Monument, the Jefferson Memorial, the Vietnam Memorial, and the Lincoln Memorial. Like millions of visitors before them, they were stirred that tranquil evening by the dramatically lit statues of a resolute Jefferson and a pensive Lincoln, and the more than fifty-eight thousand names etched in the black marble wall that is the Vietnam War Memorial.

The three felt safe, even at the late hour. "Who's going to pick on a pair of six-foot-tall women?" Janet joked. She and Maggy were bundled against the chill in layers of sweaters under raincoats, two Floridians clearly out of their element.

In fact, the Renos attracted no attention at all on their walk. Maggy and Bobby advised Janet to enjoy her anonymity while she could. Once she won confirmation—that morning's newspapers had predicted a cakewalk—she would soon be trailing aides, FBI agents, and reporters everywhere she went.

The Renos stopped to rest on the steps of the Lincoln Memorial, at the foot of the Mall. Before them rose the Washington Monument, its image mirrored in the Reflecting Pool. At the far end of the Mall, they could see the splendid Capitol dome.

They talked about the past and the future, sharing patriotic thoughts inspired by the dramatic vista before them. Each wondered aloud how Jane and Henry would have reacted to this scene, this night, and Janet's imminent Senate hearing. Then they envisioned the possibilities. "Just imagine . . . " one would start, another would finish the thought, and they roared with laughter.

It was a break Reno sorely needed. She had been probed, prodded, and prepped virtually nonstop for weeks. Her head was crammed with material from thick briefing books and sessions with experts. She admitted to a touch of homesickness for Florida's sunny warmth.

"I will never forget those February days," Reno said later. She had fielded the expected questions: " 'What are you going to do about minimum mandatories?' 'How are you going to handle your personal opposition to the death penalty?' 'What about career criminals?' 'How are you going to handle Bureau of Prisons issues?' "

But there were other matters—details of pending investigations, controversial cases left over from the Bush era, and national security concerns—she had not been briefed on. Until confirmed, and accorded the proper security clearance, she would not have access to such sensitive matters.

The White House staff "shook their heads at me and looked at me almost pityingly and said, 'You just don't know what you're in for yet. There is a whole realm of issues that you haven't even begun to consider.' "

Reno had been home to Miami just once before the confirmation process began, for five days. She returned immediately after Clinton announced her nomination so she could speak to her employees in the state attorney's office. She also needed to pack up more clothes and other necessities, and to make temporary arrangements for her office and house.

When Reno landed in Miami, the local press was waiting at the airport. In contrast to the crowd of Washington journalists she had faced the day before, the reporters who rushed toward her on the concourse were familiar to her, and she felt more comfortable with them.

But she also had been warned that every word she uttered would be studied more closely than ever before. So she was miffed when she got hit again with the question about her sexual orientation inspired by Jack Thompson. Reno kept her cool, smiled ruefully, and referred to herself as "an old maid who prefers men."

Her confidence shone when she was asked whether she could handle the job of attorney general. Yes, she said, thanks to the training she had received in Miami. She would draw on her experience with urban problems, including riots, to develop "national policies that I hope can be effective for local government."

When she got to her cramped offices on the sixth floor of the Metro Justice Building, she was welcomed like a general bearing the laurels of victory earned in a far-off war. Employees who had worked with her for years cried and cheered. A switchboard operator called the mood "happy and sad, because we hate to see her go."

Reno, who had been sucking lozenges to soothe her weary throat, did her best to be heard. Tears brimming in her own eyes, she told the assembled staff that her nomination "is a tribute not just to me, but to every single one of you."

She shook hands, accepted hugs, kissed cheeks, and traded reminiscences into the evening. So as not to jinx her chances of winning confirmation, she decided not to remove any mementos from her office just yet, not even her favorite plaque, a cross-stitch of an Adlai Stevenson quotation: "The burdens of the office stagger the imagination and convert vanity to prayer."

She spent most of the weekend trying to pack, but the phone rang incessantly, late into the night. Family and friends, political supporters, reporters and job seekers, and people she didn't know called to offer congratulations. That's what happens when the president of the United States announces on national television that your home phone number is listed, which is just what Clinton had done in the Rose Garden press conference.

When she returned to Washington on Wednesday, February 17, Reno brought with her from Miami her own small team to provide moral and logistical support.

Old friend John Edward Smith was designated to provide personal background information. He could relay requests to his wife, Sara, a longtime confidante of Reno's who had helped care for Jane in her final months. Sara knew the family tree, had spent hours at the Reno house, and could put her hands on just about anything in minutes.

A trusted assistant from the state attorney's office, Trudy Novicki, came along to coordinate research into cases Reno had handled that could be of interest to inquisitive senators.

Smith and Novicki moved into the venerable Hotel Washington, just around the corner from the White House. They were instructed to direct any calls, especially those from reporters, to Ricki Seidman, who worked in the White House press office.

Reno moved in temporarily with a cousin in suburban Maryland, where she could avoid reporters and have some privacy. But she was rarely there, as her preparations for the confirmation hearings immediately went into high gear.

"I would pick her up every day to take her downtown, but she wanted to be dropped off a ways away from the Old Executive Office Building so she could walk a few blocks," said Bettina Dudley, her former college roommate. "In retrospect, it had to be stressful, but we would just talk as we usually do."

Dudley and others began scouting furnished apartments in downtown Washington; Reno decided she wanted to live within walking distance of the Justice Department. By Saturday, they had

located a furnished one-bedroom apartment in the newly reno-
vated Lansburgh Building, just off Pennsylvania Avenue, where
rents start at $1,045 a month. The landlord agreed to rent to Reno
on a weekly basis, pending her confirmation.

Reno's primary White House handlers were Ron Klain and Ricki
Seidman. Klain, from the White House general counsel's office,
and Seidman, who handled legal affairs in the press office, were
bright, intense, and overworked lawyers. Both had long experience
as staffers on Capitol Hill, which made them invaluable guides for
nominees crossing the political minefield otherwise known as the
Senate confirmation process.

Seidman had made her reputation as legal director of People
for the American Way, a liberal lobbying organization founded by
television producer Norman Lear, which had worked to derail
Judge Robert Bork's nomination for the Supreme Court in 1987.
Seidman then joined Senator Edward Kennedy's staff, where she
helped convince Anita Hill to go public with her story of sexual
harassment by Clarence Thomas.

Klain served as chief counsel to the Senate Judiciary Committee
during the Hill-Thomas hearings. As one of the White House's associate counsels, he remained close to Senator Biden and kept in
contact with former colleagues on Capitol Hill.

The White House also recruited outside advisers led by Jamie
S. Gorelick, the Washington lawyer who had been on some early
lists for attorney general. She joined the administration as general
counsel at the Pentagon, but she later went to work for Reno at
Justice.

The nominee began "courtesy calls" on Capitol Hill on February
18, drawing stares, smiles, and the occasional smattering of applause as she headed for Senator Graham's suite in the Hart Senate
Office Building. As her home state's senior senator, Reno's old

friend would ceremoniously escort her to Judiciary Chairman Biden's office.

Reno's real escort was Klain. He made sure she visited the offices of all eighteen members of the Judiciary Committee and other key lawmakers. Some private meetings were barely more than a handshake and a how-do-you-do; others required Reno to listen patiently to laundry lists of complaints and concerns, including South Dakota Republican Larry Pressler's lecture about problems on Indian reservations.

With the slightest touch of sarcasm in her voice, Reno later referred to these rounds as "an excellent introduction to the ways of Washington." But she said they helped put her at ease when she went before the committee as a whole.

Knowing well the behind-the-scenes influence of legislative staffers, Klain also arranged a two-hour, informal lunch where Reno could schmooze with legal-affairs aides to members of the Judiciary Committee over sandwiches, sodas, and potato chips. She scored points by recalling her own days as a committee staff director in Tallahassee and expressing her appreciation for how tough it could be serving the strong egos of politicians. She took questions and showed her sense of humor. One aide described her as "warm" and "homespun."

During her first afternoon on the Hill, Reno and Graham chatted excitedly as they strolled from the Hart Building to the Russell House Office Building. Klain trailed a few paces behind. They boarded a "Senators Only" elevator, where Graham introduced Reno to New Mexico Senator Pete Domenici. While pumping her hand, he unexpectedly went on record as her first Republican supporter.

"The sooner you get to work over there, the better. From what I've read, you'll have my vote," Domenici said. It left Klain with a wide grin.

A few minutes later, before their private seventy-five-minute chat, Biden appeared briefly with Reno in his conference room for the traditional "photo op" of the committee chairman greeting the important nominee and her home-state senator, posing in front of an ornate marble mantelpiece. Biden was one of the few lawmakers equal to Reno in height, but both stood three inches taller than Graham. Reno stood between the senators, her peach-colored wool suit providing a dramatic contrast to their somber business suits.

As strobes flashed and twenty-six different cameras zoomed in, Biden smiled his trademark bared-teeth grin. Reno looked nervous and smiled tightly. Except for the moment when she shook Biden's hand, she kept her hands anchored behind her back. As instructed, she kept her comments short and simple, saying she looked forward to getting to know the senators. Typically, Biden offered a wisecrack. "The only criticism I have so far is that everybody likes her," he said, "and that always makes me worry."

In fact, Reno did have some opponents, some old, some new, who were already setting in motion their strategy to defeat her. For the Free Congress Foundation, a conservative organization whose advisers included former Judge Robert Bork, that strategy called for undercutting Reno's credibility with moderate and right-of-center lawmakers. Leading the effort was a young lawyer named Thomas L. Jipping, head of the Foundation's Center for Law & Democracy. Jipping's track record included coordinating the conservative lobbying effort on behalf of Clarence Thomas a year earlier.

In one attack, Jipping claimed Reno was guilty of "rampant abuse of Dade County's grand jury" to advance her political agenda. He cited a 1992 grand jury report that looked at regulation of firearms. The grand jury noted that, between 1985 and 1992, Dade County averaged 474 deaths a year due to firearms versus 337 a year due to automobile accidents. The jury's final report stated, "The only difference in our minds between being hit by a vehicle traveling at sixty miles an hour and being shot with a firearm is that one is more likely to survive the vehicular accident."

Under Florida law, grand juries are permitted to pursue public-safety issues and make recommendations for changes in the law. This jury called for statewide gun registration, licensing of firearm owners (including a proficiency test), and special liability insurance coverage for guns.

Jipping claimed that Reno, through her assistants, had misused her prosecutorial powers and steered the grand jury to its conclusions. Reno had favored some forms of gun control for years. In 1988 and 1989, she supported the "Cool It, Florida" petition drive that forced a state referendum on a five-day cool-off period for handgun purchases.

Assistant State Attorney Katherine Fernandez Rundle, who presented cases before the grand jury, denied that Reno had steered the grand jury's conclusions. "A grand jury has eighteen independent minds. They read, they have their own opinions, and they represent the community," she said.

If Reno had hoped the grand jury report would lead to legislation imposing tighter controls on handguns, she was in for a disappointment. In Miami, where drug-related violence had become a daily occurrence, the report got brief media coverage but not much more. In Tallahassee, where conservative legislators dominated, it was barely noticed.

The Center for Law & Democracy also circulated postnomination articles from the *Miami Herald* showing that Reno's office had the second-highest acquittal rate for felony trials in the state.

Figures collected by the Office of the State Courts Administrator from all twenty court circuits found that from 1989 through 1991, Reno's office lost nearly 40 percent of its felony cases, more than all but the Broward County state attorney's office, which lost 42.2 percent. The statewide average was 30.2 percent. The Orange County prosecutor lost just 19 percent.

But Reno aides and supporters—including some criminal defense lawyers—were quick to point out that Dade County suffered a much higher rate of serious crime, saw far more arrests, and generated the most complex cases in the state. Only a small percentage of those arrested on felony charges get to trial, which is the lengthiest and costliest way to resolve cases. Nor did Reno shy away from letting difficult cases go to trial, which underscored her confidence in her attorneys. Greater use of plea bargaining (Reno settled only 55 percent of all felony cases through pleas or diversion into pretrial programs, compared with a 64 percent statewide average) could have improved her conviction rate.

"A credit to Janet Reno is that she never really cared about those statistics," said Richard Sharpstein, a former assistant state attorney who became a top defense lawyer. "If she thought a case should be tried, if she thought there was probable cause, she never really cared that it was an absolute winner. She would let the people decide."

At her confirmation hearing, Reno offered her own statistics: For all cases handled by her office, both felonies and misdemeanors, "If you consider pleas, convictions and successful diversions, we are successful in 89.9 percent of the cases compared to the statewide (average of) 86.7 percent of cases."

Longtime Reno adversary, self-styled antismut crusader Jack Thompson continued his attempts to discredit Reno, sending fax messages to journalists and calling radio talk shows to announce his willingness to travel to Washington to testify against Reno. Some national reporters profiling Reno used a critical quote or two from Thompson, but their newspapers shied away from his more outrageous and unprovable claim that she was a lesbian.

Thompson got support from Andy Martin, a Republican gadfly from Palm Beach and a perpetual—and perpetually unsuccessful—candidate for political office in Florida. Martin was then running for governor and spearheading a petition drive calling for a referendum that would ban any law extending civil-rights protections to Floridians based on their sexual orientation.

The *New York Times* quoted Martin's characterization of Reno as "a high priestess of political correctness" who would pander to groups like the National Organization for Women. Encouraged by the attention he received, he staged a press conference on Saturday, February 13, at the Palm Beach post office—the nearest federal facility—to demand that Reno "make a full disclosure of her sexual orientation and views on gay rights in the U.S. military." He simply ignored her "old maid" comment made the day before at Miami International Airport.

Two days later, Thompson and Martin picked up an unexpected ally in a radical gay-rights group with a decidedly divergent viewpoint. A small group of demonstrators from Queer Nation appeared on the sidewalk in front of the Justice Department to demand that Reno "come out of the closet" as a model for young gays and lesbians. "Obviously, our motives are different," organizer Margaret Cantrell said, referring to Thompson and Martin and their tirades. "We think being gay's a wonderful thing."

The press ignored the event after Cantrell, a Washington schoolteacher, admitted she had no proof that Reno was anything other than heterosexual. "I can't give you one hundred percent proof. I haven't slept with the woman. I don't have photos. And I don't have the names of anyone who's slept with her." But she claimed that, in Florida, "Everybody knows it. It's generally accepted. It's common knowledge."

Cantrell complained that the media had "an impossibly high standard" of proof before it would publish or broadcast such charges. Queer Nation had earlier claimed to have "outted" another unmarried Clinton cabinet member, Health and Human Services Secretary Donna Shalala. After Shalala denied that she was a lesbian, the story died.

Maggy confronted the rumors about Janet head-on: "Is she a lesbian? No. Has she given up love for her career? Bullshit.

"We Renos don't bother messing with people we're not madly in love with. She just hasn't met anybody she's fallen madly in love with. It was sheer luck I met my husband."

Potentially more ominous for Reno were allegations that she had been stopped several times for drunk driving and had used her position to avoid arrest. Jipping's tracks were evident when that unsubstantiated rumor was shot down, as were those of a lobbyist for the National Rifle Association, whose deep pockets and populist power were legendary in Washington.

Dave Gibbons would eventually leave his job as an NRA lob-byist after revelations about his role in spreading the rumor. Officially, the NRA opposed Reno on the basis of her support for handgun control. In an alert mailed to members days after her nomination, the NRA called Reno "a hard-core anti-gun zealot, and she is sure to continue her gun-banning crusade once she is confirmed."

The rumor circulated among Senate staffers and then raced up Pennsylvania Avenue to the White House. It was promptly dismissed by Reno, who said critics like Thompson had circulated such "garbage" for years. Klain sent word back to Capitol Hill to ignore it.

But Senator Trent Lott, the wily Mississippi Republican who was the GOP's point man on Clinton nominees, fanned the flames during a February 28 appearance on CBS-TV's "Face the Nation." Lott was asked about rumors that "derogatory personal information" was coming forward about Reno.

Lott replied that "very derogatory" articles in the *Miami Herald* had raised some questions, adding, "They are of concern to us, but at this point, they are allegations and nothing more." Neither Lott nor the interviewer identified the allegations. The *Herald* had published no story about drunk-driving rumors.

Senate Majority Leader George Mitchell, a Democrat from Maine who followed Lott on the program, was astonished by the Republican's remarks. "I do not know anything about it," he said sharply and indicated he planned to ask Lott for his information.

Later that week, *Roll Call,* a feisty insiders' tabloid newspaper that covers Capitol Hill, broke the story of the whisper campaign against Reno on its front page. It identified two primary sources of the drunk-driving rumors as Gibbons and Jipping, who had met with a group of Republican senators' staffers shortly after Reno's nomination. Following that meeting, Republican senators had asked the FBI to pursue the drunk-driving allegations.

Although Gibbons's boss at the NRA, Legislative Affairs Director James Jay Baker, insisted his group had only offered information about Reno's record on gun issues, both Gibbons and Jipping admitted passing on the drunk-driving rumors to Senate staff.

An angry Reno wanted to personally denounce the rumors, but Seidman and others convinced her to stay above the fray. "How would it look to have the attorney general–designate stoop to their level?" one White House adviser said.

Instead, friends and White House officials put out the word that she vehemently denied any drunk-driving incidents. She did acknowledge "a couple of traffic stops" over the years, but neither involved alcohol or drugs. In one instance, she had a broken taillight; in the other, she hadn't come to a complete stop at a stop sign.

With encouragement from the White House, Senator David Pryor, a Democrat from Clinton's home state of Arkansas, condemned Jipping's Free Congress Foundation on the Senate floor. He suggested that as an "educational organization" with tax-exempt status, the foundation might be violating the law with its lobbying activities. "Since that is the case, what is the Free Congress Foundation doing raising unsubstantiated allegations with the Senate Judiciary Committee concerning a presidential nominee?" Pryor asked.

Jipping responded with a yelp of anger. "Senator Pryor is trying to intimidate individuals and organizations from discussing matters of public concern," he said in a statement faxed to news organizations that afternoon. "This leads us to think that the Clinton administration knows something Americans do not about Janet Reno and is trying to keep anyone with important information silent."

Within days, the FBI background check of Reno found no credible evidence of drunk driving. Some Republican senators and their aides complained privately, and angrily, that they had been sent off on an embarrassing chase for nothing.

On the day Reno's Senate hearing opened, the NRA announced that Gibbons had quit. His boss called senators to tell them Gibbons "was acting as a free agent in this matter." But for the NRA, the damage was already done. The controversy over the false charges had undermined the NRA's opposition to Reno.

Jipping was not similarly chastised. In fact, he was asked to develop plans for the conservative movement's new National Empowerment Network, a cable-TV outreach effort. "I have nothing to apologize for," he said months later. "I would do it again." He noted that Pryor and others who condemned his tactics had been glad to get similar information about former Texas Senator John Tower that contributed to his defeat as President Bush's nominee as secretary of defense.

He claimed bitterly that he had been victimized because he had spoken to the *Roll Call* reporter "off the record," meaning he wasn't to have been identified as a source of the Reno rumors.

Aside from the plots and schemes that entertain Capitol Hill, the rest of the nation was warming to a refreshingly different presidential nominee. This was no rich corporate attorney but a woman who had coped with a colorful, outspoken family; faced down drug lords and street punks; and maintained a square-jawed integrity that seemed decidedly inspirational. In the constellation of media celebrities, Reno's star was soaring.

For Reno, prepping for the Senate hearing brought back memories of cramming for the bar exam. She was given thick briefing books, and Gorelick and Klain assembled volunteer experts to coach her on federal issues with which she wasn't familiar.

Some fields of law within the Justice Department's purview, like antitrust, Reno admitted she had rarely thought about since law school. There wasn't time for a refresher course. To avoid embarrassing mistakes before the Judiciary Committee, she and her advisers concluded that she would apologize for what she had forgotten, remind the senators that she'd been a busy state prosecutor for fifteen years, and promise to make it a priority to study up as quickly as possible. She also would say she would be naming well-recognized experts in each field as assistant attorneys general to oversee specialized divisions within the department.

Then, one coach advised, "shut up and wait for the next question."

Reno also met with Stuart Gerson, the Republican holdover who was acting as attorney general, as well as with Webb Hubbell and other Justice officials, to be briefed on other issues that might come up. Of pressing national concern was the bombing of the World Trade Center in New York City on February 26, a stunning and unprecedented act of terrorism on U.S. soil.

In addition, the Justice Department had just become involved in a tense standoff with a little-known religious cult outside Waco, Texas, that started February 28 with a botched raid. The Bureau of Alcohol, Tobacco and Firearms, a Treasury Department agency, had been trying to serve a warrant when a gun battle left four ATF agents dead and sixteen wounded. FBI hostage negotiators were called in and the FBI, a branch of the Justice Department, took on official responsibility the next day. No one could predict how long the situation might last or how it might end.

On such controversies as the Waco standoff or the fate of embattled FBI Director William Sessions, who continued to resist calls for his resignation, it was decided that Reno should avoid taking positions. She could say she needed time to thoroughly examine the situation. She also could beg off because, as a nominee, she didn't have access to sensitive data and secret files, especially about national security matters.

Dress rehearsal demanded two moot court–style practice sessions staged in a large conference room in the Old Executive Office Building. Reno sat at a table facing her inquisitors, bereft of her briefing books and note-filled yellow legal pads. White House lawyers fired questions, she riposted, then Klain, Seidman, and others dissected her responses.

If she talked too long, they cut her off. If she wandered, they steered her back to the point. Their mantra: Avoid controversy whenever possible. Edging toward exhaustion, Reno chafed at some orders. If asked, she wasn't going to hide her support for a woman's right to choose abortion or her opposition to the death penalty. She would heed their advice where she could.

Ultimately, it was the handlers who gave in. Her unadorned,

unaffected, plain-speaking self just might be the ticket. "She'll do great," Klain predicted.

Meanwhile, additional case summaries and biographical materials were flown up from Florida, checked and double-checked, then handed over for Judiciary Committee review. A lengthy committee questionnaire, which included a personal financial-disclosure statement, had to be completed.

Many nominees are shocked and angry to discover they must reveal all their assets and liabilities, then calculate a net worth. Not Reno. For fifteen years, she had complied with Florida law, which demanded that she file detailed annual disclosure statements.

Reno reported that she earned $91,122.53 in 1992 from the state of Florida. The house and land she inherited from her mother in December were worth $342,946, her Chevrolet sedan, $15,000. She had $13,133 in cash on hand or in the bank. Her state pension plan, valued at $154,751, would pay her $4,038.18 a month if she retired at sixty-two. She had a life insurance policy with a current cash value of $31,963. She listed no debts, not even a credit card balance. So her net worth was $557,793.

Among the three-inch-thick stack of supporting documents that Reno handed in were reports from the American Bar Association task forces on which she served; five past speeches, including one to the International Society of Barristers; three sets of testimony on drugs and crime she had given to congressional committees, including Senate Judiciary; a half-dozen law review articles and newspaper columns she had written; and the chapter on prosecuting she had written for a 1984 book on female lawyers.

The Judiciary Committee questionnaire asked whether Reno belonged to any clubs or organizations that discriminate on the basis of race, gender, or religion. Such memberships, especially in country clubs that have lily-white, all-Christian rosters, can mean trouble for nominees.

Reno responded: "I have been a member of the National Society of the Daughters of the American Revolution [DAR] Coral Gables chapter since 1964. I have heard some concern that the Society might have discriminated, but upon checking several years ago and today, I have been told that the Society does not discriminate."

Reno had joined the DAR at the insistence of her maternal grandmother, Daisy Sloan Hunter Wood, who had proudly traced her ancestry to Henry Hunter, a Revolutionary War fighter from Mecklenburg County, North Carolina.

Biden set the Judiciary Committee hearings for Tuesday, March 9, and Wednesday, March 10. Reno's guests began arriving in Washington the preceding weekend. With the fifty or so family members, including second and third cousins, and a platoon of friends from Florida, New York, California, and Maine, Reno was amassing an impressive cheering squad.

They camped out in more than a dozen locations: hotels, the homes of cousins and old college roommates, Janet's one-bedroom apartment, and another, larger apartment in the same building that was borrowed for the week. Adults slept on couches, kids on floors. "It was exciting, like a big family reunion," said cousin Sally Wood Winslow. Throughout the week, "there was an overwhelming sense of her wanting to include the entire family, and we all felt included, like her partners."

Though their partying ran late on Sunday and Monday nights, family members ordered Janet to bed shortly after ten on the eve of her hearing. "The candidate ought to get some sleep," Maggy declared.

About eleven-thirty, when the small group that was sleeping in Janet's living room returned to her apartment, they shushed each other and prepared to tiptoe in. But when they opened the door, the lights were blazing and Janet was pacing about in a bath-robe. She was aglow.

As she was trying to get to sleep, she explained, the phone had rung. "This is Bill. You nervous?" The president of the United

States had called to wish her good luck. She repeated his opening line several times, trying to mimic his accent. It took more than an hour for everyone to settle down and for Reno to get back to bed.

Just after nine on the morning of Tuesday, March 9, the audience in Room 106 of the Dirksen Senate Office Building burst into applause when Reno entered the ornate chamber. People who lined the walls craned their necks to see her as she worked her way to the witness table. It wasn't hard; Reno, wearing her best dark-blue dress, towered over nearly everyone in the room.

Chairman Biden rapped his gavel and asked the audience to "please refrain from any show of emotion." Nonetheless, it took several minutes for the hubbub to die down.

Reno took her seat at the witness table and carefully folded her hands. Camera shutters clattered and motor drives buzzed like amplified mosquitoes as photographers recorded the moment. Biden asked those who clustered near Reno's table to stay down so the committee members could see the nominee.

Biden triggered a big laugh when he sighed loudly, "You have no idea how happy we are to see you here today. You have none."

It wasn't just Zoë Baird's hearing that had given the committee members heartburn. Fourteen members of the committee were veterans of the Clarence Thomas–Anita Hill confrontation and had suffered its profound political fallout.

Since then, two newly elected female senators, Democrats Dianne Feinstein of California and Carol Moseley-Braun of Illinois, had been recruited for the committee. Feinstein had been the first committee member to endorse Reno.

Biden had been badly burned by the Hill-Thomas fiasco. He had worked hard for respect since he was first elected in 1972, just meeting the Senate's minimum age requirement before being sworn in. He proved to be the comeback kid, surviving both a charge of plagiarism that forced his withdrawal from the 1988 presidential race and a near-fatal brain aneurysm.

Now fifty-one, Biden relished the opportunity offered by high-profile hearings to show off his mastery of issues like crime and drug policies. Though decidedly taken with his own opinions, he could demonstrate his painstaking fairness and impartiality.

His official welcoming remarks to Reno mentioned the broad range of issues to be faced by the next attorney general, from juvenile crime to international terrorism, and stressed the hope that the Clinton administration and the Democrat-controlled Congress could show a new spirit of cooperation on criminal-justice issues. He praised Reno's record in Miami.

Orrin Hatch of Utah was new to his role as top-ranking Republican on the committee. A senator since 1977, the stiffly formal Mormon had moved into the seat next to Biden just ten weeks earlier when Strom Thurmond, the venerable South Carolinian, relinquished the position to gain a more powerful position on the Armed Services Committee.

Hatch set the tone for the rest of the Reno hearing. Under a prearranged deal with Biden, it was Hatch, one of Clarence Thomas's chief defenders, who officially announced that the rumors and allegations against Reno had been dismissed by the FBI and committee investigators. But Hatch went on, calling the charges "unfair" and "scurrilous." His voice quaked.

"This hate-mongering campaign is despicable in my eyes. And until now, no one has been immune to specious charges that serve only to degrade and discourage. No one, not Democrats, not Republicans. Hate crosses both party lines, it's no respecter of persons."

With that out of the way, Biden called on three Florida lawmakers to formally introduce Reno to the committee. They spoke less than twenty-five minutes in all and turned out to be the only witnesses to testify at Reno's hearing. Since no allegations of wrongdoing could be substantiated, Biden, with the acquiescence of the Republicans, sought no testimony from Reno's critics.

Senator Graham introduced her "with absolute confidence that she is superbly qualified to be our nation's lawyer. She is an innovative, straightforward, and brilliant prosecutor—tough, firm, and honest . . .

"Janet also has the human touch. She is sensitive, responsive, and accessible. Have you ever known the chief prosecutor in a major metropolitan area of high local and international crime to have a published home telephone number? That is Janet Reno."

Graham referred to Reno as "part social worker, part crime fighter" and concluded, "The people of Florida have greatly benefited from her courage and leadership. We are proud to share her with America."

Senator Connie Mack was next, and in somewhat of an awkward spot. Mack simply didn't know Reno, except by reputation. He was a Republican, not a Democrat. A banker, not a lawyer. From the west coast of Florida, not the east. He had never served in Tallahassee. The grandson and namesake of the famous Philadelphia Athletics manager, Cornelius McGillicuddy Mack, had had no political experience when elected to the U.S. House in 1982. And Reno had supported Mack's Democratic opponent in his 1988 Senate race.

But it was clear she was headed toward confirmation, and Mack wanted to be part of the parade. So he attributed his accolades to "a number of individuals, Republicans and Democrats alike, whose opinions I greatly respect."

"The overwhelming opinion," Mack said, "is that Janet is a talented prosecutor who is tough on crime yet fair in the administration of justice. . . . By her ability to get things done and inspire those around her to reach their full potential, Janet epitomizes what a public servant ought to be."

Representative Carrie Meek, who knew Reno well, was up next. The first black elected to Congress from Florida since Reconstruction, Meek was an educator and a divorced grandmother who had served in the state legislature. She bore a grudge against the Judiciary Committee for its handling of Anita Hill, and if she hadn't been afraid of embarrassing Reno, she would have given the committee "a good, big piece of my mind," she said later. She limited herself to one subtle dig:

"The introduction of Janet Reno to you today, as I scan your faces, renews my faith in the process," Meek said. "It makes me know this process does work. And it works for a woman who has worked for years and years and years for everyone without regard to color or creed, sex or gender, or whatever. Janet Reno has been there."

Meek directed the committee to ignore the "outright lies" about Reno, dismissing them as "heifer dust."

That brought howls of laughter. "That's the best I've heard in a long time," Biden told Wyoming Senator Alan Simpson, legendary for his own colorful Western lingo.

The accolades finished, Reno pushed her glasses up her nose and adjusted the microphone to deliver her opening statement. She had it memorized, but she added some thoughts as she delivered it. Simple and straightforward, it took her less than ten minutes.

Reno recalled her parents, the family home, her life in Florida, and some of her priorities as a state prosecutor. The statement had touches of humility as well as flashes of indignation. She told of being denied a summer internship at a Miami law firm because of her gender—and then becoming a partner there fourteen years later. "I know what it's like to finally have opportunity."

Reno went on to spell out her agenda: "I'd like to use what I have learned in my community, in my background, and I want to remember it if you confirm me.

"I want to remember what I learned as a front-line prosecutor and join forces with state and federal law enforcement agencies around this nation in making sure we work together in the most effective manner possible, to use our resources as wisely as possible, to once and for all show that together we can do something about crime.

"I want to remember the splendid skies of the city I love, and the Everglades and the coral reefs that I've explored all my life, and I want to see that the laws of this country are enforced in every way possible to protect the environment.

"I want to remember what it was like on a Sunday night on several occasions to receive a call from a lady who had not received her child support for that month. She didn't know how she was going to pay the rent the next day, and she didn't know how she was going to care for her children.

"I want to remember her plight, and the plight of so many other children and families, and do everything I can to see that children in America are given an opportunity to grow as strong, constructive human beings.

"I want to remember what it was like not to be able to get a job because I was a woman, and I want to make civil rights enforcement one of the high priorities of the office and do everything I can to see that Americans have equal opportunity.

"I want to work with the dedicated men and women at the Department of Justice to establish as hallmarks of that department excellence, integrity, and professionalism. There is an inscription on the Department of Justice building which says, 'Justice in the life and conduct of the state is possible only as it first resides in the heart and souls of the citizens.'

"I want to remember the countless citizens who have touched my life over all these years, who believe so deeply and yearn so fiercely for justice. And I want to do everything I can, if you confirm me, to work with them as their lawyer to seek justice."

The statement was vintage Reno and pulled out all the emotional stops. Gorelick was crying when Reno finished, as were several of Reno's relatives. At the first break, Hatch walked over to Reno's family, offering effusive praise for their values. (By the time the hearings concluded, Maggy said later, he had shaken her hand eight times in two days.)

Biden paused to let Reno's poignant closing words resonate in the high-ceilinged room, then he began the questioning. It was clear from the outset that this would be a lovefest. Reno would not be challenged. Instead of probing the nominee's mind, motives, and qualifications for high office—the stated intent of such hearings—committee members would eschew dramatic confrontation for the opportunity to get their pet priorities on the record.

For her part, Reno proved the consummate politician, flattering every position and stirring up no controversies. Her White House advisers couldn't have been more delighted.

Biden asked if Reno would support his Violence Against

Women Act, which for two years had failed to win passage. Reno hedged, saying she wasn't familiar with the bill's fine points but pledging to examine it as "one of my first priorities." Biden pressed: "Based on what you know about the act, do you have any inclination at this point . . . ?"

"Senator, in my review of the legislation I will be very supportive, and I know the president will," Reno said.

Biden wouldn't let her off the hook quite so easily. The act would make gender-motivated crime a violation of federal civil-rights law, he said, although Chief Justice William Rehnquist had expressed concern about federalizing another section of the law.

Reno tried yet again. She told Biden his initiative was "very appropriate. There should be no distinction between gender-motivated crimes of that type and racially motivated crimes, and I would look forward to working with you on that effort."

It was Hatch's turn. And, though he had condemned the tactics of Thompson and others, he now pursed his lips and raised their underlying issue head-on. "Do you intend to continue the Justice Department's priority on the prosecution of obscenity in our society?"

Reno was prepared for this one. In less than a decade, she said, her office in Miami had prosecuted 146 cases under the Florida obscenity statutes. "Child exploitation is one of the major problems that we have tried to focus on," she said. "It is one of my highest priorities." That satisfied Hatch; he moved on.

And so it went for two days, each committee member angling for a second chance to speak with her before the television cameras.

Reno covered all the political bases. She referred repeatedly to her knowledge of big-city problems, yet assured senators from rural states that she could relate to farmers because her mother once planted an avocado grove. She didn't mention its abbreviated existence.

To a question from Ohio Democrat Howard Metzenbaum about cracking down on environmental crimes, Reno promised "an effective, vigorous, but fair environmental effort."

To Vermont Democrat Patrick Leahy's complaint about the use of civil forfeiture statutes to take the homes of small-time marijuana growers and other nonviolent offenders, Reno assured, "I think we can spell out guidelines that address that from a commonsense point of view, Senator."

To Illinois Democrat Paul Simon's admonition that the president consult more with Congress in making Supreme Court appointments, Reno offered, "I share your view of a wide-ranging, thoughtful search."

To Maine Republican William Cohen's query about her interpretation of legal provisions requiring the president to notify Congress when he engages in covert actions, Reno dodged, saying, "I have not had the opportunity" to study the issue.

On a few key issues, including calls for reform of the appeals process that delays the implementation of death sentences, Reno was sufficiently vague to satisfy both ends of the political spectrum. She told the conservative Strom Thurmond, of South Carolina, she favored strict limits on appeals in such cases to make punishment "swifter and surer." But she assured the liberal Metzenbaum that she wanted to guarantee competent counsel so the accused would have the best representation possible before being sent to death row.

She told Pennsylvania Republican Arlen Specter—as she had told many others during her career—that she had never seen research proving the death penalty was a deterrent to crime. But she then suggested that the death penalty, "carried out in a fair, reasoned way, without delay" might demonstrate deterrence "to everyone's satisfaction."

Asked by Hatch about her priorities in the war against drugs, Reno said, "I want to do more in terms of early intervention, but I do not want to relax the fight against drugs on our streets." She favored "vigorous enforcement against traffickers, against anybody who would deal in this human misery."

Reno even covered her geographical bases, pointing out to Feinstein that she had relatives in California and to Cohen, an uncle in Maine.

And she proved her stamina. Reno repeatedly turned down Biden's suggestions that she might like a break. Senators and spectators came and went; Reno stayed. (She once boasted that as chair of a governor's task force in 1990 she allowed just one brief recess during a public hearing that lasted nearly fourteen hours.)

When the hearing concluded, both Democrats and Republicans were delighted to be able to vote for a woman with a clean reputation and a tough law-and-order background. The committee voted 18 to 0 to recommend her approval to the full Senate, and the Republicans agreed to waive the normal ten-day wait between committee action and Senate debate.

The next day, March 11, senators lined up on the Senate floor to praise Reno while her crowd of family and friends watched from the gallery above. Following tradition, Reno did not attend herself, but she watched C-SPAN in her temporary office in the Old Executive Office Building, adjoining the White House.

Fourteen senators spoke; another twelve inserted statements of support into the Congressional Record. "I would respectfully suggest that President Clinton, albeit not the first time at bat, has hit a home run," Biden said.

The most unusual endorsement came from Senator Jesse Helms, the archconservative from North Carolina. He posed a series of questions to Hatch.

Helms: "This lady favors gun control, did she say that much?"

Hatch: "I believe that is correct."

Helms: "And she is against the death penalty . . . is that correct?"

Hatch: "She is against the death penalty. But she has been a very decent and honorable prosecutor who has enforced the death penalty better than one hundred times in her career down there. So she has abided by the law, regardless of whether she disagreed with it or not."

Helms: "She favors abortion? She is pro-choice, I will put it that way."

Hatch nodded.

Helms: "But I did like what she said when she was accused of something which I believe, and trust, was absurd in the nature of a rumor. She said something to the effect that she was an old maid. I have not heard that expression in a long time. And she lives with her mother, does she not?"

Hatch: "Her mother is deceased now. She lives in the family home."

Helms: "In any case, some of my friends have called and said, 'You must not vote for this lady.' I said, 'Why not?' And they said, 'She's pro-abortion.' I said, 'Well, do you think President Clinton is going to send up a nominee who is opposed to abortion?'

"I think this lady is absolutely honorable. . . . Now, I say to the senator from Utah, that counts with me. I can get along with people who disagree with me, just so long as they have character. And I believe Ms. Reno is a lady of character. Do you agree with that?"

Hatch: "I surely do. . . . I think she will set standards that will be long followed by others who may succeed her in the future."

Moments later, the full Senate confirmed her by a roll-call vote of 98 to 0. Reno's family and friends rushed out to a Capitol hallway, in a flurry of hugs, kisses, and tears. At the White House, staffers cheered and applauded Reno. She thanked them for their help.

"I'm elated," Clinton said with a broad smile during a photo opportunity with state legislators that afternoon. "That may be the only vote I carry 98 to 0 all year."

Reno was due to be sworn in the following week, but a snowstorm was heading toward Washington. With forecasters predicting it could turn into a major blizzard, and relatives and friends anxious about getting snowbound, the ceremony was quickly rescheduled for nine the next morning, Friday, March 12, 1993, in the Roosevelt Room of the White House.

Reno invited her exuberant contingent, and the White House guest list included Senate and House Judiciary Committee members, Nussbaum, Foster, Klain, Seidman, and others involved in the confirmation. Notably missing were Mrs. Clinton and Senator Graham, who were conducting a health-reform hearing in Tampa.

In opening remarks, the president said the hearing demonstrated Reno's "qualities of leadership and integrity, intelligence and humanity." And he told her, "You proved to the nation that you are a strong and independent person who will give me your best legal judgment—whether or not it's what I want to hear." After the laughter settled, Clinton added, "That is the condition upon which you accepted my nomination and the only kind of attorney general that I would want serving in this cabinet."

Just before Supreme Court Justice Byron White administered the oath of office, Reno poked her glasses up her nose and straightened her shoulders. She put her left hand on the Bible held by her niece and namesake and raised her right hand. Grinning with satisfaction, Clinton watched over her right shoulder as the nation's seventy-eighth attorney general, the first woman to hold the job, swore to preserve, protect, and defend the Constitution.

Clinton had been in office fifty-one days. Finally, his cabinet was complete.

That afternoon, Webb Hubbell found Reno in her new office at the Justice Department. He had been out of town when the ceremony had been quickly rescheduled and had missed the swearing-in. He got on the first plane to Washington and found Reno "ready to work," asking about pressing matters and seeking material to read over the weekend.

She also began a series of thank-you calls to her key supporters, including Hugh Rodham.

"I thought to myself, how great it is that we can be sure she will remain that kind of person, not too big or too important to pick up the telephone and call someone who had a small part to do with her success and say thanks," Rodham said of the phone call "I will forever keep in my memory."

Friday evening, at one final celebration with her family, Janet and Maggy got together to concoct a column for Bob, a columnist for *Newsday*. They suggested he might wish to tell the truth about his oldest sister:

"Reno talks about being a person of principle and keeping politics out of her office. But have you ever seen such a hack politician? Reno no more said where she stood than she flew to the moon! And she got Metzenbaum and Thurmond agreeing with her on the death penalty! She's just a wishy-washy political hack, nothing more."

The Renos convulsed in laughter. The Honorable Janet Reno, attorney general of the United States? Madam General? To them, she would be General Janny Baby.

When a twice-burned president found his straight-arrow, law-and-order attorney general, it seemed a match made in heaven. In a five-week campaign, the new general had clearly taken Capitol Hill. Janet Reno comfortably negotiated the often-treacherous political rapids of the confirmation process, demonstrating just the right mix of independence and loyalty, spunk and savvy. Expectations soared for her performance as the nation's first female attorney general.

PART FOUR

Taking Charge at Justice

CHAPTER 8

Siege at Waco

During the second weekend of March 1993, while FBI agents faced a third week standing vigil in Waco, a freak blizzard blanketed the eastern seaboard with snow. But duty called—public relations duty. So on her third day in office, Reno trudged to work, throwing her trusty raincoat over an old sweater and jeans, and pulling on loud argyle socks and her well-worn Everglades hiking boots. "They weren't meant for snow, but they served me well," she said.

Seeking maximum exposure, the White House had decided that Reno's first interviews as attorney general should be with *Parade* and *People* magazines and the irreverent *Washington Post* "Style" section, whose sometimes-biting personality profiles were read by most Washingtonians, from the lowliest Capitol Hill aides to the most venerable power brokers. Eager for a first crack at the new attorney general, reporters from the three publications also trudged that snowy Sunday to Reno's new office at the Justice Department. The White House got what it wanted, glowing portraits of a sometimes quirky but forceful agent of change. Tougher questions would come later.

Most Justice employees had to rely on the media for information about their new boss as Reno had decided to learn the agency's business before making her first speech to employees on April 6. She scheduled a round of meetings with acting division directors and other key personnel, toured the headquarters building, and burrowed through urgent piles of reading material.

But she did mingle with the staff at the end of her first week, when she went to lunch in the department's basement cafeteria. Her guest was Ricki Seidman, one of the White House aides who had guided her through confirmation. The worker bees in the lunchroom were abuzz, as were the reporters who had covered the Justice Department for years. No one could remember a similar scene.

Cafeteria management had declared Reno Appreciation Day. The regular menu had been dropped in favor of dishes like Key West Hot and Spicy Shrimp, Miami Seafood Jambalaya, and Coral Gables Fried Seafood Platter. Reno picked the jambalaya, hush puppies, and a carton of skim milk, then declined the cafeteria manager's offer to pick up the $4.52 tab. Eager to do something special for Reno, the manager slipped an orange onto the corner of her tray, but Reno left it there untouched. Bypassing the only table with a white tablecloth and a small "Reserved" sign, she and Seidman settled in at one of the plain, Formica-topped tables.

Fawning over celebrities, by Washington's unwritten rules, is déclassé. But Justice Department employees, like the rest of the nation, were fascinated by their new boss, and few could resist stealing glances at Reno as they waited politely for her to finish lunch. Then they began filing past her table, introducing themselves and shaking her hand. The boldest, a quartet of young attorneys from the Civil Rights Division, invited her to visit their offices. "I'd like very much to do that," she said earnestly.

As Reno worked her way to the exit, pumping hands as she moved, a half-dozen reporters approached. How did she want to be addressed? one asked. General? Ms. Reno? "Don't call me general. Generals don't belong in the law. Call me Ms. Reno or just Janet," she fairly snapped.

Months later, however, Justice staffers were still having trouble with the preferred form of address. On July 21, Reno's fifty-fifth birthday, at a late-afternoon surprise celebration in her office, there was an awkward pause during the singing of "Happy Birthday" when the revelers came to the honoree's name. Traditionalists stuck with "Dear Janet." The politically correct warbled "Dear Ms. Reno." Others adhered to the hard-line "Dear General."

Reno later said she learned that the title attorney general was first applied to the lawyer hired as in-house counsel to the British crown who handled general matters. It had nothing to do with the military and was hardly a title of much grandeur.

The imposing granite headquarters of the Department of Justice covers an entire block between Constitution and Pennsylvania Avenues and Ninth and Tenth Streets N.W. Authorized by Herbert Hoover in 1931, the building was a Works Progress Administration project that cost $12 million.

The inspiring words etched into its cornices set the Department apart from other federal buildings in downtown Washington. Reno would read them when she walked to work and especially admired the lines high above Ninth Street: "The common law is derived from the will of mankind, issuing from the people, framed by mutual confidence and sanctioned by the light of reason." She memorized the passage and frequently invoked it in speeches.

Colorful murals of heroically muscled laborers lend a Depression-era motif to the interior of the building, which was completed in 1934. Other murals, high above the fireplace and the walnut paneling in the vaulted conference room of the attorney general's fifth-floor office suite, symbolize *Justice Granted* and *Justice Denied.*

Reno noted that as visitors pass through the room to enter her small private office, they can see the mural of *Justice Granted,* which depicts a benevolent judge (Harlan Fisk Stone) in a black robe surrounded by satisfied supplicants. As they depart, however, visitors encounter *Justice Denied,* depicted as the grim reaper. Reno called it "one of the bleakest murals I have ever seen in all my life. I'm thinking about turning my office around so that we can assure people that we can achieve justice."

Only one of Reno's predecessors, Robert F. Kennedy, ranks among her political heroes. Bobby's huge desk had sat in the large conference room on the richly colored Oriental carpet that still covers the hardwood floor three decades later.

Kennedy had been known to grill hot dogs in the large fireplace, Reno would tell visitors. It's a wonder she hadn't been tempted to do some cooking herself. One of Reno's first official acts was to shut down the private dining room with its personal staff that sat at the north end of her office suite. She had been shocked to learn of its existence when, she reasoned, there was a perfectly good cafeteria right in the basement.

Reno turned the formally decorated dining room into a small conference room, and she occasionally has food brought in for working lunches. But she insists on paying for the meals out of her own pocket, even when an aide "catered" by buying a loaf of bread, a can of tuna fish, and a jar of mayonnaise. (Always a stickler about paying her own way, Reno keeps rolls of her own postage stamps in her office so secretaries won't use federal funds to mail her personal correspondence.)

The attorney general's private office reflects the essential Reno. Behind her desk, in a place of honor, she hung the cross-stitched dictum that had hung in her Miami office, "The burdens of the office stagger the imagination and convert vanity to prayer." Contrasting with the formal certificate of appreciation signed by the judges of Florida's Eleventh Judicial Circuit is a bright green egg-carton alligator—a gift from schoolchildren—and a woven creation known as a "dreamcatcher" that was given to her by a Native American tribe.

Over the fireplace hangs a portrait of a tousled Robert Kennedy walking on a New England beach, the collar of his jacket turned up against the wind, his hands deep in the pockets of his khakis. It had been moved to her office just before Reno arrived, and she likes the idea that "some kindred spirit" had rescued it from the exile to which it had been banished during the Republican hegemony.

A hidden stairway off a small sitting room in Reno's suite leads upstairs to a tiny hideaway for reading and resting. The sparsely furnished room offers a recliner chair, a daybed, a small

This, the earliest photo of Janet Reno from 1939, shows her getting an outdoor bath in a tin washtub. (© *The Miami Herald*)

Reno's father, Henry Olaf Reno, joined *The Miami Herald* in 1925 as a police reporter, a beat he would own for forty-three years. (© *The Miami Herald*)

Reno's mother, Jane Wood Reno, was also a journalist, alternating between *The Miami Herald* and *The Miami News.* Here, she testifies before the Kefauver Committee in 1955 at hearings to investigate baby-selling practices in Miami. (Photo by Mike Freeman © *The Miami Herald*)

Jane and Henry Reno see their daughter Janet, then thirteen years old, off to spend a year at school in Germany, where she lived with her uncle in the old Danube town of Regensburg. (© *The Miami Herald*)

From the *Cavaleon 1956,* the Coral Gables High School yearbook. The caption for Reno's senior year photo (left) read: "JANET RENO . . . debater and scholar. In both, extraordinary." (Photos by the Pilkington Studio, Coral Gables, Florida)

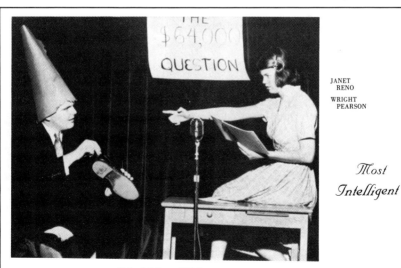

JANET
RENO

WRIGHT
PEARSON

Most
Intelligent

He thought he knew awl (?) the answers.

Janet Reno on the day in January 1978 when she was appointed Florida's first female state attorney. (Photo by Bob East © *The Miami Herald*)

Janet Reno chats with her prosecutors, shortly after taking office as state attorney in 1978. (Photo by John Pineda © *The Miami Herald*)

Janet Reno lived with her mother for forty-five years in the house Jane built and took care of her until her death in December 1992. Here they are shown together in 1984. (Photo by Albert Coya © *The Miami Herald*)

On election night in 1984 after defeating Jose Garcia-Pedrosa, Janet Reno shows her appreciation to some of her youngest supporters, Jamie and Stephanie Ramsey. (Photo by Carol Guzy © *The Miami Herald*)

President Bill Clinton points to a reporter during the brief question-and-answer period that followed his announcement, February 11, 1993, in the White House Rose Garden that he had nominated Janet Reno as his choice for attorney general. (Copyright © 1993, Martin H. Simon)

Janet Reno faces the Senate Judiciary Committee at her confirmation hearings in March 1993. (Photo by Patrice Gilbert)

Janet Reno holds her first press conference as attorney general, March 1993. (Photo by Patrice Gilbert)

Janet Reno relaxing on the porch of the quirky, slant-roofed bungalow her mother built that remains her true home. (Photo by David Walters © *The Miami Herald*)

bureau with a mirror, and a window air conditioner. Reno uses it infrequently.

Reno rises about six each morning to scan the newspapers, then, between seven and seven-thirty, she walks to work accompanied by two FBI agents. Her routine rarely varies: She reviews the day's schedule and attends to high-priority paperwork before beginning her meetings at eight-thirty or nine.

She spent much of her time in those first weeks simply trying to get a handle on the department, its divisions, and the people who work for her. It was a daunting task. She may have run the equivalent of the largest law firm in the South for fifteen years, but the state attorney's office never had more than 950 employees.

The Department of Justice was a hundred times as large, with more than 93,300 employees spread around the world and an $11.2 billion annual budget. Agencies within her vast domain include the familiar, such as the Bureau of Prisons, the FBI, the Immigration and Naturalization Service, and the U.S. Marshals Service, as well as the unfamiliar, like the Community Relations Service. In Washington, the department maintains its own shuttle bus system to serve the far-flung fiefdom of offices.

Within days of her swearing-in, Reno launched internal reviews of budgeting, purchasing, and hiring and promotion practices. Among other things, she wanted more data on the number of women and minorities in each division and agency. And she asked that the department's Equal Employment Opportunity office be given a more prominent berth at headquarters to demonstrate her commitment to greater diversity.

Reno found the range of responsibilities exciting. As a local prosecutor who saw convicted criminals winning early release from overcrowded prisons, she had often wished for control over the prisons. Now she had it.

She quickly ordered a study of the inmates in federal prisons: What charges put them there? Were they violent or not? Did they have drug or alcohol problems that weren't being treated?

Previously, Reno had been shocked to learn that 26 percent of the inmates enjoying bed and board from Uncle Sam were foreigners convicted for crimes committed in the United States. Couldn't they be sent home to serve their sentences? Reno wondered.

During her first month at the Justice Department, Reno developed her agenda by asking such questions. But persistent questioning didn't help avert her first major disaster. Indeed, some critics said that if she had questioned her advisers more tenaciously and skeptically, the tragedy at Waco might have been avoided.

Reno awakened at five on the morning of Monday, April 19, thinking about the children at the besieged Branch Davidian compound—the Ranch Apocalypse. Halfway across the country, final preparations were under way for the FBI raid she had authorized. She dressed quickly and hurried out.

It was her thirty-eighth day as attorney general. She would later call it the worst day of her life. It also was the day that made her a star.

She headed straight to the FBI's Strategic Information Operations Center on the fifth floor of the J. Edgar Hoover Building, a block north of Justice. From there, she could monitor events 1,450 miles away on the dusty prairie outside Waco, Texas. At the Center, there are the ubiquitous wall clocks tracking time zones around the globe, highly detailed maps, and several large-screen televisions. But specialized electronic monitoring equipment, along with high-powered computers and skilled analysts, do the Center's real work. A vaultlike door seals the Center off to unauthorized personnel.

Two days before, Reno had approved an FBI assault on the seventy-acre compound, where for fifty days the cult's messianic leader, David Koresh, had been barricaded. Koresh claimed to have ninety-four followers by his side, including two dozen minors, seventeen of them aged ten or younger.

It was a crisis that the Justice Department—and Reno—had inherited. The Bureau of Alcohol, Tobacco and Firearms (ATF), a division of the Treasury Department, had badly bungled its attempt to serve a search warrant at the compound on Sunday, February 28. Local police alerted the ATF to reports that the cult was stockpiling an arsenal of guns, ammunition, and explosives—including semiautomatic assault weapons illegally converted into automatics—for Koresh's predicted doomsday confrontation with nonbelievers.

The showdown was triggered by a loose-lipped TV cameraman, one of dozens of media people drawn to the scene by publicity-seeking law enforcement authorities. Unthinkingly, the cameraman told a postman about the ATF plan. The mail carrier turned out to be a cult member, and he rushed back to the compound with the news. Although an undercover agent inside the compound warned ATF officials that the Branch Davidians had been tipped off and were preparing for battle, the ATF decided to proceed. In the ensuing shootout that shocked the nation, four ATF agents were killed and sixteen were wounded; six cult members apparently died as well.

After the ATF's rout, President Clinton ordered the FBI to take over. He also approved deployment of the bureau's elite Hostage Rescue Team, which, unlike the ATF, included highly skilled hostage negotiators. Agents set up a defensive perimeter around the compound on Route 7 to keep back delivery people, journalists, and the curious.

The FBI quickly learned what they were dealing with in David Koresh, aka Vernon Howell. Wounded in the initial battle, he would rant and rave for hours about the evil of the government's agents and the world ending in a massive inferno.

Attempts by FBI negotiators to reason with Koresh over the telephone ended in rambling religious lectures. Though he was a high school dropout, the self-proclaimed prophet could dazzle the impressionable with his prodigious knowledge of the Bible. Once lured in, followers were kept in line by threats and violence. Koresh designated a group of top lieutenants as enforcers—the "Mighty

Men." His rules required cult members to report misbehavior by others or face punishment.

Koresh was subject to violent spells in which he threatened his followers and beat children until their buttocks were bruised and bloody. He claimed that, as the messiah, he had a divine right to have sex with every woman in the cult, including girls as young as twelve. He ordered married couples not to have sex, saying husbands should remain celibate while he used their wives. Indeed, he had fathered more than a dozen children with women other than his wife; some were as young as fourteen and sixteen.

Through a lawyer hired by his mother, Koresh promised to surrender when he was told by God that the time was right. But then he would stall, saying first that he would surrender after Passover, then that he wanted to finish a manuscript about the Seven Seals from the Book of Revelations. But he wasn't writing.

A growing contingent of media ringed the FBI encampment, portioning out regular updates to feed the public's insatiable curiosity about the standoff. Satellite dishes beamed their reports to the world beyond Texas, ratcheting up the tension as everyone waited for the payoff.

Official concern grew as agents gathered more intelligence. Departing cult members reported that sanitation was worsening, with garbage and human waste accumulating and the corpses of cult members killed in the initial shootout decaying. But they also said Koresh could hold out for weeks, even months, because he had stockpiles of food and water.

The FBI verified some of the reports using sophisticated eavesdropping technology. Agents sent in cartons of milk for the children and blank videotapes, asking Koresh to send out video proof that the children were healthy. He refused. But almost every object carried a hidden, wafer-thin electronic bugging device that allowed FBI agents to monitor some conversations inside the compound.

Agents waged psychological warfare, shutting off electricity and phone lines. At night, they aimed high-intensity lights at the compound to disrupt sleep. At all hours, grating music and deafening sounds from loudspeakers boomed across the prairie. The loudspeakers also broadcast appeals from cult members' relatives.

Armored military vehicles pulled cult members' cars and trucks away, including Koresh's beloved Camaro. No one budged.

Reno, sworn in on the twelfth day of the standoff, fretted about the children from the start. During almost-daily briefings on the situation, she pressed the FBI experts for as many details about the children as they could collect.

When the assault plan was presented to her during the second week of April, she grilled agents about tactical details, particularly whether the tear gas to be used would harm the children.

As state attorney, Reno had never been involved in a hostage situation and now felt intense pressure. Moreover, she barely knew those giving her advice—and what she knew of their leader, FBI Director William S. Sessions, she didn't like. Aside from darkening ethical clouds hanging over Sessions, he had further wounded his reputation by proposing to go to Waco to personally resolve the standoff. Reno's predecessor, Acting Attorney General Stuart Gerson, had ordered Sessions not to go. The image of Sessions riding into town like John Wayne would have been funny if his scheme wasn't so dangerous.

To reassure herself, Reno insisted on speaking to military experts who had reviewed the FBI's plan. She met with Dr. Harry Salem, a toxicologist at the army's Edgewood Arsenal. Salem told Reno that the tear gas the FBI planned to use, actually a fine CS2 powder to be sprayed with compressed air, would sting the eyes, nose, and throat. The powder would settle, but any movement would disperse it again, so it would outlast the use of a gas mask and cause temporary distress but no lasting damage. It also posed no danger of fire or explosion. Reno said later she found Salem to be "careful and scientific."

Reno also spoke directly with the past and present commanders of the army's crack Delta Force, General Peter Shoomacher and Colonel Jerry Boynkin. They pronounced the FBI's strategy sound, with one exception: They recommended blitzing the entire compound with tear gas at once, rather than introducing it gradually in one section at a time. But Reno stayed with the FBI plan, hoping to keep injuries to a minimum. If it took two or three days to get people safely out, she said, that was fine with her. She didn't want a "D-Day."

The Delta Force commanders did agree with the FBI about one crucial point: The Hostage Rescue Team, on full alert for more than a month, was in danger of wearing down. Sharpshooters would strain for hours at a stretch to keep watch through high-powered scopes. Other agents could spell the HRT, but they wouldn't be as skilled.

Reno agonized all week. She lay awake at night thinking, "Oh my God, what if he blows the place up? What if he holds children up in the windows and threatens to shoot them?" FBI officials told her that if Koresh wanted to blow up the compound, he could do it at any time. But they said the experts considered the likelihood of mass suicide "remote," based on Koresh's assurances to negotiators that it would violate his teachings.

It was later revealed that one FBI analyst had foreseen the possibility of mass suicide, but he was overruled by his superiors. His report never reached Reno.

She was alarmed when someone with the FBI—no one remembers who—said Koresh was continuing to "beat babies" during the standoff. She assumed the FBI's listening devices had picked up the information.

On Thursday, April 15, Reno had Associate Attorney General Webb Hubbell call Byron Sage, the FBI's lead negotiator in Waco. Sage said his team felt that negotiations had ground to a halt since the last cult member had left the compound on March 23.

But on Friday, Reno still wasn't ready to proceed. That frustrated those who were recommending an assault. Deputy Assistant Attorney General Mark Richard, who had twice been to Waco to review the scene for Reno, said he thought that to delay action would anger FBI agents to the point that they would prefer to withdraw.

But Richard said that Carl Stern, director of the Justice Department's public affairs office, worried about a public outcry over the use of tear gas. Stern compared it to Saddam Hussein's gassing of the Kurds in Iraq.

Later that day, though, Reno met again with Sessions and other top FBI officials and indicated she was more inclined to authorize the use of tear gas. She ruled out immediate action because hospital emergency rooms might not be able to handle large numbers of injured people on a weekend. Instead, she asked that the individual reports she had seen be compiled into a detailed written report outlining the situation in the compound, the conclusions of the FBI agents on the scene and outside experts, and the merits of using tear gas versus other options. She wanted it Saturday.

FBI officials and lawyers from the Terrorism and Violent Crimes Section at Justice worked virtually all night to assemble their evidence. A rough draft was ready when Reno convened a meeting in her fifth-floor conference room late Saturday afternoon. Those in the room included Hubbell, Richard, Stern, deputy chief of the Terrorism and Violent Crimes Section Mary Incontro, and Sessions and his two top assistants, Floyd Clarke and Larry Potts.

The meeting opened with a surprise. Overnight, Reno seemed to have made up her mind to proceed with the tear gas. She gave the new compilation only a cursory review, reading a chronology and scanning the various field reports and experts' opinions. "The documentation was there," she said later.

She announced that she was ready to authorize the plan for Monday. "Short of allowing David Koresh to go free, he is not coming out voluntarily," she said. Waiting would only make matters worse. "The circumstances are deteriorating. And we have to make a balanced judgment. Here are children whose health and safety are in danger."

She turned to operational details, saying she would let commanders on the scene execute the plan. But she insisted that they be given some basic "rules of engagement," two of which she dictated herself: FBI agents would not fire at the compound, even if fired upon. And if children were in any way threatened—held up at a window by a gun-toting cult member, or pushed out a door as a military vehicle approached—the agents would "back off."

The go-ahead was conveyed to the top FBI agent on the scene, Jeffrey Jamar, a burly special agent in charge of the San Antonio office. He ordered his team to begin final preparations. That included moving remaining vehicles away from the front of the main building at the compound on Sunday.

White House aides had been told by Hubbell and others that the FBI was proposing a tear-gas assault. On Sunday, Reno called President Clinton to tell him she had approved it. Their conversation lasted less than fifteen minutes.

She sketched out the plan and told him she had satisfied herself that it could work. She said she had consulted with military experts, as Clinton had ordered early in the standoff. She said the FBI agents would not return fire.

Clinton asked whether it wouldn't make sense to wait a while longer. She said she was convinced that as the situation dragged on, conditions continued to worsen and chances increased that the cultists would harm themselves. "Well, OK," he said.

Reno believed that the operation would proceed in an orderly fashion. On Sunday afternoon, she called Sam Dubbin, a lawyer and friend from Miami she had hired to join her top staff, and told him to report to her office at eight on Monday morning to get his first assignment.

Dubbin wouldn't get to see her until Tuesday.

Before dawn on Monday, April 19, Reno and others assembled at FBI headquarters to watch the attack unfold. They followed video from CNN but had an audio feed from the FBI's operations center in Waco, a specially outfitted recreational vehicle parked beside Route 7.

At five minutes before six (central time), an announcement blared from the loudspeakers around the compound: "This is not an assault! Do not fire! Come out now, and you will not be harmed!"

The announcement was followed by an attempt to reach Koresh by telephone. Koresh ripped the phone from the wall and had it tossed out the front door.

At 6:04 A.M., a modified tank moved in and used its boom to crash through a first-floor window in the compound's front wall. The CS2 "gas" was sprayed in through a hose attached to the boom. The cultists fired seventy-five to eighty rounds, but no one fired back. The waiting began.

At about nine, the tank moved in again and pounded through the wall and front door as it spewed more CS2. Agents thought that would give doubters inside an escape route. No one came out.

At a ten-thirty briefing in Waco, FBI spokesman Bob Ricks insisted, "Today's action is not an indication that our patience has run out. The action taken today was, we believe, the next logical step in a series of actions to bring this episode to a conclusion."

At about the same time, Reno had a brief conversation with Clinton to update him. The action seemed to be progressing according to plan, she said. Then, shortly after eleven, Reno left the FBI headquarters to make a previously scheduled speech to a judicial conference in Baltimore. She checked in from her dark-blue Lincoln as the FBI agent at the wheel drove north, only to be told there had been no response from Koresh.

Then, while she ate lunch, the armored vehicle moved in again, crushing much of the flimsy facade of the main building. More CS2 was sprayed, but the wind had kicked up. Gusts of nearly thirty miles per hour quickly dissipated the powder.

Shortly after the third attack, one of the fifteen FBI sharpshooters on the scene watched through a scope as a cult member wearing a gas mask cupped his hands around something and knelt down. A flame shot up. Soon, a dark spiral of smoke came from that corner and two other sections of the building, later discovered to have been soaked with kerosene and lamp oil. In just fifteen minutes, flames fed by the prairie winds engulfed the building.

There were no firefighters at the scene; Jamar and other FBI officials believed the cult's weapons, especially the fifty-caliber guns with a range of three thousand yards, posed too great a threat to local fire crews.

The initial reaction of those watching in Waco and Washington—and the rest of the nation—was stunned silence, then shock. "Oh my God, they're killing themselves!" the FBI's Ricks blurted in Waco. Clinton later recalled, "I was sick. I felt terrible."

Reno learned of the fire as she left the Baltimore hotel. Horrified, she called from her car to find out what had happened and ordered her driver to hurry back to Washington. She asked repeatedly whether any children were getting out.

Only nine cult members, all adults, fled the inferno, four of them badly burned. One man, with his clothes on fire, fell from the burning roof. FBI agents pulled off his flaming clothing as they dragged him to safety. A woman ran out, then turned to go back in. An agent leaped from his armored vehicle and pulled her clear. Authorities eventually found seventy-five bodies in the charred ruins, including twenty-five children.

A few minutes after five P.M., with plumes of smoke still rising from the ashes, Reno strode to the lectern in the Justice Department briefing room before a hastily assembled crowd of reporters and a bank of television cameras. One camera carried the scene live for CNN. Reno's jaw was set and her eyes narrowed. She kept her voice tight to rein in the emotion as she read a brief statement defending the operation.

"I think the FBI acted professionally and with remarkable restraint," she said. Her voice softened as she reached the conclusion: "These are the hardest decisions in the world to make. My heart goes out to the families of the agents killed and those injured, as well as to those children and the families of those who perished in the compound today. We must all reflect how we as a society can in the future prevent such a senseless, horrible, tragic loss of human life."

The first questioner asked whether Clinton had approved the

plan. Reno responded sharply. "I approved the plan, and I'm responsible for it. I advised the president, but I did not advise him as to the details." Then she misspoke, saying she hadn't spoken to the president all day, a gaffe that fueled the impression that she and the president were out of touch. Actually, she had updated him midmorning. But she hadn't spoken to him since the fire broke out.

The questions came quickly. She repeated her defense of the FBI and her ultimate responsibility. She offered no sugar coating.

"I think it's an extraordinarily tragic and horrible situation," she said, adding, "I have absolutely no doubt at all that the cult members set [the fires], based on all the information that has been furnished to me."

Asked once again whether Clinton had approved the plan, and whether she was attempting to distance him from the operation, Reno got angry. "I made the decisions. I'm accountable. The buck stops with me, and nobody ever accused me of running from a decision that I made based on the best information that I had."

People watching in Miami immediately recognized the Janet Reno of 1980. She was putting into practice the lessons she had learned after the McDuffie riots in Liberty City, Overtown, and Coconut Grove. As soon as the rioting ebbed, Reno took her medicine. She went to the African-American community, accepted responsibility, and listened to every gripe lodged against her.

Here, she was facing potential critics via the media. It was an act of fortitude rare in Washington and served to preempt much of the criticism she could have received.

Reno doesn't engage in self-analysis, at least not for public consumption. "I've not compared McDuffie to Waco," she said later. "In my mind, each case is a different situation."

Reno saw the reporters she faced that afternoon as "a bunch of hungry wolves" whose questions, at first, "came fast, furious, angry." But then something happened.

"About halfway through that press conference, I suddenly started looking at faces that had changed, and there was care, there was understanding, there was sensitivity, there was support, there was encouragement. The questions were still hard questions, but they weren't angry questions, because it was almost as if we had become together immersed in one horrible tragedy to which, in many cases, there were no answers. . . .

"For as long as I live and as I deal with the press, I will never forget that afternoon."

Or that evening. For nearly seven hours, she repeated her Trumanesque "the buck stops with me" line like a mantra on every television network. Her appearances included a previously scheduled hour on CNN's "Larry King Live." King, who knew Reno from his days as a radio talk show host in Miami, was the most sympathetic journalist she faced all day. He closed with, "Thanks, Janet. The first of many visits, I hope."

She finished the evening with her first appearance on ABC's "Nightline," where she embarrassed herself by mispronouncing host Ted Koppel's name. The notorious non–TV watcher called him "Mr. ko-PELL" instead of "Mr. COP-pull."

When told of her error during the first commercial break, Reno was mortified because Koppel had come into the "green room" before the program to introduce himself and to ask, "May I get you a cup of tea? And you need some lemon." But, she said, "I received the nicest letter from him later." Koppel wrote that he didn't mind if she had mispronounced his name, and he invited her back.

Koppel said some viewers appeared to have misunderstood his line of questioning that evening, but "she got it right away."

At one point during the show Koppel said, "Believe me, I ask this question with sympathy, but in other countries and in other governments, when a minister takes full responsibility for an unfortunate action, even if it was not entirely his or her fault, sometimes they resign."

Reno replied, "If that be the case, if that's what the president wants, I'm happy to do so. But I think in these situations, what's done is, if somebody makes the best judgments they can, if they review everything carefully, if they are accountable to the people, if they proceed in an open and accountable way, people will know what they have tried to do and the reason they have tried to do it."

During a press conference the next day, Clinton dismissed Koppel's question: "I was frankly—surprised would be a mild word—that anyone would suggest that the attorney general should resign because some religious fanatics murdered themselves."

It was the first defense of Reno directly from Clinton. His near-silence for the previous twenty-four hours had been deafening. In fact, all he had managed was a weak attempt to shift the blame. During a Monday morning photo session before the fire broke out, Clinton was asked about the FBI's assault. "I knew it was going to be done, but the decision was entirely hers," he said.

White House spokesman George Stephanopoulos also seemed to point the finger at Reno. Late Monday, he issued a two-paragraph statement in Clinton's name, saying the president was "deeply saddened by the loss of life" and "my thoughts and prayers are with the families of David Koresh's victims."

It went on: "The law enforcement agencies involved in the Waco siege recommended the course of action pursued today. The attorney general informed me of their analysis and judgment and recommended that we proceed with today's action given the risks of maintaining the previous policy indefinitely. I told the attorney general to do what she thought was right, and I stand by that decision."

In a cutthroat political town like Washington, where the perception of a fall from grace can quickly become reality, it appeared as though Reno had been abandoned by the White House.

It wasn't until after midnight, when Reno had turned in her stoic media performances, shouldered all the blame and appeared likely to survive the political fallout, that the president finally called her. Exhausted, she had returned to her apartment and dismissed her FBI escort. "It was twelve-twenty at night." Her voice breaks recalling that night. "I don't think I've ever been so . . . I guess lonely is the word."

The phone rang twice. "The first call I got was from my sister. She said, 'That-a-girl.' The second call I got was from the president of the United States, saying, 'That-a-girl.' "

Clinton said he told Reno "she had done a good job under tough circumstances and that she should get some sleep."

Clinton spoke publicly about Waco the next day, after a teacher-of-the-year award ceremony in the Rose Garden. Since the honoree was from Florida, the audience included a number of prominent Reno friends, among them Senator Bob Graham and state education commissioner Betty Castor.

Clinton described Koresh as "dangerous, irrational, and ultimately insane." He added: "He killed those he controlled, and he bears ultimate responsibility for the carnage that ensued."

During his phone conversation with Reno on Sunday when she presented the plan, Clinton said, "I asked the questions I thought it was appropriate for me to ask. I then told her to do what she thought was right, and I take full responsibility for the implementation of the decision."

The president said he had ordered full investigations of both the original ATF raid and the FBI's final assault, with independent experts reviewing the agencies' decision making. "We must review the past with an eye to the future."

And he endorsed Reno. Asked why he kept saying it was her decision, Clinton recalled the end of their Sunday afternoon conversation. "She might have made a decision to change her mind. I said, 'If you decide to go forward with this tomorrow, I will support you.' And I do support her. She is not ultimately responsible to the American people. I am. But I think she has conducted her duties in an appropriate fashion, and she has dealt with this situation, I think, as well as she could have."

That restored Reno's confidence. At eight Tuesday evening, she called Norman Early, president of the National Black Prosecutors Association, at his office in Denver and accepted an invitation to speak to the group in August.

Early had called Reno's office Monday morning, before the fire broke out in Waco. When he saw the events unfolding, he thought, "I probably will not hear back from her." But she called and told him, "Just tell me the date, the time, and the place, and I will be there."

Clinton's initial timidity earned him well-deserved reproof. The *Wall Street Journal,* in an editorial headlined "In Defense of Janet Reno," was the most pointed. "We suspect this Everglades native never misunderstood Tammy Wynette," said the *Journal.* "Yet the president's lack of grace in the face of the Waco tragedy raises anew issues about his instinct on matters of personal responsibility. And with these issues of character come issues of competence."

Some Republicans on Capitol Hill also criticized the president, along with Reno, for the whole operation. Senator Arlen Specter and others called for immediate hearings. But it was clear that some in Congress preferred to let the ashes cool first. On Wednesday, Senator Biden announced that he would let the investigations ordered by Clinton run their course before he scheduled any hearings.

On Thursday, April 22, Reno kept a previously scheduled appointment with the Senate Appropriations subcommittee that oversees the Justice Department's budget. It was a subdued session in one of the opulent, high-ceilinged meeting rooms on the first floor of the Capitol where Senate budget writers make billion-dollar decisions.

She was unprepared to do much more than sketch out some of her priorities, such as ending turf battles between federal agencies. "If we had approached World War II," she told committee members, "and Dwight Eisenhower had gone into Normandy with the fragmentation and the division that we have in terms of law enforcement, we wouldn't have been as successful."

Reno needn't have worried about not having final numbers

for the subcommittee. She was to discover that the budget discussion would drag on for another six months.

Waco bubbled to the surface as soon as the senators started their questions. But the courtly chairman of the subcommittee, South Carolina Democrat Ernest "Fritz" Hollings, made sure no one got too tough. He himself was extremely sympathetic, observing in his distinctive drawl, "With respect to fifty-one days, that was a gracious plenty of time" to wait for Koresh.

Reno told the senators, among them hard-nosed Texas Republican Phil Gramm, that she was anxious for the internal review to get under way. She hoped to find "improved, nonlethal means of ending something like this. I kept wishing that there was some magic weapon as we developed this plan."

Gramm expressed cautious support, and both Democrats and Republicans ended up complimenting Reno for shouldering the blame.

That afternoon, a visibly weary Reno hosted a long-scheduled reception for several hundred people in her office suite. It was a debut of sorts, the new attorney general presenting herself to justices of the Supreme Court and other judges, members of Congress, and lots of Washington lawyers.

Few members of the White House staff were there, because most were busy with the foreign heads of state attending the dedication of the U.S. Holocaust Memorial Museum. Reno stood for a couple of hours just inside the door of her conference room shaking hands and greeting people, as a long line snaked out in the hallway. To anyone who mentioned her post-Waco performance, Reno said a simple "Thank you."

(Among the visitors was Supreme Court Justice Byron White, who stopped to greet a short, elegantly dressed woman wearing oversized glasses, her dark hair neatly pulled back. She had been waiting in the line with several law clerks. "Ruth!" White said warmly, bending over to buss Ruth Bader Ginsburg on the cheek and exchange greetings with the highly regarded jurist who would soon replace him on the court.)

During the party, Reno encouraged visitors to wander into her private office, where guests admired the RFK portrait and her growing collection of mementos. People had been sending Reno gifts for weeks, ranging from books to a huge inflatable alligator complete with bright green scales. One group of guests marveled at her perfectly clear desktop—until someone leaned behind the desk to deposit a damp cocktail napkin in the wastebasket. Reno's paperwork, six thick piles, had been discreetly stacked on the floor.

Atop one pile was a stack of photocopied news clippings about Waco.

The second-guessing of the Waco operation continued for days. In a number of TV appearances, Texas lawyer Dick DeGuerin, who represented Koresh, criticized federal authorities for their lack of patience. He said they should have waited "as long as it took" for Koresh to surrender. And he pointed the finger at Washington, saying agents on the scene had told him, "We have as much time as it takes to end this without bloodshed."

On April 28, the House Judiciary Committee convened the first full-blown congressional hearing on Waco. Such hearings, it often seems, are designed to humble witnesses and inflate members of Congress. Indeed, Reno and the other witnesses—William Sessions and ATF Director Stephen E. Higgins—found themselves seated at a table as Judiciary Committee members looked down on them from their three-tiered dais, like gods perched on Olympus.

Chairman Jack Brooks, a seventy-year-old lawyer from Beaumont, Texas, and a forty-year veteran of Congress, lorded over the committee from top row center. Sometimes the shiny top of his bald, white-fringed head was all that could be seen. But Brooks couldn't be missed. His raspy twang, sharp wit, and impatience that verged on surliness, and the ever present scent of his smoldering cigars, commanded attention.

Waco wasn't in Brooks's district, but it was close enough. Besides, as chairman he could call a hearing any time, on virtually any subject he wanted.

He opened the hearing by declaring, "I don't relish playing

omniscient second-guesser when there are still facts to be ascertained and evidence to be adduced. Given the instant experts that pop up everywhere in the press, I may be in a distinct minority.

"What I care about is whether we have in place the capability and, yes, the creativity to deal with the increasingly disturbing situation of terrorism, whether in the high office towers of our urban centers or in small, entrenched pockets of alienated citizens who operate separate and apart from a larger society."

But some Republicans on the committee saw this not as a sociological exercise but as a chance to set up a partisan scrap. Texas Republican Lamar Smith and others accused Reno of protecting Clinton and failing to tell the whole story. Representative Carlos Moorhead, another Texan, asked whether cost had been a consideration, quoting an oft-repeated but erroneous estimate that the operation had cost a million dollars a day. (It was closer to half that.)

"Congressman, you don't consider dollars when you consider human lives, and that was not a factor that I considered at all," Reno replied.

Others were more realistic. Representative James Sensenbrenner, a senior Republican from Wisconsin, said Koresh, and Koresh alone, was responsible for the tragedy in the compound. "He was the one that brought them there, he was the one that kept them there, and he was the one that led them to their deaths in that fire. . . . Anybody that seriously says that the FBI or law enforcement was at fault really didn't know what was happening down there or cared not to listen."

By television news standards, Reno's three grueling hours of testimony before a dozen TV cameras yielded two memorable moments. In one, cameras captured a rare display of emotion as she confessed the lonely hours she had spent rehashing the tragedy in her mind; her eyes welled with tears and her voice cracked as she recalled the "That-a-girl" calls from her sister and the president.

The second was an angry confrontation that blew up in the face of Detroit Democrat John Conyers. A senior member of the Congressional Black Caucus, Conyers, a sixty-three-year-old lawyer, enjoyed being a rabble-rouser. A well-known publicity hound, he used his position as chairman of the Government Operations Committee to issue screaming press releases and stage showy hearings about bureaucratic bumbling.

Comparing Waco to previous showdowns with armed zealots, including the MOVE disaster in Philadelphia, the mass suicide in Jonestown, Guyana, and the Wounded Knee confrontation with Native Americans, Conyers asked, "When in God's name is the law enforcement at the federal level going to learn that these are very sensitive events, that you can't put barbed wire, guns, FBI, Secret Service around them, send in sound twenty-four hours a day and night, and then wonder why they do something unstable?"

He called the Waco fire "a profound disgrace to law enforcement in America." He snapped at Reno, "You did the right thing by offering to resign. You did exactly the right thing. I commend you for it." He told her, "I'd like you to know there is at least one member of Congress that isn't going to rationalize the deaths of two dozen children."

Reno, eyes flashing behind her oversized glasses, bit off every word as she spat out her response: "I haven't tried to rationalize the deaths of children, Congressman. I feel more strongly about it than you will ever know. But I have neither tried to rationalize the death of four ATF agents, and I will not walk away from a compound where ATF agents have been killed by people who knew they were agents. . . .

"But most of all, Congressman, I will not engage in recrimination. I will look to the future and try to learn everything I can from this situation to avoid tragedies such as this in the future."

Disregarding the signals, Conyers continued to bait Reno, dismissing her statement as "a nonresponsive answer." Reno leveled a steady gaze at her antagonist and challenged him, in effect, to step outside. She would meet him, she asserted, "anytime and anywhere" to respond to his questions.

From then on, Reno faced no challenges. Other panel members quickly disavowed Conyers's comments; one colleague apologized on behalf of the committee.

Within hours, Conyers's office was flooded with calls of protest. After watching how the confrontation played on the evening news,

Conyers decided to reposition himself. In a statement faxed to reporters, Conyers said his comments had been misconstrued, especially his reference to Reno's offer to resign.

"In no way am I calling for or seeking that resignation," he said. "The fact that we have an attorney general willing to take the heat for that decision is a breath of fresh air after a decade in which attorneys general sought to avoid accountability."

That evening, Reno kept a dinner appointment with visiting friends from Florida, including Lieutenant Governor Buddy MacKay. She took them to The Peasant, a Pennsylvania Avenue restaurant that had become her favorite, conveniently situated between her apartment and the Justice Department.

While the small group dined, patrons recognized the attorney general but ignored her, as decreed by Washington etiquette. Then, when Reno and her party got up to leave, one patron started to clap. In seconds, the whole restaurant joined in. People stood at their seats, dropping the linen napkins from their laps and applauding. "In all my years in Washington, I'd never seen anything like it," said Leslie Woolley, a veteran Capitol Hill aide dining at The Peasant with two friends.

Reno smiled, nodded, and gave a timid, self-conscious wave to acknowledge the applause as she went out the door. Outside, she briefly shook her head in amazement. "How about that?" she said, clearly touched.

Reno was hot, and Clinton and his image makers moved to capitalize on it. On Thursday, his symbolically significant one hundredth day in office, the president decided to join Reno in the media spotlight by visiting her at the Justice Department.

"When Janet Reno was confirmed, she said she never wanted to be called General, but only Janet. But somehow I feel I should call her General. She certainly seemed in command to me yesterday up on the Hill," he said, to cheers and applause from Justice Department employees.

The ostensible reason for Clinton's visit was to announce a series of appointments to Reno's staff, including that of assistant attorney general for civil rights, his old friend, Lani Guinier, a University of Pennsylvania law professor.

From the embers of Waco, Reno's phoenix rose. She was already a media phenom, but her take-charge stance had catapulted her to stardom. The headlines glowed:

"GUTS: Feisty Reno Defends Waco Decision"—*New York Daily News*

"Hurricane Reno an Improbable Superstar"—*USA Today*

"Reno's Popularity Rises from Ashes of Disaster"—*New York Times*

"General Reno Captures the Capital"—*Newsweek*

"STANDING TALL: The Capital Is All Agog at the New Attorney General's Outspoken Honesty"—*Time*

There were dissenters, but only a few. Mickey Kaus, in a *New Republic* column titled "Local Hero," asked,

> Am I alone in thinking there's something perverse, even a bit obscene, about the current lionization of Attorney General Janet Reno? . . . What exactly has Reno done to merit this glory? She made a disastrous decision that resulted in the loss of more than seventy lives. In a bizarre bit of political alchemy, this somehow protected her from suffering any of the consequences that normally attend disastrously handled responsibilities. Far from restoring accountability, Reno seems to have hit on the formula for avoiding it. Make a dreadful mistake? Go immediately on "Nightline." Say the buck stops with you. Recount in moving terms the agony of your decision. And watch your polls rise. Truman + "Donahue" = Absolution.
>
> Reno is an outsider who serves Washington's politic need to revolt against Washington politics.

Reno herself recoiled at the glowing media notices. She turned down dozens of interview requests, including a personal appeal from Jay Leno to appear on "The Tonight Show." And when she opened the *Washington Post* on July 1, she was aghast.

Cartoonist Garry Trudeau included Reno in that day's episode of his "Doonesbury" series. It featured a dream in which Joanie Caucus, a lawyer, had a visit from the ghost of a friend, Andy Lippincott, who had died of AIDS. Over coffee at one of their old haunts, they discussed Caucus's recent hiring at the Justice Department.

"So what do you think of your new job at Justice, Joanie?" Lippincott asked.

"I love it—especially working with my boss. Reno has this amazing command presence. She walks into a room, and she OWNS it," Caucus said.

"Man . . . she sounds pretty amazing," he replied.

"So," Joanie asked. "What's God like?"

"Similar deal," he said. "Remember what 'awesome' meant before it applied to pizza? That's him."

Reno was not amused. And she had a bully pulpit that day to lecture the press.

"I want to be myself, and it doesn't help to have something like 'Doonesbury' start the morning. I'm sure God is at this point very angry with Garry Trudeau," she declared in a speech at the National Press Club.

As is her habit, Reno wrote the speech herself after discussing ideas with aides, including Carl Stern, the lawyer and veteran NBC legal affairs correspondent hired by Reno as director of public affairs. But it was her decision to make the speech a pointed demand that the press quit mythologizing her.

Her emerging image as the eccentric character in the Clinton administration, and the very paradigm of principle, threatened to overshadow serious attention to her agenda, she asserted. In a fine piece of political strategy, Reno spoke to the media but aimed her remarks at her critics in the Clinton administration and on Capitol Hill. With her sermon to the press corps, she undercut any possibility of complaint from either source that she sought to upstage them by engendering press attention.

Reno was determined not to change her style to satisfy anyone's opinion. During the Press Club lunch, Reno grabbed her fried soft-shell crab, stuck it on a dinner roll, and ate it as a sandwich while other diners delicately dismembered their crabs with knife and fork.

"I know you," she told the overflow crowd in the National Press Club ballroom. "And I know that you care so passionately about your country, about your Constitution, about the First Amendment. But I know more than anything else, because I have known you, that you care passionately about the people of America and how we reach the solutions to the problems that we all face in this extraordinarily complex time."

So cover those issues, she said, and don't expect any more cooperation for fluff pieces or inside-baseball political stories. "I don't do spin," she proclaimed.

Nor would she retreat behind Washington doublespeak: "I want to try to use small, old words that everyone understands. I want to say 'No' when I can't do something. I want to be as honest and direct as I can."

Reno sought to dispel a caricature created by media profiles, "a myth of this lady from the swamps," but she nonetheless fueled the personality machine when she declared, "I'm not anything different than what you see. I am a fifty-four-year-old awkward old maid who is not a great speaker. I can be impatient. I do have a temper. My mother accused me of mumbling. I am not a good housekeeper, I don't put much priority on housekeeping. I have trouble delegating sometimes, and that becomes difficult when you come from an office of nine hundred to ninety-five thousand [at the Justice Department].

"People have told me already in my office that I am too trusting about Washington. My fifth-grade teacher said I was bossy. My family thinks I am opinionated and sometimes arrogant and would be happy to supply you with other warts I have, too."

She recalled her June 20 appearance on David Brinkley's Sunday television talk show. The chief topic was illegal immigration, but the panelists, as usual, covered a broad range of issues. No matter the subject, no matter how they poked and prodded, Reno refused to supply pat answers. She declined to discuss Justice Department policies under study or pending decisions. She simply stonewalled Brinkley, Sam Donaldson, and George Will on live national television.

Par for the course for Reno. But she had been caught off guard by the makeup that program producers insisted she wear for the cameras. "I said, 'But I don't wear that stuff.' 'Well, you have to have your hair done.' 'Well, I don't do it. I just look myself.' 'Well, it won't look that good on TV.' Like I can't go on their TV network unless I look good!"

But Reno added, "So as not to offend the person who did my makeup and fixed my hair, I want to tell you I never got so many glowing comments—not about the stuff and substance I said on the Brinkley show, but how magnificent my hair looked!"

She had other bones to pick with the press. "You love short-hand issues. You want instant answers, you want instant solutions, you contribute to the hype and the spin."

Reno told the reporters: "You've got to make sure you dispel the myth and engage in revisionist history before it gets too far down the line. You have got to ask me hard questions. You have got to help puncture the myth."

Reno and her press advisers should have foreseen the response. *Time* put her on its cover the next week, with a story full of hyperbole. "Reno: The Real Thing." The article effused, "Reno is pure oxygen in a city with thin air, and she has gone to its head. . . .When fans surround the table where she's eating dinner with Barbra Streisand, it is Reno's autograph they want."

She was profiled on ABC's "20/20" eight days after her Press Club speech. Reporter Catherine Crier, granted the interview because she is an attorney and a former judge from Texas, opened with the question: "How does it feel to be Janet Reno, superstar?"

Reno grimaced and replied, "I don't really feel like a superstar. I try to remember who I am and where I came from and understand that approval is a fleeting feature of one's life. . . ."

One offhand comment by Reno in that interview excited *USA Today* gossip columnist Jeannie Williams and similar purveyors of puffery. Crier asked why Reno had never married. Reno said, "I wanted to get married and have lots of children when I was young. And I always looked for the right person, and what I wanted I hope I can still find. And I think my mother was the person that described this to us as we were growing up: 'Don't marry anybody unless your heart goes potato-potato-potato and your mind also thinks it's the right thing to do.' "

Wrote Williams in *USA Today:* "Kids may be out, but surrounded by men as she is in her job, Reno may well find what she wants."

(There was a flurry of excitement when Reno's public affairs office claimed ABC's transcription service had misunderstood Reno in its written text of the interview. She couldn't possibly have said "potato-potato," several aides insisted, but must have said "pitter-pat, pitter-pat." But scrutiny of the tape proved the transcription accurate.)

Reno's popularity with the public skyrocketed. Virtually unknown just five months earlier, she got a 47 percent approval rating in a *USA Today* poll published May 13. Just 12 percent expressed disapproval. Her boss, President Clinton, had a 61 percent approval rating, but a sizable—32 percent—disapproval rating.

By late July, when *USA Today* published another poll, Reno's positive rating had climbed to 54 percent (versus 14 percent unfavorable), whereas Clinton's favorable rating had dropped to 51 percent after a series of missteps with Congress. His unfavorable rating had grown to 45 percent.

In a list published by the *National Law Journal* in August, Reno made the top five in a survey of the country's most-admired lawyers—and one of only two living, nonfictional attorneys on the list. She tied with Abraham Lincoln for fourth place. Number one was flamboyant litigator F. Lee Bailey, second was TV's suave Perry Mason, third was the late Supreme Court Justice Thurgood Marshall, and fifth, after Reno and Honest Abe, was Matlock, the seersuckered Southerner portrayed on television by Andy Griffith.

Reno may have hit a peak when she was interviewed by political correspondent Tabitha Soren for a profile on MTV, the rock music video channel. When Soren asked Reno about her post-Waco surge in the polls, Reno replied somberly, "The tragedy of Waco, as I've said, will live with me for the rest of my life. And it hurts when I think of that to think that people should judge popularity on that."

Soren asked, "Do you understand why you were a hero on that awful day?"

"I think people desperately want people to take responsibility, and I don't think any of us understood how much the American people want that to happen," Reno answered.

And she dismissed her poll ratings: "I know better than anybody else, after being state attorney in Dade County for fifteen years, what roller coasters [approval ratings] can ride."

Profiles appeared in fashion and lifestyle magazines. July's issue of *Lear's* ("Janet Reno: How She Got Her Grit") praised Reno's relationship with her mother. August's *Vogue* ("The Unshakable Janet Reno," illustrated with striking close-up photos of Reno's face and hands by Annie Liebowitz) maintained that Reno had "generally outclassed the president." September's *Elle* ("Janet the Great") quoted her as saying, "Who needed feminism when your mom wrestled alligators?"

In its August issue, *Esquire* named Reno one of the "Women We Love," putting her in the category of "Women Who Give Till It Hurts." (The same issue crowned Hillary Rodham Clinton as Woman of the Year.)

Caricatures abounded, too. Reno's favorite appeared in *Spy* magazine; it pictured her as "Mother Justice," with Reno's head atop a machine-gun-toting, Ramboesque body. Several editorial cartoonists portrayed her as Dirty Harry, daring adversaries to "Go ahead, make my day."

She also was parodied by two resident Washington comedy troupes, Gross National Product and the Capitol Steps, each casting a male dressed in drag as Reno. The Capitol Steps transformed

Jan and Dean's sixties hit, "The Little Old Lady from Pasadena," into "A Middle-Aged Lady Named Janet Reno":

> She's a riddle, this lady all the crooks have cussed is,
> Go Janet, go Janet, go Janet go.
> This wild, crazy lady is the head of Justice,
> Go Janet, go Janet, go Janet go.
> She can act persnickety if you're fresh
> If you doubt that just ask David Koresh.
> They're saying in Miami there is nobody meaner
> Than the woman with muscles like Dan Marino.
> If you mess with her, she will mess with you,
> She's the terror of Pennsylvania Avenue,
> She's the middle-aged lady named Janet Reno.

Privately, Reno withstood endless teasing from her siblings and closest friends, who take personal responsibility for puncturing any swollen ego. Brother Bob went public with their strategy when he introduced her to a conference of editorial writers in Philadelphia: "It is not true that we were all raised on the edge of a swamp and had to swim to school—except that Janny could walk on water."

Some of the adulation evaporated, however, when the reports on the handling of the Branch Davidian showdown were released in October. The Treasury Department's review slammed its Bureau of Alcohol, Tobacco and Firearms for the botched raid on February 28. Planning was inadequate and two line commanders lied and altered records to try to cover up the flaws, investigators said.

ATF director Stephen Higgins, fifty-five, a career employee who had headed the agency for eleven years, announced his retirement effective October 30. Two other top ATF officials also quit, and others were demoted and reassigned.

The Justice Department review was far less critical, and no one lost his or her job. Koresh alone deserved the blame for the fiery conclusion and deaths, both internal and outside experts concluded.

By sifting the ashes and conducting meticulous autopsies, Texas authorities were able to find seventy-five bodies in the compound, including twenty-five of children under the age of fifteen. Twelve children were later identified as Koresh's. He reportedly fathered children ranging in age from one to four by six cult members other than his wife, Rachel.

Fourteen adults and six children were dead before the fire, from gunshots, stab wounds, or bashed-in skulls, suggesting murder-suicides. And the fires that killed the others were deliberately set by the cultists, investigators concluded. A panel of arson experts said the fire was started from within in three different locations.

"David Koresh held the fate of his followers in his hands," said Edward S. G. Dennis, Jr., a former Pennsylvania prosecutor who led the independent probe. "In the end, being unsuccessful in maneuvering law enforcement to bring about the prophetic martyrdom he sought, in a last and fatal act of manipulation, he choreographed his own death and the deaths of most of his followers.

"This was the final act of a man who held himself out to be God."

Of the FBI and Justice Department, Dennis said, "There is no room in this evaluation for blame and no place for fault."

But the reports concluded there had been confusion and crossed signals that should have been avoided, including conflicts at the scene between those FBI agents acting as negotiators and the agents making tactical decisions to increase pressure. For example, the power was cut off to the compound, enraging Koresh, just as negotiators were attempting to secure additional releases.

Significantly, the reports dismissed the two primary reasons cited by Reno as justification of her decision to use tear gas. First, there was no evidence that abuse of children continued after the standoff began, and that was made clear in the final report prepared for Reno, the FBI said.

Second, it would have been possible to rotate in relief agents to spell the exhausted Hostage Rescue Team, though the replacements wouldn't have been as well trained.

So Reno had been wrong. But there was no stronger criticism of her in the report than the mention in a footnote that, on the Saturday she authorized the use of tear gas, she "did not read the prepared statement carefully, nor did she read the supporting documentation." In fact, the report said the statement wasn't actually completed until that Sunday, when Mary Incontro, deputy chief of the Terrorism and Violent Crimes Section, cleaned up the first draft.

The *New York Times* leaped on the findings. In an editorial headlined "The Waco Whitewash," the *Times* said Reno might have misunderstood the discussions about ongoing abuse of the children, but she couldn't and wouldn't explain "the dodge about tired forces."

"So much for the 'buck-stops-here' attitude that won her the nation's approval last spring," the *Times* said, condemning "the lack of judgment at the top and the reasons for it."

Reno said she didn't consider the report a whitewash. "I wasn't looking for vindication." There was no single reason she decided to authorize the assault, she said; it was an accumulation of factors.

Times columnist William Safire heaped on more criticism a few days later, saying Deputy Attorney General Philip Heymann had enlisted Dennis to head the probe because he wouldn't be too critical. Safire called Dennis "Mr. Heymann's longtime protégé."

Heymann, who headed the Justice Department's Criminal Division under Jimmy Carter, had brought Dennis to Washington from Philadelphia to manage the Narcotics Section in the early 1970s, Safire noted. Though Heymann left town when Ronald Reagan was elected, Dennis rose quickly at the department and served as acting deputy attorney general before moving into private law practice.

Dennis not only handled controversial matters at the department, he and his law firm, Morgan, Lewis & Bockius, frequently have cases before the Justice Department, Safire noted. Dennis's role in investigating Waco amounted to a "Mutual Protection Society," he said.

Heymann flatly dismissed the criticism, saying he hadn't known Dennis well when he hired him and had had no influence over his career since. He called Dennis "a man of honor, integrity, and talent, and I was prepared to live with whatever he came up with."

When she attended the thirtieth reunion of her Harvard Law School class in late October, Reno was challenged on Waco by Charles Nesson, a classmate who now teaches at the law school. The Los Angeles riots and the Koresh confrontation "were the two most powerful messages that people have received about the legal system in the last year," he said. "When can we expect the Justice Department to be truly frank about them?"

Reno replied, "I'm going to try my level best, Bill Safire not-withstanding."

The most critical analysis of the government's conduct was written by Alan A. Stone, a physician who served jointly on the faculties of the law and medical schools at Harvard.

Stone was a member of the investigating team assembled by Heymann, but he broke away, insisting that he needed more time to complete his study than the rest of the group wanted. He felt the FBI had not been totally forthcoming in its presentations to the experts, he said.

Stone lambasted FBI leadership for allowing its tactical managers to make decisions that overrode the agency's highly qualified negotiators and behavioral specialists. "Unfortunately, those responsible for ultimate decision making at Waco did not listen to those who understood the meaning and psychological significance of David Koresh's 'mania.' Instead, they tried to show him who was the 'boss,' " Stone wrote.

He said that the FBI's "noose-tightening tactics might well have precipitated Koresh's decision to commit himself and his followers to this course of mass suicide."

That FBI mind-set convinced Reno that gas had to be used, Stone concluded. Even the information they gave her about the CS2 was faulty. Studies in England had shown that CS2 could have long-term effects on infants and others with weak respiration, especially in closed spaces. She was "ill advised and made an ill-advised decision."

The FBI's new director, Louis Freeh, said that he and Reno

would participate in a "crisis management exercise" at the FBI training academy in Quantico, Virginia. He said it was one of a number of "substantial changes" being made in the way incidents such as Waco would henceforth be managed, led by better integration of negotiations and tactical decisions.

Defense lawyers representing cult members probed the flaws in the government's handling of the Branch Davidians during the trial of eleven surviving members who had been in the compound during the February 28 raid.

Prosecutors thought they got a break when cult member Kathryn Schroeder, thirty-four, pleaded guilty to forcibly resisting Treasury agents. Like the others, she had been charged with conspiracy to murder a federal officer, firearms violations, and other offenses, but she was allowed to plead guilty to the lesser charge in exchange for testimony against the other cultists.

During the six-week trial, prosecutors portrayed the surviving cultists as warriors who spent more than $225,000 on "weapons of war and devices of death." Assistant U.S. attorney Ray Jahn said the Davidians were "not mere biblical students" but were trained and equipped for the "physical acts of an army." Defense lawyers countered that federal agents had overreacted in storming the compound, forcing the Davidians to shoot in self-defense. "The ATF declared war on its citizenry," attorney Steven Rosen said.

Schroeder's testimony backfired. Although she identified which of the defendants had been shooting from the compound, she smiled warmly at them and denied any preconceived plan to murder ATF agents.

The Texas jury deliberated for four days. On February 26, 1994, just two days short of the anniversary of the ATF's original raid on Ranch Apocalypse, the jury cleared all eleven cultists of the murder conspiracy charges. Five were convicted of less serious charges of voluntary manslaughter, and two of illegal weapons charges. Four went free.

Defense attorneys said the verdicts should force law-enforcement officials to reconsider their tactics.

But Reno, saying she considered the verdicts "thoughtful," insisted that they did not validate defense claims that the cult only fired in self-defense. "It is clear by this verdict that the jury found that the deaths [of the ATF agents] were not justified," Reno said.

However, she didn't believe the verdicts excused federal actions. "I have always said that I didn't look at this in terms of vindication." She added: "I will never forget Waco. The ghost of Waco will be with me all my life."

Reno weathered Waco, but the sweeping changes she planned at Justice proved more politically difficult. She struggled to get her own team in place for over a year, causing rifts with the White House and Capitol Hill that raised serious and damaging doubts about her administrative abilities.

CHAPTER 9

The Politics of Justice

When Edwin Meese was confirmed in 1985 as attorney general during Ronald Reagan's second term, his predecessor, William French Smith, told him, " 'Ed, there will be days
when you feel a lot like the captain of the Olympic javelin team
who won the toss and elected to receive.'

"It wasn't quite that bad," Meese wrote in his autobiography,
"but I soon discovered that taking charge of the Department of
Justice . . . was a colossal responsibility."

Unlike Meese, who was following in the footsteps of another
Reagan appointee, Janet Reno became the first Democrat to head
the department in twelve years. Hers was the daunting task of
redirecting the Justice Department to reflect the vastly different
policy positions of a new administration.

She confronted not only an enormous management challenge
but also the question of just how much management freedom she
would have. Speculation was widespread in Washington that lawyers in the new administration—including the president and first
lady—wanted to call the shots from the White House.

The chief executive wields considerable influence in the workings
of the Justice Department through the appointment process. The
president appoints, with Senate confirmation, 227 of the department's
top-level executives, far more than any other department.

Clinton's transition team began interviewing candidates for

these positions immediately after the November 1992 election. As the president's third choice for attorney general and last cabinet appointee, Reno entered the process late. By the time she was sworn in on March 12, 1993, lists of favored candidates for key Justice Department jobs had been circulating for weeks.

Reno told close friends that the president had assured her she could veto anyone she didn't want working for her. But she realized that as a Clinton team member, she was expected to accept many White House referrals. If need be, she would pick her battles once she figured out how to maneuver amid Washington's political power struggles.

On March 23, her eleventh day as attorney general, Reno made political waves with her announcement that she was requesting the resignations of all Republican appointees who sat as U.S. attorneys across the country.

Reno's boldness was a shock: Although it was standard practice for new administrations to replace U.S. attorneys, most attorneys general don't plunge into a wholesale changeover, for fear of disrupting ongoing prosecutions across the country. Adding to the impression of abruptness, Reno made the announcement at her first press conference before word reached all the U.S. attorneys through official channels.

There are ninety-three U.S. attorneys nationwide. At the time Reno fired them, seventy-seven incumbents had been appointed by President Reagan or President Bush. In the other sixteen jurisdictions, the U.S. attorneys already had quit. Reno acted "at the request of the president," she said, aiming to "begin to build a team that represents my views and the views of President Clinton."

"All these people are routinely replaced, and I have not done anything differently," Clinton said the next day. "We waited longer than most of our predecessors have [to begin the process]. . . . It took us longer because of the delay in getting an attorney general confirmed."

Neither Clinton nor Reno anticipated the reaction. Republi-

cans called Reno's move a ham-handed partisan power play—
"Reno's March Massacre," in the words of Senate Minority Leader
Bob Dole—aimed at saving the skin of a prominent member of
Congress.

Chicago Democrat Dan Rostenkowski, chairman of the House
Ways and Means Committee, was widely known to be the target
of a federal grand jury investigation of financial irregularities at
the House Post Office, directed by Jay Stephens, the U.S. attorney
for the District of Columbia.

A central charge was that post office employees, who worked
for the House of Representatives, not the U.S. Postal Service, had
illegally allowed some members of Congress to cash in official expense vouchers made out for postage, or to trade in postage stamps
previously obtained with a voucher. Between May 1991 and July
1993, seven post office employees, including former postmaster
Robert V. Rota, agreed to plead guilty to federal embezzlement
charges.

Rota admitted to personally providing more than thirty thousand dollars in cash to two congressmen. They were identified in
court papers as "Congressman A" and "Congressman B," but there
was no doubt that the first was Rostenkowski and the second was
former Representative Joe Kolter, a Pennsylvania Democrat who
had retired with the 1992 election. House records of postage purchases by the two congressmen correlated precisely to the dates
and amounts referred to by Rota. Both Rostenkowski and Kolter
angrily denied any wrongdoing.

The replacement of Stephens by Democrat J. Ramsey Johnson
delayed action on the case for months, according to Stephens and
other Republicans. They accused the administration of buying time
for Rostenkowski, an important ally in Clinton's battle for passage
of his tax plan and his health-reform package.

After Rota's guilty plea, House Republicans tried to force the
release of materials gathered during the investigation. But Johnson
said public release could jeopardize the ongoing investigations, and
on July 21, House Democrats prevailed in a 244–183 vote that
defeated a resolution calling for full disclosure in the case.
Rostenkowski, unindicted, filed for reelection in early December.

Neither Rostenkowski nor Kolter had been charged with any crime at the time this book went to press.

Throughout the summer, Reno and White House officials denied any connection between their call for the resignations and the Rostenkowski case. Indeed, it would have been overkill to dump every top prosecutor across the country to justify firing Stephens. But Reno did not include Stephens when she allowed twenty-four other Republicans to remain in office until their replacements could be named; in those cases, she said major ongoing cases in their districts justified retaining them. (One Republican U.S. attorney whose stay was extended was Roberto Martinez, with whom Reno had worked in South Florida. Although Martinez applied to remain in the job, he was replaced in November 1993 by Kendall Coffey, a Democrat with no prosecutorial experience who was recommended by Senator Bob Graham.)

In the remaining sixty-nine jurisdictions, career assistant prosecutors were named acting U.S. attorneys. It took more than two months for Clinton to begin to nominate new top prosecutors. The White House didn't act until Democratic lawmakers had made their recommendations to Reno's office, the FBI had completed background checks, and Reno had had personal interviews with the finalists. Unlike previous attorneys general, she insisted on meeting each finalist before he or she could be nominated.

By November 22, when Congress adjourned for the holidays, fifty-seven U.S. attorneys had been confirmed and twenty nominations were pending. Reno and the president had failed to nominate candidates for the other sixteen vacancies.

One nominee, Janet Ann Napolitano of Arizona, proved to be the most controversial. Several Republican senators tried to block the appointment of Napolitano, who had provided legal advice to University of Oklahoma law professor Anita Hill during her testimony against Clarence Thomas's nomination to the Supreme Court.

Citing attorney-client privilege, Napolitano refused to answer questions about her discussions with one of Hill's character witnesses, Susan Hoerchner. The Republicans wanted to explore allegations that Hoerchner had changed part of her testimony. But the Senate voted 72 to 26 to cut off a GOP filibuster, and Napolitano was approved by a voice vote on November 19.

Reno brought only a handful of trusted assistants and friends from Florida to work in Washington; most joined her staff as special assistants.

For example, Ray Havens, her chief investigator in Miami, became her personal liaison to state and local law-enforcement agencies. Shay Bilchik, a lawyer who had been her chief administrator, has taken on budget and management issues. Sam Dubbin, who had been a partner at Steel, Hector & Davis, works on criminal-justice reforms, including the issues that grew out of Vice President Al Gore's effort to "reinvent government." Richard Scruggs, a former assistant U.S. attorney in Miami with wide experience in drug cases, serves as a special legal adviser.

John Hogan, one of Reno's most trusted assistants in Miami, despite his penchant for bargain suits that had nearly cost him his career, arrived at Justice in early June after completing the prosecution of police officer William Lozano. His loss in that case ended a string of seventy successful prosecutions in a row before that. "He is one of the best trial lawyers I know, and he is absolutely committed to justice," Reno said of Hogan.

Hogan became a troubleshooter for Reno, and his first big assignment was a doozy. Reno asked him to reinvestigate a complicated case involving allegations that the Bush administration had conspired with the British and Italian governments to provide more than five billion dollars in secret loans to Iraq to finance arms purchases.

The money had gone through the Atlanta branch of an Italian bank, the Banca Nazionale del Lavoro (BNL). At the time, the U.S. government was covertly supporting Iraq in its war against Iran. But the arms purchased by Saddam Hussein were later used in Iraq's invasion of Kuwait and the subsequent Persian Gulf War, and the source of the money became a hot political issue for Bush.

Six employees of the Atlanta branch, including manager Christopher Drogoul, were charged with illegally lending money to Iraq—

technically, defrauding the parent bank in Italy by making loans without authorization. But U.S. District Judge Marvin H. Shoob had persistently raised questions about a broader conspiracy.

Hogan spent four months reviewing the case and interviewing people from the Justice Department, the CIA, and other agencies. When Hogan appeared before Shoob in August to report that he had found no evidence of a cover-up, the judge expressed disbelief. He said he was convinced the Atlanta bankers were only "pawns and bit players in a far more wide-ranging conspiracy." Hogan's conclusion was possible only "in Never-Never Land," Shoob said.

The judge underscored his disdain for the government's case by letting five of the six codefendants off easy. He sentenced them to probation in late August. Then on December 9, prosecutors allowed Drogoul to plead guilty to just three charges—one of wire fraud and two of making false statements to bank regulators. Shoob, still convinced that Drogoul was the pawn of a larger conspiracy, sentenced him to a minimal thirty-seven months in prison.

Then early in 1994, as congressional investigators continued to press on BNL, Hogan and his task force reopened the case. Another judge—not Shoob—granted immunity to Drogoul for testimony before a grand jury that could implicate higher-ups.

Reno hired Lula Rodriguez as her administrative assistant, to be responsible for scheduling and office operations. Rodriguez, a buoyant, gregarious contrast to her reserved boss, had been Senator Graham's South Florida coordinator.

Finding Reno's personal staff overwhelmed with an unprecedented volume of mail and phone calls, Rodriguez set up a correspondence office and had a voice-mail system installed to allow callers to leave a comment or question for Reno.

Reno often gives out her office number—(202) 514-2001—and urges people to call with questions or comments. She has apologized that the FBI won't let her give her home phone number to the public. "But it wouldn't matter," she admits. "I'm never there anyway."

Reno insists on receiving samples of her calls and letters daily. Rodriguez offers a diverse selection, including some from children and senior citizens, politicians and Justice personnel. Rodriguez also assists Reno with more personal matters, as when she helped her boss shop for a dress to wear to the White House congressional holiday ball in early December. Rodriguez vetoed Reno's plan to wear a suit, insisting that she get a gown for her first formal evening at the White House. Much to Rodriguez's chagrin, Reno chose to go to the ball unescorted.

Rodriguez got in hot water when she returned to Miami for a long weekend in early November 1993 and agreed to help out at the campaign headquarters of her brother-in-law, Raul Martinez, who was running for reelection as mayor of Hialeah, the second-largest city in Dade County. His campaign was complicated by his recent conviction on federal extortion charges, for which he had received a ten-year sentence. He was convicted of shaking down land developers and others who needed city permits.

While free during his appeal, Martinez won reelection by a scant 273 votes, the margin of victory provided by absentee ballots. When his challenger contested the results, and federal investigators began looking into the possibility of vote fraud, it was discovered that Rodriguez had signed as a witness on thirteen absentee ballots delivered to Martinez's headquarters.

Rodriguez denied any wrongdoing. Reno, who stood loyally by Hogan through his designer suit scandal and Adorno after his loss of the McDuffie trial, was willing to let her assistant stay. But Rodriguez resigned in late January to avoid causing Reno embarrassment. She took a job at the U.S. Agency for International Development. Martinez's appeal resulted in a reversal of his conviction in February 1994; the appeals judges ordered a retrial.

On April 6, Reno announced the first four presidential nominees for her top assistants at Justice. A communications gap between the White House and the Justice Department resulted in both issuing press releases on the nominations that day, each with its own telling perspective. The Justice Department headlined its release: "Attorney General Reno Announces Her Team." The White House announced: "President Clinton Names Four to Top Justice Posts." It wouldn't be the last time Clinton and Reno seemed out of touch.

Reno made the announcement from the stage of the department's Great Hall, the aptly named three-story atrium at the center of the headquarters building. Its stage is flanked by massive, gold-hued statues of a bare-chested man and a partially draped woman. When Ed Meese announced a mid-1980s crackdown on pornography from that stage, news photographers couldn't resist angling their shots to show Meese standing just below the woman's naked breast.

One nominee was Clinton insider Webster Lee Hubbell. Hubbell, nominated for associate attorney general, had been a partner of Hillary Rodham Clinton's at the Rose Law Firm in Little Rock, chief justice of the Arkansas Supreme Court, and mayor of Little Rock. A mountain of a man, he played football well enough at the University of Arkansas to be drafted by the Chicago Bears as an offensive tackle. He passed up pro ball, however, to attend the University of Arkansas law school. Hubbell also was a golfing buddy of the president's, valued for his ability to keep mum about Clinton's off-duty discourse. "We never talk business on the golf course," he told one inquisitor. "And if we did, I wouldn't tell you."

Clinton wanted an inside perspective on the Justice Department and had assigned Hubbell there in mid-January. Hubbell burrowed into the operations of the department while acting Attorney General Stuart Gerson, a Bush appointee, made day-to-day decisions.

Some observers speculated that Clinton had gone too far in placing a presidential crony at Reno's elbow, that the attorney general might justifiably bristle at this intimation of perpetual oversight. But Reno warmed quickly to Hubbell, calling him "one of the best things to happen to me in these eight weeks" and "one of the great men in America."

Hubbell returned the favor. His friendship sustains Reno during tense moments with the White House. The former football star has become her blocker.

"I admire her because she takes ultimate responsibility for what she's doing," Hubbell has confided. "She studies a problem, she works at it, she takes personal responsibility for the tough decisions, and when she makes them she says, 'I did it. I don't expect you necessarily to always agree with what I did, but you'll know why I did it. And I won't duck it.' "

On the same day that Reno tapped Hubbell, she also announced three other key nominees: Philip Heymann as deputy attorney general, Drew S. Days III as solicitor general, and Carl Stern as director of public affairs.

Defense lawyer Charles F. C. Ruff, a former U.S. attorney for the District of Columbia and a Justice Department prosecutor, had been the early favorite for deputy attorney general. When his prospects sank with the disclosure that he had failed to pay Social Security taxes for a one-day-a-week housekeeper, Reno actively advocated Heymann.

Five years older than Reno, Heymann offered the Washington experience Reno and Hubbell lacked. He graduated from Harvard Law School in 1960, then clerked for Supreme Court Justice John M. Harlan. During the Kennedy-Johnson years, he worked at the Justice Department as an attorney in the solicitor general's office. One of his bosses was Archibald Cox, who later hired Heymann as an associate Watergate special prosecutor.

During Jimmy Carter's presidency, Heymann served as assistant attorney general in charge of the Criminal Division. Since 1981, he had been a professor at Harvard and a legal adviser to the lobbying group Common Cause. He consulted with emerging democracies around the world—including Colombia, Guatemala, Russia, and South Africa—about creating criminal-justice systems. In the States, Heymann provided advice on criminal-justice policy to Democratic presidential candidates Michael Dukakis in 1988 and Bill Clinton in 1992.

Drew S. Days III was a professor at Yale Law School, where he had graduated in 1966. He practiced briefly at a labor law firm in Chicago, then spent two years as a Peace Corps volunteer in Honduras. When he returned to the United States, he joined the NAACP Legal Defense Fund in New York, handling cases involving school desegregation, police misconduct, and job discrimination.

In March 1977, Days was nominated by Jimmy Carter as assistant attorney general for civil rights, a post he held through 1980. When Republicans reclaimed Washington in 1981, he joined the Yale faculty, where he developed a specialty in international human rights.

Reno met Days for the first time when both were at the Old Executive Office Building interviewing for their future jobs. But she appreciated his reputation and was eager to work with him, noting that "for most of my professional life I have been hearing about Drew Days and all the wonderful things that he has done to seek justice for all Americans."

Rumors that Days would be nominated for solicitor general had been so widely published that he told Heymann, "I've been in the *Washington Post* longer than any other human being in the history of the Justice Department."

Carl Stern, Reno's nominee for director of public affairs, had national name recognition as the NBC legal affairs correspondent, having covered the Supreme Court and the Justice Department since 1967. In addition to his master's in journalism, from Columbia, his law degree, earned at Cleveland State University, impressed Reno. Stern would "bring an understanding of both sides: of our need to be open and accessible to America so that Justice can have credibility, but to understand the law and the necessity to preserve individual rights and due process in the course of investigations and prosecutions," she said.

Heymann and Days were easily confirmed; Hubbell ran into some flak for his membership in an exclusive Little Rock country club and some past investments, but he too was confirmed by the Senate.

Her team now in place, Reno met with them twice a week to review the status of appointments, cases before the Supreme Court, and internal matters within the department.

Heymann, who taught public management at the John F. Kennedy School of Government (at Harvard) for many years, called Reno, after her first six months in office, "the most impressive public manager I've ever seen."

"She has the sense to tell the important from the unimportant. But she has another capacity that is simply remarkable: Most of us keep an awful lot on notepads and have to refer back to them all the time. That's because most people can keep about four things in their mind at any one point. She can keep thirty things in her mind."

At the meetings, "she goes down her list, which is always well chosen for its importance, and she says, 'Has this been taken care of?' 'Will you do it?' 'Will you see this gets referred to the right person?' And at the next meeting, she makes sure it was done."

Yet a behind-the-scenes clash in management styles led to Heymann's unexpected announcement on January 21, less than a year into the job, that he was resigning. He said that he and Reno "concluded that our operational and management styles are too different for us to function fully effectively as a management team at the Department of Justice." She said it was a mutual decision. More simply, Heymann said, their "chemistry" wasn't right.

Justice sources said Heymann had tired of Reno's demanding style; she once dressed him down in front of underlings when a report was delayed. Heymann's office also had been jokingly referred to as "the black hole" where assignments took months to be completed, which frustrated Reno.

Heymann disputed that; Reno publicly praised his efforts, including the investigation of the Waco debacle.

To replace Heymann, Reno turned to another Washington insider, but one with whom she was comfortably familiar: Jamie Gorelick, forty-three, the lawyer who had helped Reno prep for her confirmation hearings. Gorelick had spent the last year as the Pentagon's general counsel, overseeing six thousand other lawyers.

"I think we'll have a wonderful working relationship," Gorelick said, noting that, like Reno, "I make lists and check them off."

To bring her issues to the public, Reno travels widely, speaking to a variety of audiences around the country, from associations of police and prosecutors to female lawyers and antidrug coalitions. She makes at least three appearances a week, sometimes more. But she has sought her own place in the Washington community as well, where she can connect with "real people" as she had in her hometown.

A special opportunity appeared during her first spring in Washington. Mount Pleasant is an eclectic, down-at-the-heels neighborhood in northwest Washington where many Latin immigrants have settled among local blacks. For several tense weeks, Mount Pleasant was terrorized by a drive-by gunman who aimed his shotgun at randomly selected victims on street corners. Several people were hit, including a woman who was killed while walking her dog.

Eleanor Holmes Norton, the D.C. delegate to Congress, invited Reno to accompany her and Mayor Sharon Pratt Kelly on a visit to a neighborhood school, a visit designed to reassure students— and, through media coverage, the rest of the city—that local and federal authorities were doing all they could to catch the gunman. Reno quickly accepted the invitation.

During the visit, her heart went out to one little girl at Raymond Elementary School who looked up somberly and pleaded, "We want to go outside without no shooting, no killing. . . . When am I going to be able to go out and play?"

Not long afterward, a suspect was arrested and the shotgun attacks stopped. But Reno remained concerned about the girl and her classmates. She began making regular visits to Raymond Elementary—with no word to the media and no cameras in tow—to spend half a day as a teacher's aide, to speak to classes, to tutor troubled students. She returned to her office one afternoon marveling that there were students from four continents in the kindergarten class she'd read stories to that morning.

On December 7, at a holiday open house that spilled from her office suite to the hallway on the Justice Department's fifth floor, Reno positively glowed as two choruses from Raymond Elementary, the kids dressed in their best dark skirts or slacks and white shirts, sang Christmas carols. Members of Congress, judges, and other guests applauded enthusiastically. Reno shook hands with the performers, dispensed a few hugs, and provided punch and cookies. Many of the kids, used to Reno's presence, dashed past her to meet a volunteer dressed as Santa Claus.

Two nights later, Reno was back at Raymond Elementary. At dusk on that Thursday evening, she joined a group of parents and other activists who patrol the neighborhood on foot to "take back the streets" from drug dealers and gangs. Reno donned one of the group's distinctive orange baseball caps, strolled the streets for over an hour—and promised to visit again.

The second wave of top appointments at the department came on April 29, when seven assistant attorneys general were named to oversee specific divisions within the department. It was the day after Reno's triumphant appearance before the House Judiciary Committee on Waco, and Clinton, quick to share the spotlight, made his first visit to the Justice Department headquarters to make the announcements himself.

Before the announcements, Clinton spent nearly an hour on a tour of the headquarters, including a stop in Reno's private office. A photographer snapped a photo of the president and the attorney general standing in front of her fireplace admiring the painting of Robert Kennedy that hung above it.

Speaking to Justice employees, Clinton declared, "My goals for this Justice Department are simple: I want it to be free of political controversy and political abuse. I want it to be an innovator in crime reduction and in law enforcement. I want to create a genuine partnership with those who work with us in state and local systems of justice. I want it to set an example in the practice of law and in the protection of civil rights that will make all Americans proud."

Reno's influence in the selection of this second batch of nominees was slight. Every one had clear ties to the Clintons, their inner circle, or a powerful senator.

Eleanor Dean Acheson, named to head the Office of Policy

Development, candidly attributed her nomination to "the amazing serendipity of having joined somebody named Hillary Rodham in what passed for political disruption and civil disobedience at Wellesley College in 1969."

Eldie, as she was known, is the granddaughter of former Secretary of State Dean Acheson and had been a partner in a prominent Boston firm. Her confirmation was delayed by the Senate because of questions about her membership in a country club in Brookline, Massachusetts, that had no black members. Hubbell had faced a similar problem. Although both resigned from the clubs when they moved to Washington, such memberships still create an appearance of insensitivity, if nothing else, and Democrats on the Senate Judiciary Committee have hammered Republican nominees over discriminatory clubs for the last dozen years. In 1990, the committee adopted a rule that nominees should not belong to clubs that excluded minorities unless they had "actively engaged in a bona fide effort" to end discrimination.

Acheson's nomination finally moved when her sponsor, Massachusetts Democrat Edward Kennedy, angrily challenged South Dakota Senator Larry Pressler, a Republican who tried to delay her. "I make no defense of clubs in my city of Boston that have discriminated," Kennedy stormed, "and I don't need any lecturing from the senator from South Dakota about that."

Later, Kennedy aides reminded reporters that Pressler had belonged to a country club in the affluent Washington suburb of Chevy Chase, Maryland, that had no black members.

Other appointments announced by Clinton included Frank W. Hunger as assistant attorney general for the Civil Division. Hunger, Vice President Al Gore's brother-in-law, came from a Mississippi firm that practiced civil litigation.

Sheila Foster Anthony, nominated as assistant attorney general for Legislative Affairs, was the sister of Vince Foster, the deputy White House counsel. Born in Hope, Arkansas, the president's hometown, she is married to Beryl Anthony, an influential former congressman from Arkansas. Sheila Anthony, a former patent lawyer, was first tapped for a job at the Commerce Department but moved to Justice within several weeks.

Anne K. Bingaman, nominated as assistant attorney general for the Antitrust Division, is the wife of Senator Jeff Bingaman, Democrat from New Mexico. A graduate of Stanford's law school, she had been a litigator with a Washington firm.

Duke University law professor Walter Dellinger, nominated as assistant attorney general for the Office of Legal Counsel, is a Yale graduate who clerked for Supreme Court Justice Hugo L. Black. He had key allies in the Senate, including Judiciary Committee Chairman Joseph Biden, and had worked briefly in the White House counsel's office for Clinton.

Gerald Torres, a University of Minnesota law professor, was nominated as assistant attorney general for the Environment and Natural Resources Division. He had been a lawyer with the Children's Defense Fund, the advocacy group whose board Mrs. Clinton chaired.

And there was Lani Guinier, a University of Pennsylvania law professor who had been a classmate of the Clintons at Yale. They had remained friends—the Clintons had even attended Guinier's wedding in 1986 on Martha's Vineyard. An expert on the Voting Rights Act, she was to head the Civil Rights Division.

Despite their close association, it was Guinier's nomination that blew up in Clinton's face.

Guinier's father, an African-American labor organizer who was blacklisted in the McCarthy era, and her Jewish mother had raised her to be a "bridge person" between races and cultures. She became a provocative scholar who argued that minorities weren't getting their fair share in American politics despite decades of progress in civil rights.

In lengthy law-review articles, Guinier explored ways to guarantee equal representation. She contended, for example, that redrawing congressional district boundaries along racial lines to give viability to black and Hispanic candidates, as suggested by the Voting Rights Act, consolidates small enclaves of minority voting strength but disenfranchises those racial and ethnic minorities who live outside those districts.

A pair of conservatives—Clint Bolick, a Reagan-era Justice Department lawyer, and Paul Gigot, a *Wall Street Journal* columnist—seized on excerpts of Guinier's writings and labeled her a "Quota Queen." Their selectively focused attack so radicalized her views—she had specifically rejected the use of quotas—that Guinier later complained to a *Washington Post* writer, "I felt as if someone had moved into my brain and rearranged the furniture. I was made to embody America's worst fears on race."

The furor, fed by media reports that repeated only those aspects of Guinier's work selected by Bolick, quickly grew too intense for her old friend. Clinton admitted that he hadn't read the articles before he nominated Guinier. And after reading some of them, he decided it wasn't worth the political cost to defend her. He said he found one of her articles "antidemocratic."

Although he appeared pained to abandon a friend, Clinton announced on June 3 that he was withdrawing her nomination.

In the wake of the president's action, Reno's team spirit took a nosedive. She had recommended that Clinton stand behind Guinier and was disturbed by his retreat. Unlike the president, she had read the controversial articles long before the nomination and had decided she liked Guinier's thought-provoking style. In Reno's view, it was just what someone in academia should do: think hard and long about ways the law could be changed to improve the workings of the real world. "I had come to respect her a great deal as a person of intellect, common sense, and real commitment to civil rights," Reno later told the *Philadelphia Inquirer.*

The day after Clinton's announcement, Reno allowed Guinier to hold a press conference at the Justice Department, where Guinier said she hoped "that we can learn some positive lessons from this experience, lessons about the importance of public dialogue on race in which all perspectives are represented and in which not one viewpoint monopolizes, distorts, caricatures, or shapes the outcome."

Reno said: "I had thought she handled herself with grace and dignity, and I wanted to ease"—she paused—"the hurt."

Some White House aides were furious, saying Reno's decision to give Guinier a forum didn't show proper deference to the president's judgment. They offered caustic comments to friendly reporters, who agreed to keep their names out of print and off the air. One dubbed Reno "Saint Janet."

Reno insists she never heard any criticism directly and wasn't interested in discussing it. Her support of Guinier protected Reno from the scorn heaped on Clinton by the bitterly disappointed Congressional Black Caucus and other critics.

In the months after she was given the bum's rush, Guinier returned to Penn to teach; she also became popular on the speaking circuit and signed contracts to write two books explaining her positions. And she and Reno stay in touch. Reno accepted an invitation to speak in October at a convocation dedicating Penn's new law library. On the dais, Reno and Guinier embraced warmly.

Guinier recalled that she hadn't received much support from Reno when the firestorm began. "But once I started to fight back," she said, "when I vowed to press forward, we connected."

"I think she is an attorney general of enormous integrity," Guinier later remarked. "As she said to me during the period when my nomination was pending, 'If you stand on principle, you cannot lose. Because even if you lose, you still have your principles.' And I think that that comment, which was essentially advice she gave both to me and to the administration, is advice which she herself embodies."

The search for another nominee to head the Civil Rights Division dragged on for months. The administration sought someone with civil rights credentials but unencumbered by a controversial record, lest conservatives, emboldened by their success in scuttling Guinier's nomination, attack again.

Finally, in late September, another selection was made: John Payton, who had served since 1991 as the District of Columbia's corporation counsel, equivalent to a city attorney. A graduate of Harvard Law School, Payton had become a partner at the prestigious Washington firm of Wilmer, Cutler & Pickering. He did pro bono legal work for the Lawyers' Committee for Civil Rights Under Law and had represented antiapartheid activists who were arrested for demonstrating at the South African embassy. He had argued before the Supreme Court on behalf of contract set-asides for minority-owned businesses.

No formal announcement of the nomination was made, pending completion of an FBI background check. But Reno and the White House were eager to get the process in motion, so Payton was sent to Capitol Hill in early November to meet with the Congressional Black Caucus.

Just before that meeting, reporters discovered that Payton had not registered to vote in the District of Columbia for many years, and in the fifteen subsequent elections in which he was eligible to vote, he cast ballots only three times. He had not voted just the month before during a special election for chairman of the D.C. Council.

This man is going to lead the voting-rights fight for all Americans? Caucus members asked.

They found equally upsetting Payton's admission that he had not thought about the ramifications of a Supreme Court case challenging a so-called minority-access congressional district created in North Carolina after the 1992 Census. A dozen members of the Black Caucus owed their election to such districts.

Freshman Representative Bennie Thompson, a Mississippi Democrat, charged that Payton "has not demonstrated civic responsibility in exercising the right to vote." Another freshman Democrat, Representative Earl F. Hilliard, from Alabama, expressed concern that "we don't get another Clarence Thomas in government purportedly representing our interests."

Hubbell had been designated the department's point man on the nomination, and he and White House aides went to work, lobbying civil rights groups and the Black Caucus on Payton's behalf. The administration claimed to be making headway, but Payton's nomination still had not been announced by the time Congress adjourned before Thanksgiving.

As late as December 16, Reno was pushing for him. "I don't have any second thoughts about Mr. Payton. I think Mr. Payton is a fine, dedicated, wonderful lawyer who would make a splendid assistant attorney general for the Civil Rights Division," she told reporters.

Both Reno and the White House were embarrassed the next day, when Payton "sadly" withdrew from consideration. White House aides said they had polled the Black Caucus again and found only lukewarm support, so Payton had been warned that he would face a tough battle winning confirmation. Tired of the negative publicity, he quit.

The same day brought news that another struggling nominee, Torres, the president's choice for assistant attorney general for the Environmental and Natural Resources Division, also was withdrawing. Torres would have been the highest-ranking Hispanic at the department. His nomination foundered on questions about two former associates who had been accused of misconduct with regard to work they did for the Federal Deposit Insurance Corporation. Torres denied any detailed knowledge of their activities, but the FBI's investigation dragged on for months. He, too, ran out of patience.

Before year's end, Reno recommended that Lois Schiffer, acting director for Environment and Natural Resources, be nominated as assistant attorney general for that division. In January 1994, another candidate for the Civil Rights Division emerged. Deval Patrick, a thirty-seven-year-old partner in a Boston firm, had worked at the NAACP Legal Defense and Education Fund with Guinier, but he had no long list of academic writings that could be culled for controversial theories. He had been considered for a U.S. Attorney's post in 1993, but lost out due to a lack of experience in criminal law.

But until both positions could be filled, one-quarter of Clinton's term would pass without a chief litigator in place for either civil rights or environmental concerns, areas Clinton had declared as top priorities during his campaign. Two key Democratic constituencies, civil rights groups and environmentalists, had good reason to complain about the administration's commitment.

While political battles raged between the White House and Congress over the appointments, Reno made sure that work continued in the Civil Rights Division under acting director James P. Turner.

Among other cases, the Justice Department sued dentists who refused to treat HIV-positive patients; opened an investigation of eighteen Mississippi jails where black inmates had died under mysterious circumstances and joined a lawsuit against one county for the terrible condition of its jails; sent observers to monitor voting-rights compliance in local elections in Alabama, Georgia, and other states; filed employment-discrimination suits against cities in Illinois and Florida and against the North Carolina Department of Corrections; sued a New Mexico county for failing to provide voting information to Navajos in their native language; indicted three Ku Klux Klan members for assaulting a black couple in Indiana; and argued for the admission of women to the Virginia Military Institute.

Reno also launched a crackdown on discrimination by mortgage lenders, telling a Senate hearing on November 4, "I can think of few things more harmful to the fabric of our society than to be denied credit because of the color of one's skin."

On December 13, Reno and Federal Trade Commission chairwoman Janet Steiger announced a precedent-setting settlement with Boston's Shawmut Mortgage Company, in which the lending firm admitted discrimination but said it had launched internal reforms. The settlement required the lender to compensate past victims of bias a minimum of $10,000 per applicant. It was expected to cost Shawmut $960,000 or more but help Shawmut win approval of a pending bank merger.

Just two weeks before Clinton and Reno took off in opposing directions on the Guinier nomination, Reno's independent streak triggered a major dustup with the White House over the handling of corruption allegations involving its travel office.

On May 19, 1993, Clinton aides fired all seven staff members of the travel office, which is responsible for coordinating charter flights and hotel arrangements for those traveling with the president, chiefly the press corps. The aides said an audit had uncovered evidence of mismanagement and possibly theft. The career staffers vehemently and publicly denied the charges.

Reno entered the fray when a White House lawyer, William Kennedy III, another Arkansas transplant, seemed to sidestep Reno by going directly to the FBI to request an investigation of the travel office. After a meeting with FBI officials, White House communications director George Stephanopoulos also bypassed Reno and the Justice Department by issuing a statement that the FBI had found sufficient suspicion of criminal activity to justify an investigation.

In an outburst reported by the *Washington Post,* Reno called White House counsel Bernard Nussbaum and told him that any future contacts with the FBI would go through her office. Nussbaum insisted there had been no formal policy on direct contacts with the FBI, but he was appropriately cowed and agreed to go through channels in the future.

In a later, cooler account of her confrontation with Bernie Nussbaum, Reno downplayed her anger: "I said, 'I don't think we should do this because it causes great confusion, and I think in the future, you should call me or the deputy [attorney general] or the associate if you've got a problem.' He said OK."

Congressional Republicans and other critics, seeing a chance to skewer Clinton, accused the White House of a blatant attempt to politicize the FBI.

The *Wall Street Journal's* editorial board, which already had questioned the number of Clinton "cronies" placed in top policy jobs, especially those from Little Rock's Rose Law Firm, unleashed another salvo. "A Rose clique from Little Rock that has already shown a willingness to cut many legal corners needs adult supervision," it said.

The criticism was overblown. This was hardly another Watergate, although improper use of the FBI was a serious matter. Soon, both sides would have much to regret over the incident.

White House aides, furious that Reno had gone public, once again vented their indignation to the press under the cloak of anonymity. This time, one referred to Reno as "Snow White."

Their jabs came to a halt on orders from White House chief of staff Mack McLarty, after *Washingtonian* magazine asked, "Who's the Fairest of Them All?" A cartoon showed Reno as a beribboned Snow White with seven renamed dwarfs: Labor Secretary Robert Reich (Rhodie), Health and Human Services Secretary Donna Shalala (Doc), Defense Secretary Les Aspin (Sarge), Interior Secretary Bruce Babbitt (Fruit N' Nutty), Clinton (Sneezy), Gore (Woody), and Secretary of State Warren Christopher (Rover).

Reno repeatedly denied a feud with the White House over the travel office incident. "You love to stir up fights," she complained to the press. "You try to get Bernie Nussbaum and I to pick a fight with each other. Well, first of all, I decided that I was bigger than Bernie so that wasn't going to work. But now, I've decided that Bernie Nussbaum is one of the sweetest guys in the whole wide world, and you have just got to stop making us appear to be fighting, because we are not."

Hubbell, her ally on the inside, backed her up. "I know how close she is to Bernie . . . , and I think that [reports of a feud] hurt her, or at least bothered her. . . . We probably have had the best working relationship between the attorney general's office and the White House counsel in a long, long time. I don't know that there's ever been as good a relationship. Complete trust back and forth. Complete candor."

As for the travel office episode, the White House press corps "took a small event and tried to blow it up," Hubbell maintained.

After the initial brouhaha, both the White House and Reno were forced to admit to overreaction. The White House put five of the seven travel office employees back on the public payroll when it was determined they had no control over the office's finances. The fiasco had been triggered at least in part because Hollywood producer Harry Thomason, a friend of the Clintons and part owner of an air charter company, had complained that the travel office wouldn't consider new suppliers.

Reno was embarrassed too. It turned out she had, in fact, been informed by the FBI that it was reponding to a White House call. The Justice Department's Office of Professional Responsibility had sent her an "urgent report" memorandum, but she hadn't read it before going public with her scolding. "It seems the attorney general's big problem is with not reading her urgent mail," *New York Times* columnist William Safire chided.

The mea culpas came too late for deputy White House counsel Vince Foster. On July 20, Foster committed suicide. Six months to the day after his best friend from childhood was sworn in as president, Foster drove to a Virginia park overlooking the Potomac River and shot himself in the head with a 1913 Colt revolver.

In a note found nearly a week later, he complained about the way the travel office affair had been portrayed and about criticism leveled at him by *Wall Street Journal* editorials. "I was not meant for the job or the spotlight of public life in Washington," he wrote. "Here ruining people is considered sport."

Despite occasional rough water, Reno's increased clout with the White House was evident in her impact on some key appointments. She recruited Jo Ann Harris, an experienced prosecutor from New York, as assistant attorney general for the Criminal Division. The White House had another candidate in mind—former New York prosecutor Benito Romano—but Reno insisted on Harris.

A University of Iowa graduate, Harris worked in publishing for fourteen years before attending New York University's law school. From 1974 to 1983, Harris worked at the U.S. attorney's office in Manhattan and in the Justice Department's fraud section. Since 1983, she had been in private practice in New York City and teaching at Pace University's law school. She specialized in white-collar cases—a priority of Reno's—and was regarded as an expert on evidence and trial techniques.

Reno also picked a former Miami police administrator, Eduardo Gonzalez, as director of the U.S. Marshals Service. Gonzalez rose from patrolman to deputy director of the Metro-Dade Police Department, then was named chief of police in Tampa in March 1992.

Reno selected Loretta Collins Argrett as assistant attorney general for the Tax Division. Since 1986, Argrett had been a professor at Howard University's law school. She also served as counsel to the Opportunity Funding Corporation. She earlier had been an attorney for the Joint Congressional Committee on Taxation. Argrett's education had closely paralleled Reno's. An undergraduate chemistry major, Argrett turned to law and attended Harvard Law School, graduating in 1976.

In an interview in September, as Reno finished her first six months in the cabinet, Clinton accentuated the positive.

"I think she's done superbly well. She's obviously caught the imagination of the American people by being frank and forthright," he said.

He stated that he trusted Reno and gave her wide discretion. "If anything, some people have asked me if there is too little daily contact on a lot of the operations of the Justice Department, based on the pattern of past presidents and past attorneys general."

Clinton also maintained that he regarded Reno as a valuable adviser: "I consult her closely on many things. For example, I talked to her at length about the vacancy on the Supreme Court. And she was very strongly in favor of Ruth Ginsburg's appointment.

"Before I interviewed anybody, I asked [Reno] to come visit with me. She laid out in very cogent detail what she thought the criteria for a justice on the court should be, the kind of person I should be looking for."

As Clinton, with Reno's advice, concentrated on the search for appointees to fill out his administration, he and Reno were slow to remove a Reagan appointee who was provoking a crisis in ethics at the FBI.

CHAPTER 10

Turmoil at the FBI

Bill Sessions tripped up not once, but twice.

First, his many ethical breaches led two attorneys general and their presidents to seek his removal as director of the Federal Bureau of Investigation.

Then, after a July 1993 Saturday morning confrontation at the Justice Department where he refused Janet Reno's request for his resignation, Sessions stumbled over a curb in full view of several television cameras. He fell hard on the sidewalk and shattered his elbow.

Sessions should have taken the fall as a sign, but he was too proud and too stubborn. He wouldn't leave; Bill Clinton had to fire him two days later.

Clinton had been on the job for six months and Reno for four before they finally put an end to the acute embarrassment Sessions had caused the FBI. In the meantime, the bureau grappled with one crisis after another: the confrontation in Waco, the bombing of the World Trade Center and planned terrorist attacks on other sites in New York City, and an alleged plot to foment a race war in Los Angeles.

William S. Sessions brought a reputation for integrity to the FBI. The son of a minister, he had graduated from Baylor Law School in 1958, then practiced law in Waco, Texas, for ten years before he joined the Justice Department as a prosecutor. Through connections with Senator John Tower, he was appointed U.S. attorney in San Antonio in 1971, and three years later, he won a lifetime appointment as a federal district judge.

Sessions was known as a tough, fair, and principled jurist during his thirteen-year tenure on the bench. By the time he was picked as director of the FBI in November 1987, he had earned a national reputation for his commendable handling of two complicated trials stemming from the 1979 assassination of a colleague, U.S. District Judge John H. Wood. The trials led to the conviction of an accused drug trafficker for paying a hit man to kill Wood, known as "Maximum John," who was scheduled to preside over the trafficker's trial.

The Reagan administration was mired in the Iran-contra scandal, so when William Webster moved from the FBI to become director of the CIA after the death of William Casey, Reagan and Attorney General Ed Meese needed a successor with a spotless record.

Sessions was fifty-seven when Meese appointed him to a ten-year term with the FBI. He decided to concentrate on management, specifically the much-needed modernization of the bureau's archaic record-keeping systems and the resolution of such thorny issues as FBI discrimination against female, black, Hispanic, and Asian agents.

He left supervision of investigations to career agents like Floyd I. Clarke, appointed by Sessions as his deputy director in 1989. Clarke, once described as the personification of the G-man portrayed by television actor Efrem Zimbalist, Jr., made a name for himself in the early 1980s as head of the FBI's Kansas City office. His use of creative surveillance techniques inside the federal prison at Leavenworth had helped establish conspiracy in the plot to kill Judge Wood.

Sessions and his wife, Alice, relished the perquisites of his office, including the personal security agents, the chauffeured cars, and the planes at his disposal. He became a cheerleader for the bureau, traveling nationwide to make speeches and present awards. But many career employees were embarrassed at seeing the pair commit serious ethical breaches over the years.

Public criticism finally came on William Barr's last day as attorney general in the Bush administration. Barr released a scathing 161-page report from the Justice Department's Office of Professional Responsibility accusing Sessions of a number of ethics violations, both significant and trivial. Ironically, many allegations surfaced through the work of Ronald Kessler, a journalist who had been given extraordinary access by Sessions to write a book about the bureau.

According to the report, Sessions kept an unloaded gun in the trunk of his car so that he could claim it as a full-time "law enforcement vehicle" and deduct all mileage on his taxes. His wife sent FBI agents on her personal errands. Sessions arranged speaking engagements so the couple could take FBI planes on personal trips back to Texas and other locations. They once used an official plane to carry firewood from New York to Washington. And they appeared to have benefited from a sweetheart deal on a $375,000 personal mortgage.

In the face of the allegations, Sessions and his wife went on the offensive. While he agreed to reimburse the government for disputed travel expenses, he claimed most of the charges were trumped up by career employees—Alice Sessions singled out Clarke—who were resistant to the changes he demanded. He rallied committed defenders to his side, including Coretta Scott King, who supported Sessions's assertion that he was being railroaded by conservatives for his efforts to push affirmative action within the bureau and his outreach to civil rights leaders.

As Sessions dodged one volley after another, fed-up bureau managers suspended disciplinary actions against rank-and-file agents for similar transgressions, refusing to pursue charges of wrongdoing while the boss himself eluded accountability.

Clinton had more than ample reason to dump Sessions—an FBI director can be dismissed by the president for cause. But Clinton, preoccupied with the launch of his presidency, and more than willing to let someone else take the heat, decided action could wait until his new attorney general had a chance to review the report.

Meanwhile, as the Sessions drama was playing itself out, the FBI was embroiled in some of its toughest cases in recent memory. Agents scrambled to track down those responsible for the horrific February 26, 1993, bombing of the World Trade Center. Two days later, the bureau took over responsibility for the standoff with the Branch Davidians. In late June, the FBI cracked a larger terrorism plot to bomb the United Nations, the Lincoln and Holland tunnels, and other key sites in Manhattan, and to assassinate political leaders.

On July 15, after a yearlong investigation that paralleled the Rodney King court cases, agents in Los Angeles arrested eight neo-Nazis and charged them in a plot to "spark a holy war." The schemes included mailing a bomb to a rabbi and destroying a large black church in the heart of South-Central Los Angeles. Some of the group, members of the Fourth Reich Skinheads, also had plotted to kill Rodney King and other high-profile black figures.

While Sessions portrayed himself as personally overseeing many of these operations, to insiders his claims often were absurd. In one instance, as the nation waited tensely for resolution to the crisis in Waco, Sessions boasted of his contribution: he had put an end to the use of blaring Tibetan bell music as part of agents' psychological battle with the Branch Davidians in response to an objection by the exiled Tibetan spiritual ruler, the Dalai Lama, that this was a misuse of sacred music.

Before Reno was sworn in on March 12, interim Attorney General Stuart Gerson told her that Sessions "exhibited flawed judgment which had an adverse effect within the FBI" and recommended his firing.

For a lawyer who had built her personal reputation on ethics—and had telegraphed her standards to Justice Department employees when she refused a free lunch in her own department's cafeteria—Reno surely would have been troubled by the charges against Sessions. Yet she was also aware that firing the head of an independent law-enforcement agency could trigger political shock waves for the Clinton administration.

Seeing the FBI as troubled, but not crippled, by the Sessions issue, Reno let weeks pass while seeking more information so she could make "an independent assessment of his ability to lead." She submitted questions to Sessions and waited for him and his attorneys to respond.

Reno ignored Sessions's frequent requests to meet with her, even turning away from him when he approached her after her speech to employees in the Justice Department courtyard on April 6. For months, she froze him out, speaking with him only on official business, as during final deliberations leading up to the assault on the cult compound in Waco.

But the cold shoulder had no effect on Sessions, who refused to make it easy on Reno and Clinton by resigning. In July, Reno and the White House finally concluded what everyone else in law enforcement had recognized months earlier: Sessions had to go. In fact, her effort to be fair had caused the FBI embarrassment and sacrificed its effectiveness.

On Saturday, July 17, Sessions finally got the meeting he wanted with Reno, but she had her own agenda. She summoned the FBI director to her office where, in the presence of White House counsel Bernie Nussbaum, she told Sessions that he should resign to save himself the humiliation of being fired. Sessions stubbornly refused, saying he wanted to hear the words from Clinton himself.

It was on his way back to the FBI headquarters that Sessions stumbled and fell. He was shown on television that weekend responding to reporters' questions with his broken arm in a sling.

"It's a matter of principle," he insisted, still denying any wrongdoing.

At 3:59 on Monday afternoon, July 19, Clinton called Sessions and ordered him out, then called back at 4:03 to add that the order was "effective immediately." In the FBI's eighty-five years, Sessions was the first director to be fired.

Clinton announced the dismissal at a news conference. Reno was present but declined to elaborate on her two-paragraph letter to the president. She wrote: "I have concluded that the director has exhibited a serious deficiency in judgment involving matters contained in the report (issued in January) and that he does not command the respect and confidence needed to lead the Bureau and the law enforcement community in addressing the many issues facing law enforcement today."

Clinton described the firing as an emergency action, taken because the FBI was in "turmoil," and declared, "We cannot have a leadership vacuum at an agency as important to the United States as the FBI. It is time that this difficult chapter in the agency's history is brought to a close."

He later admitted that the decision had taken longer than he had hoped. Reno's delay in arriving at her decision, though, would help defuse accusations that the firing was politically motivated. "The attorney general was very deliberate, very thorough in this and, I think, has gone out of her way to avoid the appearance of political impropriety," he said.

The deed finally done, Reno took no chances. She sent Deputy Attorney General Phil Heymann to Sessions's office to make sure he understood his termination. As a final indignity, the former director was now considered a visitor to FBI headquarters and had to have escorts wherever he went.

Sessions held a brief press conference at which he remained defiant to the end. "It is because I believe in the principle of an independent FBI that I have refused to voluntarily resign," he stated. "I will speak out in the strongest terms about protecting the FBI from being manipulated and politicized both from inside and out."

With the Sessions imbroglio finally behind her, Reno celebrated her fifty-fifth birthday with a canoe trip on the Potomac River on

July 24. She had been invited along on an annual outing by some of the career lawyers in her department after they learned of her canoeing experience on Florida's rivers. Reno signed up and brought along her brother Bob, her sister Maggy, and one of Maggy's kids—as well as her ubiquitous pair of FBI security escorts.

The twenty-two-member expedition had a splendid time until they reached a stretch of rapids known as Yellow Falls. Reno watched from the bank as one canoe team shot the roiling waters, then declared she would do it, too. She cinched her life vest and pushed off. But Reno's canoe turned ever so slightly in the wrong direction, and over it went, dumping the attorney general in the rushing water. Alarmed, Maggy and an FBI agent jumped in, but Reno had already been swept downstream, where she emerged soaked but smiling, her baseball cap and glasses still in place.

"She was fearless to the end," said Peter McCloskey, a lawyer in the Civil Rights Division and one of the outing's organizers. He called her "just one of the gang."

"She acquitted herself well in the waters," deadpanned Barry Kowalski, who had been the lead prosecutor in the federal trial of the police officers who beat Rodney King.

When word of her spill leaked to the press the following week, Reno good-naturedly okayed the release of a snapshot of herself, river water dripping from her short-sleeved flowered shirt and baggy shorts, for the *Washington Post*'s gossip column.

Louis J. Freeh had been rumored as a likely replacement for Sessions before Reno arrived in Washington. She quickly became a fan and supported Clinton's decision to nominate him.

Freeh, just forty-three, had excelled as an FBI agent and federal prosecutor before he was named a U.S. District Court judge in New York in July 1991. A native of Jersey City and a graduate of Rutgers Law School, Freeh had been an FBI agent from 1975 to 1981. He was best known for leading an investigation of racketeering on New York's waterfront that led to 125 convictions of union leaders and others.

For the next ten years he had worked as a prosecutor in the U.S. Attorney's Office for the Southern District of New York, during which he masterminded the famous "Pizza Connection" case. He proved that the Sicilian Mafia was marketing illegal drugs through pizza parlors in the United States. After a fourteen-month trial, he won convictions of sixteen of seventeen defendants in March 1987.

In 1990, Freeh was assigned by Attorney General Richard Thornburgh to oversee the investigation of a mail-bombing case in the South. Bombs killed federal Judge Robert Vance, of Birmingham, Alabama, and Alderman Robbie Robinson, of Savannah, Georgia, who was also a civil rights lawyer active in the NAACP. Other bombs went to civil rights offices in other cities, but no one was injured. Freeh supervised about three hundred investigators during the probe, which resulted in the capture and conviction of Walter Leroy Moody.

When he was approached about becoming FBI director, Freeh initially said he wasn't interested. He feared the job would take too much time and keep him away from his family. Freeh and his wife Marilyn had four young sons.

"I did not seek the job of FBI director, and I did not campaign for it," Freeh told the Senate Judiciary Committee on July 28, at his confirmation hearing. "Indeed, I discouraged friends and associates from promoting me for the job." But, Freeh said, "I concluded that I did not have a good reason to say no if the president and his staff thought I was the right person for the job."

Indeed, Clinton, who interviewed Freeh for two hours the Friday night before Sessions was fired, called Freeh "a law-enforcement legend" when he announced his nomination on July 20, less than twenty-four hours after Sessions was canned.

"It can truly be said that Louis Freeh is the best possible person to head the FBI as it faces new challenges and a new century," Clinton said. Senators enthusiastically agreed; they confirmed him within a month. (His screening was made easier by the fact that he had undergone recent background checks to become a judge).

Freeh made it clear at his swearing-in ceremony on September 1 that although he had come from the ranks, he would not be a captive of the FBI's old guard. He ordered his troops to quit feuding over turf with other law-enforcement agencies—federal, state, and local. "Share your toys," he commanded.

Reno took that advice as the answer to another headache she suffered through her first seven months. This one was largely self-induced.

Her own complaints about turf battles between agencies, shaped by her frustrating experiences in such South Florida cases as Video Canary, drew the attention of at least one important listener.

Vice President Al Gore had been assigned by Clinton to review all agencies of government and recommend efficiencies that would cut costs and improve services for taxpayers. When Gore and his staff turned their attention to the Justice Department, Reno told them horror stories of discovering that agencies with overlapping jurisdictions didn't share intelligence data, trained agents at separate facilities, couldn't communicate over their separate radio networks, and couldn't seem to coordinate strategies even in the most crucial investigations of drug kingpins.

So Gore's Task Force on Reinventing Government recommended that the Drug Enforcement Administration be merged into the FBI, and later, the Treasury Department's Bureau of Alcohol, Tobacco and Firearms (ATF) and any other federal law-enforcement agency doing similar investigative work would be added to what was envisioned as a super-law-enforcement agency.

It was hardly a new idea. Three previous White House commissions had recommended a version of the merger idea, and the DEA administrator had reported to the FBI director for five years during the Reagan administration. But this time, the task force recommendation seemed likely to succeed, given Reno's public statements and Gore's imprimatur.

Instead, the proposal set off a firestorm of protest. To Reno's surprise, DEA employees from administrator Robert Bonner on down argued to Congress that the FBI's bureaucracy would swallow up their specialized drug-fighting mission, especially overseas, where the DEA had agents in forty-eight countries, effectively undercutting the war on drugs. The political uproar caused Reno to back off and promise to take a closer look at such a merger. And she disavowed any interest in taking over the ATF. "One thing I didn't want to do was come to Washington and say, 'Gimme,' " she said.

For weeks after the eruption over Gore's merger proposal, Reno consulted with FBI and DEA personnel, former DEA administrators, lawmakers, policy analysts—even her friend Tom Cash, the DEA special agent in charge back in Miami. In her travels, Reno made it a point to visit the local offices of the FBI, the DEA, and U.S. attorney to solicit views from the front lines.

When the House Judiciary Committee opened a hearing on the proposal September 29, most committee members and witnesses panned the concept, although no one disputed the wasteful duplication among agencies. Deputy Attorney General Phil Heymann indicated that Reno was considering another approach that would compel agencies to cooperate.

Three weeks later, Reno announced that the DEA would remain independent, but its investigations and its purchases for investigative efforts—cars, radios, computers, sophisticated eavesdropping equipment—would be reviewed by a "Director of Investigative Services" to avoid duplication with the FBI.

The same oversight would be imposed on the U.S. Marshals Service and the Border Patrol, both smaller agencies with some overlapping law-enforcement roles. For example, the Marshals Service pursues federal fugitives, as do the FBI and DEA.

According to Reno's plan, responsibility for oversight would rotate among the presidential appointees who head the agencies involved. Her choice to initiate the process, though, was Freeh.

"I think he can very easily resolve disputes," she said. As a prosecutor and judge, he "knows and appreciates the good work that has been done over the years by the excellent and professional and very dedicated agents in the department."

Gore endorsed the Reno plan. Their shared goal had been to end duplication and improve efficiency, Reno said, adding, "I think we've been on the same wavelength all along." And she admitted that she had been a bit overzealous her initial talk of reform.

DEA officials, having dodged a bullet, reacted enthusiastically when they first heard the plan. Tom Cash called it "a rather brilliant move. I applaud it. Janet is on track again."

But, ten days later, DEA administrator Bonner admitted that he was less than pleased. His plan had been to stay with the agency until Reno's decision was made. That done, he announced his resignation to return to private law practice in California, where he had been a prosecutor and judge before being brought to Washington by George Bush. In a round of departure interviews, he complained that Reno's choice of Freeh to oversee joint agency operations was "comparable to telling the chairman of the board of IBM to resolve disputes between IBM and Apple."

But Freeh called his new assignment "a great innovation." He said, "Through successful coordination and the avoidance of petty infighting and squabbling, we will on a broad basis make more meaningful use of our agents in the field where they can best serve the nation's interests."

More than twenty years after his death, legendary FBI director J. Edgar Hoover still casts a long shadow over the agency he dominated for nearly half a century. One legacy, an outright ban on homosexuals as agents, was supposedly dropped in 1979, but Reno and Freeh confronted a lingering institutional bias against gay men and lesbians.

FBI policy for screening employees permitted homosexuality to be a determining factor in hiring, retaining, or promoting an agent or granting a higher security clearance. The bureau argued that an agent's hidden homosexuality could be used as blackmail. Of course, it was the FBI's institutional pressure that created that bind; if agents were allowed to openly acknowledge their sexual orientation, they couldn't be subject to blackmail.

The change in policy was forced by a lawsuit brought by Frank Buttino, an agent in the San Diego office who was fired in 1990.

In twenty years with the bureau, Buttino had won numerous awards and received excellent evaluations. For all those years, Buttino had kept his homosexuality a secret. So he lied when confronted with a copy of a letter—sent anonymously to his boss—that he'd written in 1988 in response to an advertisement in a gay publication. Although Buttino later told the truth, he was suspended and his clearance was lifted because his misleading statements allegedly had made him a security risk.

Without clearance, Buttino couldn't do his job, and he was fired in June 1990. Buttino sued, and his lawsuit was expanded into a class action on behalf of all gay agents who were forced by the bureau to stay in the closet.

Reno's change in policy came as the trial on the lawsuit opened in U.S. District Court in San Francisco in early December 1993. She announced that sexual orientation would not be given special scrutiny during security checks at the FBI or anywhere else in the Justice Department.

"The department may investigate and consider any matter that would reasonably subject the applicant or employee to coercion, but no inference concerning susceptibility to coercion may be raised solely on the basis of . . . sexual orientation of the applicant or employee," Reno said.

Within days, there was a settlement in Buttino's case. It did not call for Buttino, then forty-eight, to be rehired, but the government agreed to give him a financial award—amount undisclosed—that would qualify him for a pension. The settlement did call for the FBI to hire Dana Tillson, an applicant who claimed she was turned down for a job in 1988 because she was a lesbian.

Reno had gone further in altering FBI employment practices than Clinton was willing to go with regard to the admittedly much larger issue involving the U.S. military. The president had sought her legal review of constitutional issues as he developed a liberalized policy regarding gays in the military. When opponents voiced howls of protest, Clinton sought middle ground with a "don't ask, don't tell" compromise.

Reno and Freeh further demonstrated their commitment to new sensitivities when they led an observance of World AIDS Day in November at the Justice Department. Reno condemned "vicious stereotypes and blind ignorance" and declared that her employees should lead the way in dealing sensibly with issues of HIV infection in the workplace.

Repeatedly during her first year in office, Reno expressed her admiration for the talented career employees at the FBI and other Justice Department agencies, who enforced the law without regard for the politics and personalities that changed from administration to administration.

Indeed, what appeared to be the biggest undercover FBI investigation at the end of that year—code named "Operation Lightning Strike"—had been launched by the previous administration in the spring of 1992. It centered on allegations of kickbacks and overbilling among contractors working for the embattled National Aeronautics and Space Administration (NASA).

The case centered on NASA's Johnson Space Center in Houston, with agents posing as businessmen willing to pay bribes to obtain a five-hundred-thousand-dollar NASA contract to build equipment for the space shuttle. To gain credibility, the scam enlisted former NASA administrator James Beggs as a consultant.

The sting ensnared two NASA employees and seven contractors' agents who took kickbacks and sold inside information, according to indictments issued in February 1994. Two employees of a Martin Marietta unit were fired. Martin Marietta and General Electric, which sold the unit to Martin Marietta in April 1993, agreed to pay one million dollars to the federal government for the cost of the investigation.

Before it could run its course, the sting was revealed by two Houston newspapers and a television station that broke stories on the day that NASA launched its shuttle mission to repair the Hubble space telescope. An irate Reno and her federal prosecutors fumed privately that the leak ended the covert investigation and jeopardized their case. Some NASA observers speculated that if the probe had continued, it could have rivaled Operation Ill Wind in the 1980s, which revealed widespread contractor fraud at the Pentagon.

Even more explosive was the FBI's arrest on February 27, 1994, of a mid-level officer from the Central Intelligence Agency. In perhaps the most damaging espionage case ever because of the sensitivity of the material to which he had access, Alrich Hazen Ames and his Colombian-born wife, Maria del Rosario Casas Ames, were charged with spying for the Soviet KGB and its successor Russian agency since 1985.

For his work as a "mole," investigators said Ames—the son of a veteran CIA agent—had received more than $2.5 million and even the promise of a prime piece of Russian real estate for his retirement. Critics said the CIA's internal controls should have detected his lavish lifestyle, including the Jaguar he drove and the $540,000 in cash he paid for a Virginia home.

It took the FBI to catch Ames.

"The FBI is to be commended for its tenacious efforts and the CIA for its complete support no matter where the difficult trail led. As the filed charges show, it is an extremely serious espionage case," Reno said.

Louis Freeh said, "FBI agents worked doggedly on this case, not for months but for years, with the CIA's unwavering assistance every step of the way."

In quick order, a senior Russian "diplomat" was expelled from the United States for his alleged role in the Ames case, and an American assigned to the Moscow embassy was kicked out of Russia in response. The long-term damage to American intelligence, and to United States–Russian relations, was impossible to predict.

Such white-collar crime and espionage carry enormous cost to society, but it is the growing threat of violent crime that galvanizes public emotion. While lawmakers debated death penalties and mandatory sentences, the nation's chief law-enforcement officer draws on her experience in Miami to preach a holistic crime-prevention message about nurturing and protecting children.

CHAPTER 11

Standing Up for Children

Passengers on a cross-country flight out of Washington's National Airport in June 1993 were treated to the sight of the attorney general of the United States bouncing a toddler on her knee and chatting earnestly with the young mother seated across the aisle from her. Janet Reno was quizzing the woman about day care, immunizations, and other matters.

As attorney general, Reno has the FBI's Sabreliner jet at her disposal. But she prefers to fly commercially—coach, never first class—although it gives fits to her security detail. To accommodate their concerns, her reservations are made under assumed names, and one FBI agent sits in the row with Reno and a second sits in the row behind. Reno generally catches up on paperwork while flying, but she can rarely resist a young child, or a friendly mom.

"His mother was wonderful with him," Reno recalled. "She played with him and she talked to him. And I was thinking, 'Here is an eleven-month-old, and look how much he has learned already.' "

The encounter confirmed for Reno her oft-stated belief that the best way to prevent crime is to raise a child right from the beginning, even before birth. Every dollar spent on prevention would save three or more down the road. "You can trace so many behavioral problems back to lack of preventative health care," she says.

Such attitudes are hardly revolutionary. Yet talk of family, health, and home are traditionally the province of the departments of Health and Human Services or Housing and Urban Development. The nation's top cop is expected to talk law and order, à la Edwin Meese. But Reno is Reno. Her experience on Miami's mean streets, with welfare moms, deadbeat dads, and crack babies, developed in her a holistic approach to crime prevention that leads her to embrace positions seemingly far removed from her portfolio.

Interested in results, not notches on her gunbelt, she became an early and outspoken advocate for President Clinton's health-care reform plan.

Though the Justice Department has a narrow role in health care, Reno served on Hillary Rodham Clinton's health-care task force, squeezing hospital visits into her already crushing schedule. To get a firsthand view on the subject, she even stopped off at a Washington trauma center over a busy Thanksgiving weekend.

The Justice Department plays a role in two major health areas: First, it prosecutes all cases of fraud involving Medicaid and Medicare, which provide health insurance coverage for the poor and the elderly. And second, its Antitrust Division reviews hospital mergers and joint ventures in the medical industry, going to court to break up anticompetitive deals deemed in violation of antitrust laws.

In mid-September, Hillary Clinton made her first visit to the Justice Department. She joined Reno, antitrust chief Anne Bingaman, and Federal Trade Commission chairwoman Janet Steiger in announcing that the federal government would simplify six rules to make it easier and more cost-effective for doctors and health care executives to complete deals, so long as they don't drive up consumer prices.

For example, smaller hospitals would be allowed to merge to gain economies of scale in treating patients. And hospitals would be allowed to jointly buy expensive equipment such as a CAT scanner, provided they could prove that a joint venture was necessary to afford the purchase.

Mrs. Clinton hailed the changes as exemplifying the way the government should react with speed and efficiency in handling health care issues. She said she was pleased "to know that Attorney General Reno is at the helm" of the Justice Department.

Although Reno is a team member, she avoids speaking about specifics of the health reform plans. She focuses on the big picture—adequate preventative health care for all Americans, especially children. Reno alludes frequently to the rationing of health care that is inherent in the current system. She complains that Medicaid, like welfare, cuts off coverage for low-wage parents trying to work their way up from poverty. Once a family's income exceeds a mandated income threshold that varies from state to state, they lose benefits. Yet, she notes, insurance coverage—both government and private—offers the elderly high standards of care.

"Something is terribly wrong with a nation that says to a person of seventy years of age, 'You can get an operation that will extend your life expectancy by three years,' and tells the child of a working poor person, 'You can't get preventative medical care,' " Reno believes.

The considerable publicity Reno has received for her outspoken views on children, education, health reform, and other issues has angered some aides to other cabinet members, who complain privately that Reno is intruding on their turf. They accuse her of being a publicity hound, reaping abundant press coverage while their bosses toil in relative obscurity.

Grousing from cabinet agencies was behind some of the media backlash against Reno that began to appear about six months into her term, although most of the anonymous put-downs were attributable to White House aides. Typical was an item in *Newsweek*'s Periscope column: "Reno: Rambo or Bambi?" It quoted "one administration source" as saying, "She's not like you guys in the press have portrayed her—tough on crime. She seems more interested in sociology."

Reno denies any friction between her and her cabinet colleagues. She admitted some initial trepidation about encroaching on others' territory, but she said she has been encouraged to speak out on children's issues by Health and Human Services Secretary Donna Shalala.

"When I met her for the first time, I said, 'I hope you don't mind me fussing around in this area,' " Reno related later. "[Shalala] said, 'You go right on and fuss because it is so desperately needed.' " She feels she has the same support from Education Secretary Richard Riley, Housing Secretary Henry Cisneros, and others.

"I thought, 'They'll run me out of town because they'll think I'm taking over their department.' . . . But Governor Riley said, 'No, Janet, you just keep on talking because this is the first time I've had a prosecutor that can talk about it and not get accused of being liberal or soft-hearted or something like that.' "

Cisneros has praised Reno, saying she "has really brought the Justice Department the support of the other departments. Her experience at the local level as a prosecutor puts her in a position to understand the relationship to HHS, Labor, Education, and HUD and others of us.

"The attorney general has such an important and broad-ranging portfolio—civil rights, community policing, community relations, so many other things—that she has really been a leader in helping bring the other departments together."

At the top of Reno's social agenda is her concern that "America has forgotten and neglected its children," a situation she calls "the greatest single crisis in American history since World War II." She considers youth violence "the greatest single crime problem we face," and doubly tragic because so many of its victims are youths as well.

"I used to think that being a parent was the toughest job I could imagine," she often says. "But I think maybe being a child in America today may be more difficult than raising children."

Like peeling layers off an onion, Reno worked down to the root causes of juvenile crime during her association with Miami's juvenile court. She quickly realized that society couldn't afford to delay intervention until sixteen- and seventeen-year-olds had wound up in juvenile court, dropped out of school, or, as she puts it, "until they had gone through so terribly much in growing up."

Considering the twelve- and thirteen-year-olds brought into court, she found that intervention still came too late. "Already they had fallen behind two grade levels, they had lost self-esteem."

In Miami, she supported the community policing concept—getting teams of police, social workers, school counselors, and public health nurses working together—to attack truancy among elementary-age children and to help their families through crisis, but saw that intervention even at that early age was not enough.

When the crack cocaine epidemic hit Miami in 1985, and Reno held pitiful, drug-addicted newborns in her arms, she saw how even prenatal intervention can be essential. "I began to understand that you have got to make the investment up front," Reno said.

"The most profound lesson that I learned is that zero to three is the most formative time of a person's life. The conscience is developed during those years, the concept of reward and punishment. What good are all the prisons in the world if, at eighteen, a child doesn't understand what punishment means and is totally lacking in remorse when they commit a crime?"

When she says that, Reno is quick to insist she isn't writing off today's young people—"We cannot, either for our safety's sake or humanity's sake, give up on a generation"—but is searching for ways to provide "a continuum of care."

That care must start in the home, she argues. "Success as a child requires that the child be loved, that the child have guidance, that the child have limits and an understanding of what they can and can't do. And then, if they cross those limits, they get punished, but the punishment must be fair, it must be reasonable, it must fit the crime. But punishment by itself won't do it. The parent then has to move in and let that child know that he or she is still loved."

Early in her tenure as attorney general, Reno cultivated ties between the FBI and state and local police in the Midwest, to help track gangs from Los Angeles that were migrating in search of new territory for sales of guns and drugs. She set up pilot programs in Denver, Omaha, and Wichita not only to enable FBI and police to share intelligence but also to support community-based law enforcement and provide grant money for alternative recreational programs to get youngsters off the streets.

"When I leave office, I want to say that we did something for all Americans, including American children," Reno has said.

Reno's agenda for children is ambitious, to say the least: Every pregnant woman should have prenatal care. Every drug-addicted pregnant woman should get treatment during her pregnancy "without punishment." Every child should be immunized. Every child age zero to three should have "either proper parental supervision" or "safe, good, constructive, thoughtful 'educare' " that blends into Head Start. Head Start should be offered "in every school throughout America where it is needed."

From kindergarten through high school, students should be offered creative activities in the afternoons: computer instruction, art, music, and drama as well as athletics. Those not attending college should be assured that they will graduate from high school with an employable skill, or be eligible for a trade school.

Reno attaches no cost estimates to her social agenda but insists that society must cover the tab. If not, taxpayers will eventually pay medical, law-enforcement, welfare, and other costs incurred by unhealthy and ill-educated teenagers.

She has an argument for every constituency. She tells the business community, "Unless we make investments in children . . . we are not going to have a work force with the skills that can fill the jobs that can maintain America as a first-rate nation."

To a wealthy physician in a posh suburb who says he doesn't care about poor children, she would say that "the health care system upon which he is dependent is going to be brought to its knees unless we make an early investment in preventative care."

"Senior citizens used to tell me, 'Janet, I sent my son to college, I sent my granddaughter to college, I even helped send my great-grandson to college. I've done my duty,'" she says. Her response: "You've got to continue to do so or your pension won't be worth the paper it's written on if we don't have a work force that can maintain the economy.

"If they tell you they still don't care, then tell them that they're going to be held up in their driveways when they come home from the grocery store if we don't do something about children."

Reno expects the most support from lawyers. She lectures her fellow attorneys, from the American Bar Association's annual convention to smaller groups that visit the Justice Department, that the law must work for all Americans.

"And when we talk about access to legal services, our traditional response has been to say parents will represent their children's interests. [But] there are too many children in America for whom the fabric of society has literally fallen away and have no one to speak out and to advocate for them. And we have a great challenge to devise a system that can do that."

She urges lawyers to volunteer as advocates for a family, a school, or a city block. But she knows that pro bono services are not enough. There needs to be a new way to steer needy people through the legal system and the government bureaucracy, she argues.

"Increasing access to the justice system is the right thing to do, it is the fair thing to do, and it is the smart thing to do," she said. "After all, society pays for every family that is forced to go on welfare because there was no lawyer to help collect child support. Society must cope with every homeless person who was wrongfully evicted for lack of legal assistance. . . . Local and state taxpayers must care for every disabled person whose federal Social Security benefits were cut off because there was no lawyer to interpret complex regulations."

To provide those legal services she has proposed a radical approach, a four-year college program leading to a degree in "community advocacy." Trained and licensed community advocates would be capable of representing people now shut out of the system.

There has been no rush to endorse the idea, although her old friend Sandy D'Alemberte, former ABA president and law-school dean, calls it worth considering. No longer waiting for a job in the Clinton administration, D'Alemberte became president of Florida State University in Tallahassee in January 1994—a position where he could advocate Reno's concept, if he chooses.

"We've got to make sure that parents are old enough, wise enough, and financially able enough to take care of their children, and that they are taught parenting skills that enable them to be responsible parents."

Within this statement—Reno's mantra about the responsibilities of parenthood—lies one of the pillars of her support for the right to abortion: a woman should not be forced to bear a child if she is not ready to be a parent.

She voiced that support before and during her confirmation hearing. Then, on March 10, the day before the Senate voted to confirm Reno, an abortion protester murdered Dr. David Gunn in the parking lot of an abortion clinic in Pensacola, Florida. Gunn was shot three times in the back by a pro-life activist who had ties to a radical group called Defensive Action, which advocated violence against clinics and doctors.

In one of her first acts as attorney general, Reno called to offer condolences to Gunn's widow and daughter and endorsed the plea by abortion-rights groups for a new federal law to protect access to abortion clinics.

In Pennsylvania, Kansas, Virginia, and other states where clinic sites had become battlegrounds, federal judges had been using a 122-year-old civil rights law as the basis for injunctions against Operation Rescue and other demonstrators. But in January 1993, the Supreme Court ruled 5 to 4 that the old law applied only to abortion protests under extreme circumstances, effectively leaving state and local trespassing laws—misdemeanor offenses—as the strongest protections.

Within two weeks of being sworn in, Reno endorsed a bill introduced by Senator Edward Kennedy that would guarantee access to abortion clinics. She addressed constitutional concerns by helping to draft amendments to the bill that balance protesters' right of free speech with the right of access to clinics.

"A woman's right to choose whether to terminate a pregnancy is fundamental," Reno testified on May 12 before the Senate Labor and Human Resources Committee, which was considering Kennedy's bill. She endorsed its criminal sanctions against those committing violence against clinic personnel and patients, threatening providers, or obstructing or destroying clinics.

Though she acknowledged protesters' right of free speech and the "extraordinarily delicate balance that we have to strike between the rights of all people involved," she yielded no ground when challenged by antiabortion senators who claimed that the access law would be held unconstitutional.

For months, Reno refused to meet with pro-lifers, even when Operation Rescue staged a vigil near her office on Constitution Avenue before launching its seven-city summer campaign. She finally agreed to a meeting when confronted at a town hall meeting in Wichita, Kansas, on August 30. (Because of the violent nature of the abortion controversy—Operation Rescue organizers had labeled Reno a baby-killer—Reno took the unusual step of flying to Wichita in the FBI's jet and had extra security for her visit.)

"I would be happy to speak to a responsible, thoughtful group," Reno told a questioner. Operation Rescue's leader, the Reverend Pat Mahoney, declared a victory.

However, Mahoney and two other militants were excluded from the October 29 meeting in Washington. Though Mahoney compared himself to Martin Luther King, Jr., and other nonviolent protesters, Justice officials said his record of arrests for violating court orders at clinic demonstrations made him a security risk. During the meeting, Reno assured other abortion opponents, including representatives of the Catholic church, that she would protect their free-speech rights.

Ironically, it was during a meeting with leaders of the pro-choice movement earlier that day that Reno lost her cool. She met with a group that included Kate Michelman of the National Abortion Rights Action League and Pamela Moraldo of Planned Parenthood, to reassure them of her support for the clinic-access bill.

When they complained that clinic violence had escalated while the bill languished without sufficient backing from the administration, she bristled. Voice rising, Reno cut off what she heard as a challenge to her commitment, and the president's, and threatened to walk out of the meeting. After she calmed down, she promised to investigate the violence. No reference to the angry exchange was made when the activists emerged for an upbeat press conference.

Action on the legislation took longer than supporters had hoped. The Senate didn't pass its version of the bill until November 16, and the House passed it on November 18, leaving insufficient time for a conference committee to iron out differences before Congress adjourned for the holidays. Final action was delayed until early 1994.

Reno touched a nerve in October when she invoked the specter of censorship in her zeal to protect children from the effects of televised violence. Her populist banner unfurled, she waged a battle royal with the media, but won little support—initially, at least—from the president.

The Senate Commerce Committee had invited her to testify on October 20, 1993, on several pending bills that would regulate violent programming on network television. The bills offered several alternatives: One would have required broadcast networks to audit the violent acts shown on their programs; another would have banned violence during so-called "safe harbor" hours in the afternoons and early evenings when children were likely to watch; another would have required cable systems to offer subscribers a cable-box programming code enabling parents to block out certain shows.

Reno testified that any of the bills would pass constitutional muster; then she concluded her remarks by threatening the networks with a crackdown if they didn't begin policing themselves. She concurred with Illinois Senator Paul Simon's suggested deadline of January 1, 1994; the date ultimately came and went with no action.

From her travels around the country, Reno knew there was growing sentiment for a campaign against violence on television. And she could cite increasing evidence, most recently a study by the American Psychological Association, of a connection between what youngsters saw on television and the way they behaved.

"There is no one single answer to the problem of violence," Reno told the committee. "But television is so dominant in people's lives today that it must be regarded as a contributing factor.

"In only a half century, television violence has become a central theme to the life of our young people, as central as homework and playgrounds." She cited studies showing that the average sixth-grade child has seen ten thousand acts of violence on television, including eight thousand murders. By age eighteen, that child has witnessed two hundred thousand acts of violence and forty thousand murders.

"We're just fed up with excuses and hedging in the face of this epidemic of violence," Reno said.

It was fine for some to say that parents should better regulate their children's TV viewing, and in many households, that would be effective, Reno reasoned. But too many children live in households where working parents aren't home to supervise, especially during after-school hours. Television is the babysitter.

"In dangerous neighborhoods, television may be one of the safest forms of recreation left for children, unless it is more violent than the streets they are afraid to walk on. Indeed, in high crime areas, television violence and real violence have become so intertwined that they may well feed on each other. If this is true, television is utterly failing us."

Reno told the senators, "I'm not here to condemn documentaries which teach us the lessons of war, news programming that seeks only to accurately portray the darker side of life, or sporting events that help society channel its competitive and aggressive impulses. Violence has always been a part of our life, our history, and our culture, and television programming in a free society should not pretend that it's otherwise.

"But violence has become the salt and pepper of our television diet. Fictional shows and movies feature dozens of killings of bad guys or innocents. Made-for-TV movies glorify the most sordid examples of human behavior. The local news opens with pieces on violent crimes before proceeding to any other type of story. And so-called real life police programs portray the world of law enforcement as nothing but a violent game between America's police and its citizens."

Adults are affected as well, she said. Violent programming "hurts adults by heightening our fear and mistrust of the outside world, by convincing us that our epidemic of violence is too intractable to address, by numbing us to the plight of its victims, or by repeatedly showing us how to address the most frustrating problems of life with violence."

She complained that too many shows show "somebody killed and nobody mourning. . . . I think that when it comes to something like violence, you've got to put it in the most realistic terms possible and show the agony that it conveys."

Network executives exploded. One privately fumed at her, calling her "a major-league hypocrite. Here's someone who goes around boasting, 'I don't watch much television,' and yet she's telling us the programming has too much violence. That's not terribly constructive, to put it nicely."

The executive noted that Senator Fritz Hollings, the Commerce Committee chairman from South Carolina, had identified specific programs he didn't like—including MTV's controversial cartoon characters Beavis and Butt-head, although Hollings referred to them as Buffcoat and Beaver. (Just before the hearing, MTV announced it would drop its seven P.M. showing of the cartoon, after a two-year-old Ohio girl died in a fire started by her five-year-old brother, who was mimicking an episode that showed the twosome playing with matches.)

While Reno didn't say at the hearing what kind of programming she would like to see, at a conference on youth violence in Lincoln, Nebraska, in August, she had described her personal tastes as rather saccharine. "I'm an old sentimentalist. I like *Sound of Music*. I guess that was my favorite movie. And I guess I would like that kind of programming in the afternoon and the evening, but we can have some variations," she said, drawing laughs and applause.

She didn't threaten government regulation in August; rather, she urged her audience to complain to corporations that advertised on shows that contained violence. "Let us send a message through advertisers as to what we would like on TV afternoons and in the evening. Let us send the clear message that I am hearing throughout America, that we're sick and tired of violence."

Reno unsheathed her sword before the Senate committee because she felt she had been misled during a meeting with entertainment industry executives three days before the hearing. Though they were conciliatory, promising cooperation in crafting reforms, she later learned that the same rhetoric offered by executives in years past had produced few, if any, changes.

During her meeting with the executives, Reno presented her own plot line for a realistic but nonviolent program with an uplifting message, adding that any producer could use it for free. She described the plot during a later appearance on the "MacNeil-Lehrer Newshour" as featuring a fourteen-year-old kid "who helps raise his two siblings while his mother is recovering from crack addiction" after he gets her into treatment. Three years later, "she goes to law school, and he graduates as valedictorian." No one snatched it up.

Reno admitted that the chief obstacle to drafting regulatory language would be in defining violence, or, as most lawmakers referred to it, "gratuitous violence." Somewhere, a line would have to be drawn between news and entertainment, especially with "real-life" police dramas like "Rescue 911" and "America's Most Wanted."

Most bills pending in Congress at the time left that challenge to the Federal Communications Commission. Only one bill attempted a definition. Its sponsor, Minnesota Republican Senator David Durenberger, wanted networks to offer content warnings. Violence, as defined in the bill, was "any action that has as an element the use or threatened use of physical force against the person of another, or against oneself, with intent to cause bodily harm."

The media responded with outrage to the whole notion, accusing Reno and the lawmakers of advocating government censorship. In an editorial headlined "Janet Reno's Heavy Hand," the *New York Times* intoned, "To look back at 70 or so years of American films is to see a whole roster of things that nobody should do. Nobody should imitate the Keystone Kops running amok with fire engines, Harold Lloyd dangling off a clock hand, Charlie Chaplin eating a shoe or James Dean racing a convertible. It's foolish to try to stop a bullet like Schwarzenegger or swing off a mountain like Stallone. But most foolish of all is Janet Reno's dangerous embrace of a very seductive form of censorship."

Said a *Washington Post* editorial: "The violence is terrible; the regulation would be worse."

Detroit Free Press television writer Marc Gunther asked what would constitute violence: "Is it a barroom brawl on the CBS sitcom 'Love and War'? Is it Elmer Fudd shooting a shotgun at Daffy Duck? Is it the miniseries 'Roots'? A pie in the face? Threatening words? Pro wrestling?"

Even the *Wichita Eagle*, which had recently hailed Reno as a hero for her crusade against gangs, panned "the crescendo of official threats." It said, "Ms. Reno and censorship-minded members of Congress have forgotten what determines the content of the entertainment industry's products. It's the taste of the public, which has always tended toward trash."

Some commentators, however, were delighted by Reno's stand. Syndicated urban affairs columnist Neal R. Peirce compared Reno's new crusade to former Surgeon General C. Everett Koop's war on smoking. "The attorney general's tough warning to the entertainment industry—clean up your act or face federal controls— came like an elixir," Peirce wrote. "This is the act of courageous leadership from the top of American government that we've waited for years to hear."

Columnist Cal Thomas, a spokesman for the religious right, recalled the ridicule that had been heaped on the Reverend Donald Wildmon and other conservatives, including former Vice President Dan Quayle, when they called for crackdowns on violence and sex in the media. Would Hollywood now disown Clinton, whom they helped elect? he wondered.

That seemed unnecessary, since Clinton showed no interest in joining Reno's crackdown. On October 28, Clinton distanced himself from her stance, saying he had been unaware of how far Reno would go in her testimony. He blamed the media for exaggerating her conclusion; he understood Reno was "asking the networks to engage her in a dialogue."

He also said he wasn't sure that violence could be tied to any one program, or how violence should be defined by law. "Instead of going to the censorship bottom line, let's see what the cumulative impact is on all these kids," he suggested and called for cooperation from the entertainment industry to "see what we can do to turn away from that."

Reno herself was quick to agree that she would rather see the television industry develop and enforce standards, much like the movie industry's rating system. "The industry knows better how to do it than I do," she said. "I think the television industry in America is smart enough, shrewd enough, and cares enough about America—but more importantly, enough about its profits—to produce something that the American people are willing to buy."

That was more to Clinton's liking. He repeated the invitation to the entertainment industry at a thousand-dollar-per-person Democratic party fund-raiser in Los Angeles in early December. After criticizing violence in movies, on television, and in music, he asked the four hundred Hollywood moguls to clean up their act so government didn't have to do it for them.

Truth be told, an initial attempt at negotiations between Washington and Hollywood had sputtered to a halt. On November 18, Reno had met with a delegation from NBC, including actor Michael Moriarty, who plays a tough assistant district attorney on the crime-oriented show "Law & Order." Reno got impatient and brusque, again accusing the executives of failing to keep past promises.

The next day, Moriarty fired off a one-line letter to Reno: "The next time you call me to a meeting where only one side gets to ask the questions, send a subpoena." In a longer letter to Clinton, the actor compared Reno to Red-baiting Joe McCarthy and called for her resignation.

The January 1 deadline for industry action proposed by Senator Simon came and went, with the networks making halfhearted efforts to put warnings at the start of some shows carrying violent scenes and Congress yet to act on proposed legislation. As Reno started her second year in office, she had yet to signal her next move.

Right-wingers embraced Reno's campaign against televised violence, but they blasted her position in a high-profile child pornography case, claiming the attorney general had "opened the door" to child pornographers and pedophiles. While Reno attempted to defend her stance, Clinton pulled the rug out from under her.

Stephen A. Knox, an honors student working on his doctorate in history at Pennsylvania State University, had been convicted under a Reagan-era federal pornography statute for possessing lewd videotapes of children. The 1984 law defined child pornography as depictions of "a minor engaging in sexually explicit conduct." Such conduct includes "lascivious exhibition of the genitals or pubic area."

In April 1991, the U.S. Customs Service raided Knox's apartment after he received advertisements for pornography through the mail. Agents seized three tapes from Knox's apartment on which he had compiled excerpts from tapes purchased from a Las Vegas supplier that showed teenage and preteen girls in bathing suits, bikini panties, leotards, and similar attire. One viewer described the action this way: "The camera zoomed in on each girl's loins and lingered there."

The supplier, the Nather Company, said in its catalogue that its tapes were "completely legal" because they showed "no sex or nudity." The catalogue offered titles like "Ripe and Tender," "Young Flashers," and "Sweet Young Things." It described one of its tapes as "featuring about twenty young beauties, ages eight to fourteen, performing baton twirling, majorette and gymnastics routines, plus our usual panty-flashing shots and tight young butts in short-shorts and bikinis."

Knox was convicted in federal district court of possessing child pornography and sentenced to five years in prison. A three-judge appeals panel upheld the conviction, with Judge Robert E. Cowan writing that the ban on "exhibition of the genitals or pubic area" could occur "even when these areas are covered by an article of clothing." In these tapes, Cowan wrote, the photographer focused on each girl's "clothed genital area with the obvious intent to produce an image sexually arousing to pedophiles."

When Knox's lawyers appealed to the Supreme Court, the Justice Department first filed a brief supporting the lower court rulings. But after Drew Days was confirmed as solicitor general and reviewed the case, he withdrew that brief and on September 17 filed another that, in a highly unusual move, retreated from the government's victory in the case.

The new brief, approved by Reno, said the appeals court had gone too far. It argued that law requires that "the material must include a visible depiction of the genitals or pubic area (as distinguished from a depiction of the clothing covering those areas)" and that "the material must depict a child lasciviously engaging in sexual conduct (as distinguished from lasciviousness on the part of the photographer or consumer)."

That supported the position taken by a coalition of artists, booksellers, and civil liberties groups, which argued that the interpretation offered by the appeals court could mean a ban on pictures of cheerleaders, videos of a girls' dance class, even clothing advertisements.

Privately, senior Justice Department officials said Days made the decision because he believed the government could lose on such a broad interpretation of the law, and that the entire pornography statute could have been declared unconstitutional. To put it bluntly, said one official, "People who looked at the tapes said after a while, 'Well, when are you going to get to the good parts?' And there are no good parts. This material simply isn't child pornography. It's crazy to litigate extreme cases like this."

On November 1, the Supreme Court sent the case back to the U.S. Court of Appeals for the Third Circuit for reconsideration, given the government's change in position.

Conservatives didn't wait for a ruling. They whipped up a frenzy that succeeded in getting Reno in trouble with Congress and the White House. The opposition was led by two lawyers who had headed the Justice Department's child exploitation and obscenity section under Reagan and Bush.

H. Robert Showers, president of the National Law Center for Children and Families, had filed a friend-of-the-court brief supporting Knox's conviction on behalf of a coalition of fourteen groups. Patrick Trueman, director of government affairs for the American Family Association, said Days "succeeded in snatching defeat from the jaws of victory."

Joining the fray was Thomas Jipping of the Free Congress Foundation, who had unsuccessfully opposed Reno's confirmation. Jipping said the Justice Department's "radical departure from past practice is unwise, unwarranted, and unconscionable. It displays either ignorance or disregard for the nature of child pornography and the harm it does to children."

Beverly LaHaye, president of Concerned Women for America, accused Reno of "opening the door for every child pornographer and pedophile to legally victimize and destroy the innocent lives of America's most vulnerable citizens." She called for Reno to resign.

The outcry convinced Congress to react. On Thursday, November 4, the Senate voted unanimously for a resolution that labeled the department's interpretation "an outrage" and called for the brief to be withdrawn. And more than 130 members of the House signed a letter to Reno with similar condemnatory language.

A worried Clinton called Reno that Saturday evening to privately discuss the uproar. Then, in a rare show of public dissonance, Clinton sent Reno a letter, released by the White House on Tuesday, in which he said, "I fully agree with the Senate about what the proper scope of the child pornography law should be. I find all forms of child pornography offensive and harmful, as I know you do, and I want the federal government to lead aggressively in the attack against the scourge of child pornography."

Clinton ordered that Justice "should promptly prepare and submit any necessary legislation to ensure that federal law reaches all forms of child pornography."

Rather than cheer Clinton's move, Trueman and other critics insisted it was an effort to deflect criticism. "No change in law is needed," Trueman said. "Congress deserves no blame. Blame it on Reno."

A loyal Reno downplayed any conflict with the White House, saying she and Clinton agreed "one hundred percent. I don't know anyone—certainly not the president and certainly not me—who supports the exploitation of children." Shortly thereafter, the Justice Department sent Congress a recommendation to amend the law to ban "the lascivious exhibition of the genitals or pubic area of any person, whether clothed or unclothed." The recommendation specified that such a display would be illegal if it was clearly designed to elicit "a sexual response in the viewer" regardless of whether the child knew "that the depiction is designed for such a purpose."

That didn't stop 104 members of Congress from petitioning the Supreme Court to uphold the Knox ruling and reject the Justice Department's reading of the original law.

Little noticed in the middle of the furor was a Justice Department announcement that a million-dollar grant would be shared by twenty-six states to help them expand the use of closed-circuit television for testimony in child-abuse cases. It was a pet project of Reno's, who helped pioneer the use of such testimony in the Country Walk baby-sitter's conviction.

"This is the kind of thing we should be spending our time and resources on," one Justice official said. In truth, Reno faced myriad and competing demands for her department's time and resources, including growing security concerns at the nation's borders and beyond.

CHAPTER 12

Policing America's Borders

The deadly bomb that rocked the World Trade Center on February 26, 1993, awoke Americans to the threat of domestic terrorism. Allegedly plotted by a radical Muslim cleric living in the United States, the bombing was one of a series of crises involving the Justice Department's Immigration and Naturalization Service (INS) during Janet Reno's first year on the job.

A long-simmering problem of illegal immigration erupted on several fronts as mercenary Chinese gangs smuggled boatloads of aliens to U.S. coasts, as growing unrest in the Caribbean spurred a new flood of Haitians and Cubans seeking haven in Florida, and as economic refugees by the thousands seemed to cross the U.S.–Mexico border at will.

The year had begun with California Governor Pete Wilson asking Washington for $1.4 billion to offset the cost of federally mandated services his state provides to its escalating population of legal and illegal immigrants. By year's end, Florida Governor Lawton Chiles had announced an even more aggressive approach: Florida would sue both the federal government to seek reimbursement for costs related to illegal aliens and the INS for failing to stem the tide of immigrants.

An estimated 3.3 million illegal immigrants nationwide cost federal, state, and local governments $7.7 billion in 1992, mostly for health care, education, and public assistance, according to an estimate from the conservative Heritage Foundation. The challenge of controlling the forces that push and pull people across America's borders long ago had outgrown the capacity of the historically underfunded and mismanaged INS.

Clearly, regaining control of America's borders looms as one of the greatest challenges confronting the attorney general. In fact, it haunts Reno, who privately fears the potential for nothing less than an "immigration disaster" on her watch.

Reno, who keeps a model of the Statue of Liberty in her conference room, has seen both sides of immigration. In Miami, refugees—Cubans, Haitians, Nicaraguans, Salvadorans, and others—enrich the community economically, socially, and politically, even as they strain schools, hospitals, and courts.

Reno chose a banquet on July 21, 1993, honoring the silver anniversary of the National Council of La Raza, the country's largest Hispanic advocacy organization, to outline her views on immigration policy. Recalling her own Danish roots, Reno praised the immigrant tradition that has made the United States "splendid and strong and given it new visions" but that now burdens public services.

"We've got to understand that the problem is not immigration, it is illegal immigration. And we need to develop a system that is prompt, that is fair, that treats everyone involved with dignity. For those who belong and have earned the right and are entitled to be here, we have got to assure that with due process and dignity.

"For those not entitled to be here, we need to assure due process to them in a swift and understandable and dignified manner, with no abuse from any agency, but with fairness and objectivity."

From around the world, people flock to the United States seeking the promise of better lives, pursuing both political freedom and economic opportunity. America admits three classes of immigrants: refugees who have "a well-founded fear of persecution" because of their ethnicity, race, or political or religious beliefs;

people with desirable talents or skills; and immediate relatives of those legally here. So-called economic refugees seeking only to escape poverty cannot enter.

Despite the rules, enforcement has been difficult. Definitions of some refugee categories have gotten murky, special exceptions have been granted, and patrolling thousands of miles of border and coastline has had limited effectiveness. Three times in the last decade, Congress passed tough immigration reform bills but failed to provide adequate resources to enforce them.

In 1992, more than 1.25 million arrests were made along the U.S.–Mexican border. Because of poor record keeping and the common use of aliases, officials can't say how many of those were repeat offenders, that is, people who were picked up in El Paso or San Diego and sent back across the border, only to try again the next day.

Another three hundred thousand people entered the country on tourist visas or other short-term entry permits, but then stayed beyond their allotted time. They left late or not at all. And some thirty-five thousand refugees sought political asylum upon arriving.

By law, asylum seekers and others can be detained until their appeals are heard. Currently, the INS has a backlog of two hundred thousand people awaiting asylum hearings. But only six thousand beds are available for detention, and the average stay in those beds is twenty-six days. The New York district, which has seen a boom in asylum seekers arriving at John F. Kennedy International Airport, has room for only a hundred detainees.

So most applicants are paroled and given a temporary work permit to support themselves. The vast majority simply disappear, never showing up for their scheduled hearings.

The government's ultimate weapon is deportation. But illegals must be located to be served, and then they have the right to appeal—which can take months or even years. In 1992, fewer than thirty-eight thousand people were deported.

Reno inherited a bureaucratic disaster and chose to express her frustration during a June 20 appearance on David Brinkley's Sunday morning news program on ABC-TV. Just days before, ten

Chinese aliens had drowned after jumping into the sea when the *Golden Venture,* a freighter bringing them to a new life in America, ran aground off Queens, New York.

Reno had just returned from her first visit to the Mexican border in Texas, where she saw Border Patrol agents hamstrung by inadequate equipment. "When you see Border Patrol cars on the border not being used because they don't have radios, you understand the dimension of the problem," she fumed.

Reno vowed to shake up the INS. She told a group of lawyers who specialize in national security issues that she considers it essential to upgrade the INS "in terms of management to become a real partner with the intelligence community, with the diplomatic community, and with the law-enforcement community to address the critical issues that we face."

Two days earlier, on June 18, Clinton had taken a step in that direction by nominating Doris Meissner as INS commissioner. The first commissioner in thirty-one years to have solid experience in immigration issues, Meissner had been actively recruited by Reno after her name appeared on short lists suggested by immigration experts.

Meissner, herself the daughter of immigrants, had been director of the respected Immigration Policy Project at the Carnegie Endowment since 1986, frequently testifying before Congress and conducting conferences on immigration-reform issues. Previously, she had worked at the Justice Department and INS under both Republican and Democratic administrations. In fact, sandwiched between two political appointees in the early 1980s, she had done a stint as acting INS commissioner.

By contrast, Gene McNary, appointed INS commissioner by George Bush, had been Bush's Missouri state campaign coordinator, chief executive officer of St. Louis County, and a twice-unsuccessful candidate for Missouri governor.

Clinton was clearly proud of Reno's pick to run INS. In nominating Meissner, he ranked resolution of immigration problems as a priority due to its link to other goals of his administration.

The president declared that immigration policy "will affect our ability to create jobs for our people, will affect our ability to provide health care to our people, may affect our ability even to pass a health-care program in the United States Congress."

Clinton also announced a more rigorous campaign to stop the smuggling of illegal aliens into the country, which he called "a practice of unspeakable degradation and unspeakable exploitation." Smugglers often charge aliens as much as thirty thousand dollars each, Clinton noted, then force them to work as virtual slaves to repay the debt under threat of death.

The new interdiction effort showed signs of success less than a month later, when three ships carrying 658 Chinese aliens were intercepted in the Pacific by Coast Guard patrol boats and escorted to the west coast of Mexico. The smugglers were arrested. Only one passenger appeared to have grounds to seek refugee status; the rest were hustled aboard planes and sent home. The smugglers quickly turned to other routes.

In Meissner, Reno got an immigration expert who has her own opinions. While at the Carnegie Endowment, Meissner had criticized the 1966 Cuban Adjustment Act, which automatically allows Cubans fleeing Fidel Castro's communist regime quick entry to the United States. After just a year in the United States, they can apply for permanent residency.

Meissner and other critics said the law gives Cuban refugees an unfair advantage over other refugees because they don't have to prove "a well-founded fear of persecution" if they return home. Given the government's tough stance on Haitians, who are considered economic refugees and are seldom able to win asylum, many have called the immigration policy racist.

Governor Chiles made clear his opposition to the open-door policy toward Cuban immigrants in a letter directing Florida Attorney General Bob Butterworth to file suit against the federal government. Chiles wrote, "If the United States government chooses to selectively enforce the law, it has a corresponding obligation to incur the costs associated with this selective enforcement."

But neither Clinton, whose brother-in-law, Hugh Rodham, had married a Cuban-American lawyer, nor Reno, who knew well the political clout of exiles, especially the well-financed Cuban American National Foundation, showed signs of abandoning the dual standard of justice toward Haitians and Cubans. To avoid a head-on collision with her new bosses, Meissner agreed to enforce the law no matter how she felt about it.

Despite a campaign promise to the contrary, Clinton saw the threat of a massive and dangerous exodus from Haiti and decided to continue the Bush administration's policy of repatriating Haitians whose boats were stopped at sea. There had been an influx of refugees after the 1991 coup that deposed elected President Jean Bertrand Aristide.

Voicing concern that Haitians would overwhelm South Florida, Bush ordered the Coast Guard to stop every boat, in effect establishing floating INS offices to process asylum claims immediately and summarily return ineligible aliens to Haiti. While political turmoil raged in Haiti, only a relative handful of the thousands of fleeing Haitians, including some refugees needing AIDS treatment, won admission tickets to the United States. Then the Clinton administration tightened the screws on Haiti, imposing an economic boycott in an effort to restore Aristide to power.

As Aristide's exile dragged on and the violence in his homeland increased, the treatment of Woody Marc Edouard and Carlos Cancio Porcel underscored the inequity of the government's policy regarding Haitian and Cuban immigrants. On December 29, 1992, Cancio, a Cuban airline pilot, had flown a planeload of vacationers from Havana to Miami International Airport instead of the Cuban resort town of Varadero Beach. Forty-seven passengers, including some of his family members, joined Cancio in asking to remain in Miami. Five others, including the copilot, who had been jumped and then manacled during the flight, returned to Cuba.

The influential Cuban exile community complained loudly when Reno's Justice Department brought the copilot and other witnesses back to Miami, with the Cuban government's cooperation, to appear before a grand jury considering hijacking charges against Cancio. In September 1993, following weeks of consultations between Miami and Washington, the case was dropped. While Reno took part in the discussions, she said she left the final decision to the federal prosecutor in Miami—Roberto Martinez, a Cuban American.

Cancio, who was driving a lunch wagon in Miami to support his family, said he was grateful to be in a land where justice was done.

Edouard, a Haitian, also was involved in a hijacking, but his treatment bore little resemblance to Cancio's. On February 18, 1993, Edouard hijacked a missionary organization's DC-3 from a Haitian airstrip. Waving a .38-caliber pistol, Edouard ordered the pilot to fly him to Miami. A shot was fired, but no one was injured, and Edouard's attorney said it had been accidental. He also claimed Edouard feared for his life in Haiti and had to escape. But Edouard was charged with air piracy.

Federal prosecutors in Miami justified the disparity in the two cases this way: Whereas Cancio was the pilot and had been in control of his plane from takeoff to landing, Edouard had commandeered someone else's plane. Haitian advocates saw that as hairsplitting.

Even more disparate was the treatment accorded Cuban and Haitian refugees who landed together on Miami Beach in a twenty-five-foot boat. The nine Haitians and seven Cubans landed behind the ritzy Bath Club on December 18, 1993. The two groups had met in the Bahamas, where they pooled their resources and bought the thirty-five-hundred-dollar craft. But under American law, the two groups faced different fates. The Cubans were released; the Haitians were detained.

Reno raised eyebrows in another case. Eight Cuban refugees headed for Miami in a rickety boat drifted off course and then sank off the coast of Mexico. Exiles in Miami were in an uproar when the Mexican government immediately returned the refugees to Havana. Mexico agreed to get them back and send them to the United States when Reno, moved by their story, approved special visas for them to enter the United States.

Justice officials insisted Reno's decision was a one-time-only action, but there were fears at INS that it could establish a precedent.

Challenged as Miami is by immigration, the Los Angeles area has absorbed four times as many immigrants in recent years. In fact, California is home to 52 percent of all illegal immigrants in the United States.

Governor Wilson, who estimates that illegal immigrants cost his state $3 billion a year, wants to cap the flow of red ink by cutting off all benefits to illegal aliens and denying citizenship to the children born in the United States of illegal immigrants. In response to his request in 1993 for $1.4 billion in federal funds, he received $324 million.

In August 1993, Reno underscored her concern over the immigration issue by making a second visit to the border, this time the border between San Diego and Tijuana, in the company of California's Democratic senators, Barbara Boxer and Dianne Feinstein. She used the occasion to announce a joint effort with the U.S. Customs Service to improve processing at border checkpoints and to express optimism that a recent request by Clinton for $172.5 million in emergency funding for INS would enable the agency to boost staffing for the Border Patrol.

The funding request, a drop in the bucket for an agency with an annual budget of $1.6 billion, was later approved by Congress, and Meissner rushed to get new border agents hired, trained, and assigned.

At the press conference, Reno deflected questions about the politics of "closing" the border by means of an electrified fence or any of the other proposals that have been bandied about over the years.

"I really want to be as candid as I can with the American people about what can and can't work," she stated. "It is terribly important that we do not let bitterness or bigotry divide us on this issue. It is important that we talk through issues and come up with reasoned solutions."

In early October, Reno returned to San Diego, this time on a political mission. The proposed North American Free Trade Agreement (NAFTA) was in big trouble in Congress, and Clinton called on all his cabinet members to help lobby for passage. For Reno, support for NAFTA came easily; she saw a link between free trade and her immigration-reform agenda. In a speech to the University of California's Graduate School of International Relations and Pacific Studies, Reno shared her conviction that NAFTA would boost Mexico's economy and thus ease illegal immigration.

"Let us protect our borders with the most personnel and the best technology we can muster, but let us also face facts: A richer, more stable, more competent Mexico is the only solution, I think, to real, substantial immigration reform."

She also argued that NAFTA would "cement for decades" the already improving cooperation by Mexico on law-enforcement issues, especially drug trafficking across the border. "The trade agreement will make cooperation between our countries the norm instead of the exception. With NAFTA in place, I can work far more effectively with my Mexican counterparts to insure tough, honest enforcement of our antidrug laws."

The following week, Reno made her first foreign foray, a thirty-six-hour visit to Mexico City. On October 11, she met with President Carlos Salinas de Gortari and Mexican Attorney General Jorge Carpizo Macgregor, toured their new, high-tech drug war headquarters, and repeated her arguments for passage of NAFTA during a press conference at Los Pinos, the home of the Mexican president.

She and Carpizo announced a prisoner exchange policy that would allow the United States to ship Mexican criminals held in American prisons back to Mexico to complete their sentences. When she first took office Reno had been shocked to learn that 26 percent of the inmates in the federal prison system were aliens, including about eight thousand Mexican nationals. Freeing up that prison space wouldn't hurt with the NAFTA sales job on Capitol Hill, either.

Reno delighted her hosts when she recited in Spanish, albeit poorly accented, part of a Mexican poem about friendship. She also presented Salinas with a personal gift, a vibrantly colored quilted jacket made by Florida's Seminole Indians. (She had looked over but passed up the bookends, paperweights, and desk sets with the Justice Department seal that are the traditional gifts for such occasions.) Salinas was pleased with the jacket, telling Reno, "It's beautiful! So beautiful it could be Mexican!"

When she returned to Washington, Reno did some personal lobbying for NAFTA, meeting with immigration experts to convince them to support the pact and contacting members of Congress to answer their concerns. She found one member, Florida Republican E. Clay Shaw, withholding his support because of his concern that Mexico was ignoring existing extradition treaties.

Shaw had a specific case in mind: The four-year-old niece of one of his aides had been raped in southern California by a Mexican day laborer, who fled back across the border to elude capture. Reno won Shaw's vote for NAFTA by getting the personal assurance of her new friend, Mexican Attorney General Carpizo, that the suspect would be returned to California for trial as soon as he was caught.

Reno faced other immigration problems that began before her tenure. The most visible—involving Sheik Omar Ahman Ali Abdel Rahman—might have been avoided if the U.S. embassy in the Sudan had checked the State Department's "watch list" before issuing the Moslem cleric a tourist visa in July 1990. Based on allegations that he had fomented revolution in his native Egypt, the State Department had identified Abdel Rahman as an "undesirable" and put his name on a watch list, but the embassy overlooked it.

Abdel Rahman, who is blind, had been acquitted on a charge of inciting violent riots in a city south of Cairo in 1989, but Egyptian president Hosni Mubarak exercised his legal prerogative to reject the verdict and sought to have him retried. The sheik also made false statements on his visa application, concealing that he was a polygamist and that he had been convicted for forging a check.

A year after he first entered the country, Abdel Rahman applied for and was granted permanent resident alien status. He gained a reputation for preaching fiery political sermons to Muslim followers at mosques in Brooklyn, New York, and Jersey City, New Jersey. One of his followers, El Sayyid A. Nosair, another Egyptian, was accused—and acquitted—of the 1990 murder of a militant Jewish rabbi, Meir Kahane.

The sheik lost his permanent resident status on March 6, 1992, when the INS learned about the lies on his visa application. He then applied for political asylum, saying he faced reprisals if he returned to Egypt. That was denied because of evidence that he had traveled back and forth to the Middle East several times, making stops in Egypt.

An immigration judge ruled in March 1993 that Abdel Rahman was "excludable," meaning he had no legal reason to remain in the United States. That ruling was unrelated to the World Trade Center bombing, which had taken place just two weeks earlier. Although the suspects in the bombing were identified as followers of Abdel Rahman's, he denied any knowledge of their activities and publicly deplored the violence.

Abdel Rahman was allowed to remain free while he appealed the exclusion order. But then on June 23 came the breakup of the second bombing plot—whose targets included the United Nations, the Lincoln and Holland tunnels, and the George Washington Bridge—as the result of information given by an informant who served as Abdel Rahman's translator and bodyguard. The informant, Emad A. Salem, a former Egyptian army officer, provided secretly recorded tapes of the plotters and directed agents to the safe house where five men were mixing materials for bombs.

The case created an internal battle within the Justice Department. The link to Abdel Rahman was there, but it was a little tenuous for Reno. She initially overruled New York U.S. Attorney Mary Jo White and her assistants and investigators, who feared Abdel Rahman might flee and wanted to pick him up when they made their other arrests. Reno concurred with Criminal Division lawyers at Justice, who said evidence tying Abdel Rahman to the plot seemed too weak to justify charges against him—even though he was heard on one tape saying, "American blood must be spilled on its own soil."

Reno immediately took heat for her decision to let Abdel Rahman remain free. Senator Alfonse D'Amato, the abrasive New York Republican who was alleged to be one of the suspects' assassination targets, demanded a meeting with Reno in Washington. When a clutch of reporters and cameras also appeared at D'Amato's office, Reno stayed just long enough to hear D'Amato spout off but left without saying anything into the microphones.

As Reno continued to mull over the case, she authorized New York prosecutor White to bypass the usual chain of command and make her case for the sheik's arrest directly to Reno. In early July, as additional evidence in the case began to fall into place, Reno relented to an extent, agreeing that Abdel Rahman should be detained pending the outcome of his asylum appeal.

The sheik's lawyers promised he would surrender outside the Abu Bakr Mosque in Brooklyn on Thursday, July 8. But Abdel Rahman refused to come out for twenty hours, and at one point another bearded man dressed to resemble the sheik attempted to lead agents away. Finally, he surrendered at six P.M. on Friday. Just a few days earlier, an Egyptian judge had issued a warrant for the sheik on the riot charge, and the Egyptian government had made an extradition request.

But Egypt would have to wait. The sheik was being held in a detention facility seventy-five miles from New York City when a new, much broader indictment—approved by Reno—was handed down on August 25. Additional investigation, plus further analysis of the informant's secret tapes, led Reno to approve charging Abdel Rahman as the leader of a wide-ranging terrorist conspiracy that included the World Trade Center bombing and the other plots.

The charges, based in part on a nineteenth-century sedition law, said Abdel Rahman and fourteen others conspired "to levy a war of urban terrorism against the United States." The indictment said that Abdel Rahman's religious rhetoric "provided instruction regarding whether certain acts of terrorism were permissible or forbidden."

It also said the conspiracy reached back to Rabbi Kahane's killing and forward to a plan to assassinate Mubarak, the Egyptian president. Nosair, acquitted of state charges in Kahane's murder, now faced federal charges in the case.

Lawyers for Abdel Rahman and other defendants called it an overreaching indictment issued for political gain. "What they have done is take every allegation, every rumor, every loose end and created a vast, mythical Islamic conspiracy," attorney Ronald L. Kuby told the *New York Times.*

But President Clinton praised Reno's oversight of the case, saying the decision to wait for the larger indictment was "a tough call" that she had made without political considerations.

"I don't want to mislead you. I know she had discussions with the national security team, with the foreign policy team, on the implications of it; I know that she thought through all these things," Clinton said, adding that he himself did not discuss a possible indictment with Reno. "That was her decision, and it never occurred to me that I needed to have any contact with her. I knew I could trust her."

During the trial at which four bombers were convicted, transcripts of the informant's tapes began to leak. It turned out that Salem had been taping conversations with his FBI handlers as well as with Abdel Rahman and the other conspirators. Based on Salem's boasts, questions arose as to whether the FBI could have obtained enough early information to enable it to prevent the World Trade Center bombing. But Reno and other officials denied that there had been any missed opportunities to stop that part of the plot. Salem, who had been paid for his cooperation, was put in the federal witness-protection program.

Given the relentless pace of events, Reno works fourteen- to sixteen-hour days at Justice, varying her schedule only to make speeches to selected audiences where she wants to pitch her agenda.

In a city where power brokers lunch at The Monocle on Capitol Hill or Duke Zeibert's and The Palm downtown, then schmooze with media celebrities at Georgetown dinner parties, Reno doesn't play the game. In fact, her social events are so infrequent as to attract notice.

When she accepted a dinner invitation from Barbra Streisand, *People* magazine reported on their evening at a posh Georgetown restaurant. Of course, the popular entertainer wields considerable clout; she's a potent political fund-raiser in Hollywood. Asked later what they discussed, Streisand said, "Lots of things. Women's issues. Cooking."

On June 6, 1993, Reno appeared at a memorial service for Robert Kennedy at his grave site at Arlington National Cemetery, where she and President Clinton read selections of Kennedy's speeches. That event sparked a friendship with the Kennedy clan, and she accepted a dinner invitation to Hickory Hill, the family home in Virginia.

Other than business dinners and obligatory appearances at White House receptions, though, Reno has kept her social schedule light. She has also changed the rules of engagement with the Washington press. Uninterested in personal publicity, she doesn't court coverage or offer the kind of "deep background" that keeps the media in attentive captivity. According to Justice Department public affairs director Carl Stern, "She's never asked me to put out a story on this or that."

When she began accepting invitations for lunches with journalists in late July, she made them working affairs, sitting for interviews with the bureaus of Knight-Ridder Inc. (which publishes the *Miami Herald* and more than two dozen other papers), the *Los Angeles Times,* the Associated Press, and others, as well as the *Washington Post's* editorial board.

Yet Reno worried that she wasn't as accessible as she had promised to be. So she began holding weekly "press availabilities" in August. Every Thursday morning at nine-thirty, she sits at one end of a long, highly polished conference table and fields questions from two dozen or more reporters. A single television camera records her answers and feeds them to the networks.

Despite a barrage of questions from journalists, the sessions usually yield little news. Reno is resolute about never commenting on pending cases, so most of her replies are terse. Asked, however, about one of her favorite themes—crime prevention or children and violence, for example—she will volunteer a big smile, declare, "You give me such a pulpit!" and expound.

Occasionally reporters reveal their frustration through caustic humor. At the August 19 weekly roundtable, a reporter asked if she was "any closer" to recommending a new chief of the Civil Rights Division to replace Lani Guinier.

"Yes," Reno replied.

"Can you comment on that further, perhaps?" the reporter tried.

"No," Reno said, and some chuckling began. "I mean, I don't know how you define closeness."

"How do *you* define closeness?" the reporter asked.

Reno shook her head and said, "I'm closer to it," drawing a bigger laugh.

At another point during that same briefing, reporters tried to get Reno to confirm a new book's report that a sweeping espionage investigation was under way at the FBI. The book said identities of informants had been provided by a former Soviet KGB agent at the end of the Cold War. When she declined to comment, one journalist suggested that Reno should "steer us off" if such a report is "completely off the wall"—especially if it involves the president or someone else in high office.

With a smile, Reno declared, "There is not a pending investigation of anything off the wall about President Clinton, and therefore I can comment on it to tell you there is not an investigation of anything off the wall about President Clinton."

A bevy of New York reporters rushed to Washington for Reno's September 9 briefing, having been told that she would open with an announcement about the Justice Department's investigation of the emotional Crown Heights case.

In August 1991, a Hasidic scholar was killed by a mob of black youths. A teenager confessed to stabbing the scholar, Yankel Rosenbaum, and was charged by the Brooklyn prosecutor. But the teen recanted and was acquitted by a jury. That brought pressure on the Justice Department to take over the case using federal civil-rights statutes.

Word started to leak late Wednesday, September 8, that Justice officials had concluded there was no basis for a federal prosecution because it looked impossible to prove either a conspiracy to deny Rosenbaum his rights, or that local officials were to blame in the death. Jewish community leaders and New York politicians began to protest.

The next morning Reno, without apology, told the New York reporters that their trips had been wasted. She had agreed to a delay to give the local prosecutor time to make one more legal argument in writing, she said. She would say only that she had asked for a final report "as soon as possible" and would make up her mind "based on the evidence and the law."

Reno denied any political considerations in her decision. But New York press reports suggested that the Clinton administration had yielded to political pressures not to drop the case during the heated days leading up to New York City's mayoral election. In November, Democratic Mayor David Dinkins was defeated by a law-and-order candidate, former federal prosecutor Rudolph Giuliani. Then, in late January 1994, Reno suddenly declared that the Justice Department would take on the case after all. She had moved only after the local prosecutor said he couldn't make a case against a second suspect who emerged during the delay that Reno had forced.

Some critics, including members of New York's congressional delegation, offered lukewarm praise of Reno's decision to finally get involved. They expressed the fear that her delays would only make the case tougher to win, given the passage of time and the likelihood that witnesses would be lost or would have forgotten crucial details.

As stories of the larger New York bombing conspiracy again filled the press, Reno was asked at one of her weekly sessions if she saw a danger that Americans would get hysterical about Islamic fundamentalism and the potential for terrorism. Reno turned the question back on the reporter with a smile.

"Well, I, for one, am trying my very level best not to be hysterical about it, and I know that you and the rest of the media are going to join in a responsible effort to make sure that we are not hysterical."

She added that the worldwide reliance on increasingly sophisticated technology makes every nation vulnerable to terrorism, and "we've got to take commonsense, vigorous precautions against it." To that end, she had directed FBI director Louis Freeh "that one of his first objectives would be to satisfy himself that the bureau was doing everything that it could" to combat new forms of terrorism.

Yet for most Americans, the threat of terrorism seems remote compared to the daily—and deadly—reality of street crime.

CHAPTER 13

Crime, Punishment, and a Quest for Solutions

It was a wet, drizzly Sunday afternoon on October 31, 1993—Halloween—when Janet Reno indulged in a rare opportunity to survey her habitat. Wearing slacks, a waterproof jacket, and her old canvas boat hat with the slouchy brim, Reno roamed the streets and neighborhoods of the nation's capital. As anonymously as she could with two FBI security guards trailing close behind, Reno walked for miles, studying Washington landmarks and reading historical markers.

Far from her favorite haunts in the vast, stark Everglades, she nonetheless enjoyed her stroll. "It was a wonderful time to walk because there was a mist and a rain," she later reflected, ". . . as if Washington was kind of a magical place. . . ."

Reno needed a day off. After eight months on the job, she was learning that Washington could be a tough, decidedly unmagical town for an outsider, a place where "what if" is a long way from "what is."

It was her political savvy, not her legal skills, that was being put to the test. Her campaign to cool decades of scorching rhetoric on crime and to incorporate prevention in the national debate along with prosecution and incarceration was meeting with mixed success.

The job didn't get easier when tourist slayings in Florida, the murder of the father of basketball player Michael Jordan in North

292

Carolina, the kidnapping and murder of twelve-year-old Polly Klaas in Petaluma, California, and a murderous shooting rampage on a Long Island, New York, commuter train were in the headlines as the House and Senate began debating a tough crime-control bill.

The deaths of several children hit by stray bullets not far from Capitol Hill also shocked lawmakers. A chilling follow-up story on the front page of the *Washington Post* depicted youngsters so frightened by the violence around them that they planned their own funerals. One of the children, eleven-year-old Jessica Bradford, wanted to be laid out in her sixth-grade prom gown. "When I die," she said, "I want to be dressy for my family."

Clinton cited the November 1 article in several speeches, including an emotional appeal for involvement by the black community in addressing the causes of crime, a message delivered from the pulpit of the Memphis church where the Reverend Dr. Martin Luther King, Jr., had preached his last sermon. "The freedom to die before you're a teenager is not what Martin Luther King lived and died for," Clinton said.

The president deplored the "great crisis of the spirit that is gripping America today," adding, "I tell you, it is our moral duty to turn it around."

Practically unnoticed during this spate of national breast-beating was the fact that crime rates actually have been declining, according to data released by Reno's own department during her first year. In a survey of Americans' personal experiences with crime, the Bureau of Justice Statistics reported a 6 percent drop in the overall number of "victimizations" between 1973 and 1992.

But to the average citizen hearing the constant drumbeat of news reports about carjackings, drive-by shootings, and burglaries, the country seems beset by a crime wave. There were, after all, more than 18.8 million "victimizations" in 1992, or nearly one incident for every ten people. All told, 6.6 million, just over one-third, of the incidents were violent crimes.

Indeed, that survey and others indicate that the very nature of crime and criminals is changing: Crime is increasingly concentrated in cities, and the majority of offenders and victims are black. The average age of violent offenders is shockingly younger than it was two decades ago, dropping from eighteen years and three months to fifteen years and four months. In 1992, 4,516 juveniles were charged with murder in the United States. Gunshots, which kill more than thirty-seven thousand Americans each year, are the leading cause of death of young men.

Sociologists blame much of the crime on poverty, joblessness, single-parent households, and other grim socioeconomic factors characteristic of urban cores. There is also the corrosive lure of illegal drugs, the devastating firepower of automatic weapons, and, as Reno and others argue, the pervasive violence celebrated in popular culture. Many of the incidents appearing on the six o'clock news are all the more tragic for their utter senselessness, such as the killings over leather jackets or gold neck chains or status-symbol automobiles.

The violence continues despite the fact that more than 925,000 men and women are being held in state and federal prisons, a new record. The number of inmates under the control of the U.S. Bureau of Prisons, yet another fiefdom in the vast Justice Department that Reno oversees, grew by 8.4 percent in 1993—to nearly 87,000 inmates—almost double the growth rate for state prisons.

It's little wonder that the prison system is overwhelmed. In most states, inmates serve only a portion of their sentences, then are released to make room for new offenders. In Reno's home state, prisoners may serve as little as a third of their time.

And a national study by the U.S. Sentencing Commission found that laws requiring certain felons to serve mandatory minimum sentences, especially for drug-possession convictions, were causing even greater pressure on prison wardens to release inmates, including those convicted of violent crimes who received no mandatory terms.

Critics charged Reno with having little impact on the sweeping federal legislation that was Congress's assault on crime. Defenders countered that Reno, a latecomer to the administration, used her limited time to focus on where she could influence the debate.

At issue was the anticrime bill prepared by Democrats during the 1991–92 session of Congress, passed by the House but stalled by Senate Republicans and the ultimate threat of George Bush's veto. During his 1992 campaign, Bill Clinton endorsed the bill, and it was back on the table in 1993.

As the debate cranked up, Deputy Attorney General Phil Heymann said the bill "does good things. The thought [in the Clinton administration] is to go with a good bill and not to try to remake it. When everybody tries to remake it, you often end up with something far afield."

Reno first focused on one of the bill's most contentious sections: death-penalty appeals. Tired of delayed executions, conservatives had long sought to restrict the right of appeal based on the narrowly defined habeas corpus rules, which allow inmates to repeatedly return to court on new appeals of their cases. One proposal, dubbed the "one bite of the apple" approach, would limit felons to a single appeal to federal courts. Liberals and death-penalty opponents argued against the limit, which would preclude further appeals even under such compelling circumstances as the emergence of new evidence or inadequacy of counsel.

Using her credibility with the nation's prosecutors, Reno joined Senate Judiciary Committee Chairman Joseph Biden at meetings with proponents of an appeal limit, including leaders of the National District Attorneys Association, the attorneys general of the states, and other law-enforcement groups, where she worked to negotiate a compromise. Although personally opposed to the death penalty, she had long ago learned the necessity of finding common ground with its advocates.

At one meeting, according to William O'Malley, the district attorney in Plymouth County, Massachusetts, Reno said, " 'Okay, I know what you're against. What are you for?' It was a novel question for us, in a way. She asked us to articulate in a positive, affirmative way the legislation that we could support that dealt with the very complex, arcane issue of habeas corpus reform."

Reno also teamed up with Clinton's national drug policy co-ordinator, Lee Brown, to push for greater community policing, her top personal priority. As police commissioner in Houston and New York City, Brown had successfully put cops back on neighborhood beats.

Clinton and Congress had already included $150 million for community policing grants in a jobs bill that passed in early summer. (Reno was determined that the grants would be distributed by the end of 1993. When seventy-four recipients were announced, she, Clinton, and Gore staged a conference call to six mayors from the Oval Office just before Christmas.) Another $10 million was committed by the Labor Department to retrain newly discharged military troops for police work.

But Reno also wanted funding for new officers in the crime bill targeted to community policing. She argued for giving local and state governments as much flexibility in spending the money as possible, so long as their projects were consistent with the national goals of putting cops on the beat, not additional administrators behind desks.

Clinton announced his endorsement of Biden's core bill, plus some added features, at a Rose Garden ceremony on August 11. For the obligatory photo opportunity, Clinton, along with Gore and Reno, stood in front of a battalion of stern-looking police officers. They were flanked by state and local prosecutors on one side and Biden, House Judiciary Committee chairman Jack Brooks, and other key Democratic lawmakers on the other.

"This plan is tough," said Clinton. "It is fair. It will put police on the street and criminals in jail. It expands the federal death penalty to let criminals know that if they are guilty, they will be punished. It lets law-abiding citizens know that we are working to give them the safety that they deserve."

Reno's remarks were characteristically to the point: "As a former prosecutor, I understand how difficult the issues are on the streets. That's where the real problems develop. That's where the police have the hardest job of anybody involved in this effort, and we need to do something to actually support them and stop talking about it."

In Biden's bill, the hard-liners had won the habeas corpus issue; death-row inmates would be limited to a single appeal to federal courts, to be filed within six months of the conclusion of all appeals in state court. But Biden and Reno tossed a bone to liberals. The bill would mandate establishment of committees of defense lawyers in each state to write standards for defense counsel that would help ensure qualified representation for each defendant charged in a capital crime, the defense tab to be shared by federal and state governments.

Defense lawyers, who weren't invited into the negotiations, said they weren't sure the proposal would work and weren't ready to support it, even though Heymann convened a special meeting to try to sell it to them and others. Those who attended, including former Watergate prosecutor Sam Dash, left with the impression that Reno's team hadn't gotten nearly what they wanted but were required by their loyalty to Clinton to support the package. Given her appointment in March, Reno "simply arrived too late to have the impact that we would expect her to have, given her well-known positions on a lot of these issues," Dash said.

But Reno's influence was clear in other provisions. The bill would authorize $3.4 billion to hire an additional fifty thousand police officers over five years (an 8 percent increase in the number of sworn officers in state and local police agencies), expand drug treatment for federal prisoners, establish drug courts, build additional boot camps for young offenders, and impose a five-day waiting period for purchasing a handgun—the so-called Brady bill. Reno called the package "essential."

She also promised to pursue a full ban on assault weapons, although Biden and other lawmakers saw that as too high a hurdle to include in the bill. Clinton, by an executive order dated August 11, banned the importation of Uzis and other assault weapons manufactured overseas. It was a symbolic act; when it comes to assault weapons, most American criminals buy American. But Clinton couldn't ban domestic manufacture on his own.

In a second executive order, Clinton told the Bureau of

Alcohol, Tobacco and Firearms to draw up new standards for the federal licensing of gun dealers. More than 286,000 licenses had been issued, which enabled dealers to order weapons and ammunition from manufacturers at a discount. Many "dealers" sold out of their kitchens and car trunks, with little if any regulation.

Reno advocated passage of the crime bill on all the morning television news shows, in speeches around the country, and even in a promotion for what turned out to be a forgettable movie.

At the kickoff for National Night Out, a ten-year-old event that seeks to encourage Americans to get involved in community crime-control programs, Reno was introduced by Meteor Man, the superhero star of a new comedy-adventure movie of the same name. Meteor Man was portrayed by Robert Townsend, the writer-director of the film, which had a brief run at the end of the summer. When the costumed Townsend introduced Reno as an inspirational real-life hero, she drew a laugh when she responded, "I only hope that when I'm through being attorney general, you'll say the same thing."

The administration trotted out endorsements for its package—including one by Mississippi's attorney general, meant to suggest that even Southerners believed it was tough—but critics were equally fast on the draw.

California Attorney General Daniel Lungren, a conservative Republican and former congressman, said that any changes to the habeas corpus provisions would invite judicial scrutiny and "undermine the death penalty and promote more delay and litigation." William Barr, George Bush's attorney general, called the package a retreat from the hard-line policies of the Reagan-Bush years.

And the National Rifle Association (NRA) labeled the Clinton-endorsed bill "short on criminal justice and long on firearms restrictions." When ABC's Joan Lunden asked Reno how she would "battle the powerful NRA," she replied, "You battle 'the powerful

NRA' with common sense. America has for too long watched what guns have done to people on our streets."

But the most influential opposition came from liberal Democrats in the House, mainly blacks and Hispanics, who viewed the bill as too harsh, too determined to "lock-'em-up" without adequate efforts to rehabilitate. Shortly after Judiciary Chairman Brooks introduced the bill in the House, the black and Hispanic caucuses vowed to fight it, decrying the forty-seven new offenses that would carry the death penalty and other provisions. They represented fifty-eight crucial votes.

Opposition from Republicans and some conservative Democrats also solidified, their ranks joined by several police organizations when state and local officials discovered that the increased aid promised by Clinton, including $700 million to build ten regional prisons, had significant strings attached that would require state compliance with federal rules.

In a dramatic move, Brooks gutted his version of the bill to save it, stripping out all controversial elements, including the habeas corpus compromise. His committee passed its noncontroversial elements, broken down into four bills for tactical reasons, plus the Brady bill, on October 28 and sent that package to the full House, which passed this first version on November 3. Attention moved to the Senate.

In the meantime, Reno had landed in a political brier patch.

She had appeared at a news conference in mid-September with Democratic Governor James Florio of New Jersey, who was embroiled in a tough reelection fight against Republican Christine Todd Whitman. Under the glare of television lights, Reno and Florio stood behind a carefully arranged display of fearsome-looking assault weapons, weapons now banned under a state law pushed by Florio.

Several newspapers and Whitman's forces criticized Reno for politicizing her office. David Wilhelm, chairman of the Democratic National Committee, fed that perception when he listed Reno as one of the presidential surrogates who had campaigned on Florio's behalf. But Reno and her aides insisted that her appearance with Florio was a nonpartisan effort to build support for a national assault-weapons ban.

Ironically, Reno could have easily avoided the New Jersey quagmire. She had received an invitation to the White House for the same date, Monday, September 13, to witness the Middle East peace ceremony on the South Lawn and the historic handshake between Israeli President Yitzhak Rabin and Palestinian leader Yasir Arafat.

Reno chose to keep her date in New Jersey. Standing up Florio was one thing, but she didn't want to disappoint the children at the two elementary schools she planned to visit in Hackensack and Piscataway.

As the Senate prepared to debate the crime bill, Biden took a tack contrary to Brooks's. Rather than strip it down, he allowed the bill to be loaded up, figuring that every item then would be negotiable when House and Senate versions were consolidated in conference committee.

In a week of debate charged by the most scarifying crime stories to be gleaned from the media, senators more than doubled the price of the president's plan—to $22.3 billion over five years. To appease critics concerned about the cost, the Senate bill held Clinton and Gore to their promise to cut 250,000 federal jobs over five years and required the savings to go into a Violent Crime Reduction Trust Fund.

Senate Appropriations Chairman Robert Byrd, the wily West Virginia Democrat known for his mastery of the budget, declared that the trust fund plan assured that "spending in this act matches its rhetoric."

The Senate bill included $7.5 billion for a hundred thousand new police officers, $3 billion for alternative jails—including military-style boot camps—$3 billion for regional prisons, $1.8 billion for programs to prevent violence against women, and $500 million for institutions for violent juveniles.

Despite objections from state and local officials, the bill included Republican-drafted provisions requiring states to make those convicted of violent crimes serve at least 85 percent of their sentences or lose their eligibility to participate in the prison-building program. Other amendments made it a federal crime to belong to a "street gang" or to persuade someone to join one, which carried a ten-year mandatory sentence. The National Conference of State Legislatures estimated that complying would cost states an extra $12 billion for more resources, such as additional state courts and parole officers.

Biden and other Senate leaders had decided to bring up the Brady bill separately, but with Reno's support, California Democrat Dianne Feinstein offered an amendment banning nineteen military-style assault weapons. The 56–43 vote on that amendment reflected the waning influence of the NRA.

Most of the deals were done on November 4, just two days after elections in Virginia, New York City, and other areas reflected strong public sentiment for a crackdown on crime. One Senate amendment, approved 91 to 1, mirrored the "three strikes and you're out" statute approved by voters in Washington State, which made life sentences mandatory for a third violent felony conviction in federal court. Clinton himself endorsed the provision in his first State of the Union speech.

True to form, senators embraced the bloated bill, 94 to 4, despite concerns about the cost and the constitutionality of some provisions. It was a package that shocked Reno's friends and supporters. Some of its most-touted provisions were at odds with her personal priorities, most obviously the nearly fifty additional federal crimes given the death penalty and the additional minimum mandatory sentences. More than a few groups who had expected Reno to have her way with Congress were introduced to the painful reality of political compromise.

Reno said the administration supported the Senate bill "on balance," although she declined to discuss specific sections with reporters. Both Reno and Heymann uneasily admitted that some amendments had gotten ahead of them, that they hadn't been able to keep track of much of what was happening in time to influence the decisions. Although she was still handicapped by a less than fully staffed department, Reno could hardly have expected to track the dozens of amendments scribbled quickly in Senate offices and rushed to the floor in the final throes of debate. Reno promised to study each provision in the final package in hopes of influencing the negotiations with the House in 1994.

But it was an overstatement to accuse her, as did *New York Times* columnist Anthony Lewis and *Newsweek*'s Conventional Wisdom column, of being absent from the Senate debate. "Where Is Janet Reno?" the headline on Lewis's November 22 column asked.

Condemning some of the Senate's harsher provisions, Lewis wrote, "And where was Attorney General Reno while the Senate was tackling these retrograde, self-defeating steps? Neither she nor her aides testified on the subject. They had some private conversations with senators, but her voice was far from what we would have expected: strong and forthright."

Newsweek gave Reno a thumbs-down and summed up: "Former Waco star AWOL on crime bill. Unfireable but unloved at White House." In fact, those two perceptions were at odds: By keeping her mouth shut in public, Reno loyally protected many of Clinton's initiatives in the package and boosted her stock at the White House, despite *Newsweek*'s conclusion. She had done the job her president had wanted.

Indeed, Reno had made a strategic decision that paid off. She ignored the politically sticky issues that were likely to leave her frustrated and instead addressed realistic opportunities to make changes in policy. And there she scored some successes that she hopes will lead to meaningful change.

She helped fashion the $8.9 billion police-hiring program to emphasize community policing, worked with Feinstein to lobby for the assault-weapons ban, helped craft the $3 billion jail expansion program to include boot camps for juveniles, lobbied for a $1.2 billion program to finance drug courts like Miami's for three years, and pushed drug treatment for federal prisoners.

"Her fingerprints are all over the bill," said Justice Department spokesman Carl Stern.

While her work with Feinstein on the assault-weapons ban was highlighted at a Capitol Hill press conference, Reno worked behind the scenes on other issues, conferring privately with caucuses of lawmakers or one-on-one, often in meetings that did not appear on her schedule. She worked the phones and the citizens' groups, asking them to lobby their lawmakers during her speaking engagements across the country.

One of her forums was a Democratic Policy Committee meeting in September. Her discussion of the bill "impressed the hell out of those of us who didn't know her that well," recalled one senator. "She didn't have notes; she knew what she wanted to say; she handled questions with authority. And probably most impressive was that, when she didn't know an answer, she admitted it without any sense of embarrassment or without trying to give a facile response that would mean nothing."

The truth is, Reno couldn't have won on certain issues. A tidal wave of political fury had engulfed the Senate, capable of swamping anything and anyone perceived as soft on crime.

Biden was crushed in his attempt to head off an amendment offered by New York Republican Alfonse D'Amato that targeted for execution anyone convicted as a "drug kingpin." Biden pointed to constitutional weaknesses in the amendment, including the fact that prosecutors would not be required to prove that a kingpin's trafficking led to a specific death; rather, that responsibility for deaths could be reasonably assumed based on the quantity of drugs involved. Yet, D'Amato's amendment passed on a vote of 74 to 25.

Michigan Democrat Carl Levin offered an amendment substituting life sentences without the possibility of parole for the new death-penalty sanctions in the package. His amendment was voted down 73 to 26.

Reno "knew what direction things were going in and decided to work on what could be influenced," a top Justice Department official said. "She is, after all, a member of Bill Clinton's team, and he made it clear what he wanted to see in the crime bill. She couldn't go against the president. So she decided to spend her energy on things that mattered to her."

Biden, too, said criticism of Reno is "a bum rap." He told the *Washington Post* that "she wasn't going to change anybody's mind any more than I was or the president was." In fact, he dropped the carefully crafted death-penalty appeals provision in the face of some outspoken opposition.

Reno did abandon her effort to repeal some minimum mandatory sentences. She had long listened to the complaint by some judges and many defense lawyers that the more than one hundred mandatory sentences put in sixty different federal statutes between 1986 and 1990—the first era of the drug war—removed discretion from sentencing and locked away minor offenders. Both Biden and Utah Senator Orrin Hatch, the top Republican on the Judiciary Committee, had agreed that the consequences of minimum mandatories should be studied. Reno had ordered a study in April and found relatively few cases where nonviolent offenders with no prior record were being given stiff sentences for minor involvement in a drug deal.

Reno regrouped for negotiations on the crime bill in February 1994. When Jamie Gorelick came to the Justice Department, Ron Klain—the associate White House counsel who managed Reno's confirmation—also moved to the Justice Department as Reno's "counselor."

His first priority was to coordinate dealings with Capitol Hill, as when Criminal Division chief Jo Ann Harris urged the House Judiciary Committee in March to temper the popular "three-strikes-and-you're-out" provision to target the most seriously violent felons. Still, the bill was more favorable to hard-liners' views than Reno's. She privately feared that the three-strikes mandate would lead to housing old-timers no longer a threat to society.

On a parallel track with the crime package, the Brady bill represented the first change in federal gun-purchase laws since Congress banned mail-order sales of rifles in 1968 after the murders of Robert F. Kennedy and Martin Luther King, Jr.

The bill is named for James S. Brady, the burly, garrulous press secretary wounded in the 1981 assassination attempt on President Reagan. Brady remains confined to a wheelchair; his wife Sarah became the chief lobbyist for the legislation, which requires a five-day waiting period between purchase and delivery of a handgun. The wait allows for a police background check of the buyer and a cool-down period for those who might use the weapon in the heat of passion.

During the Bradys' seven-year crusade, several states—including Florida, thanks in large part to Reno's support—adopted some version of the law. But given the NRA's vehement opposition, Congress repeatedly shot it down.

Ultimately, the public, outraged by years of gun-fueled violence, convinced a majority of lawmakers that sports enthusiasts and gun collectors could wait five days for legitimate gun purchases. Even Ronald Reagan, a longtime friend of the NRA, came to support the bill.

The Senate, fresh from passage of its crime-control package, took up the bill the week before Thanksgiving. Conservative opponents, led by Minority Leader Robert Dole, threw up roadblocks with a series of obstructionist tactics and difficult amendments. What finally propelled senators to act was Senate Majority Leader George Mitchell's threat to bring them back for a vote after Thanksgiving, during the annual holiday recess. After the House passed the final version of the bill by a vote of 238 to 187 on November 23, the historic Brady bill passed the Senate late on November 24 by voice vote.

Supporters agreed to several amendments, including a commitment of two hundred million dollars a year to help state law-enforcement agencies upgrade and computerize their criminal record-keeping systems. The bill also phases out the waiting period after five years on the assumption that record checks will then be accomplished instantaneously over phone lines, much the way stores check the validity of credit cards.

Dole and other opponents promised to bring up other

modifications to the Brady bill in 1994, even though President Clinton signed it into law at a November 30 celebration at the White House. The Bradys vowed to press on for even stricter gun controls, with the support of Clinton and Reno.

Anyone who doubted Reno's contribution to the bill's passage needed only to hear Sarah Brady at the ceremony. After Reno lauded Mrs. Brady for her perseverance during the crusade, Brady said there was "one other woman" in the fight, "the attorney general herself." Brady enthused, "We've been fortunate enough to have her in Washington. She's been right along with us."

As Reno waged her battles on Capitol Hill, she was never far from the media spotlight. In its October 11 issue, the *New Yorker* ran a full-page cartoon of "The Janet Reno Collection," five no-nonsense outfits for a paper-doll figure that sported her distinctive haircut and oversized glasses. The outfits ranged from business attire ("Rayon acetate one-piece dress with knit bodice and back-zipped pleated skirt with attached slip," plus briefcase) to the Weekend-at-Camp-David look ("Mustard stone-washed cotton canvas barn jacket. White cotton shirt. Boots by Dr. Martens.")

Reno's attire did provoke collective head shaking among amused friends back in Miami on one significant occasion. Television cameras picked Reno out of the crowd on the floor of the House chamber when Clinton delivered his health-care reform speech to a joint session of Congress on September 22. She had been caught committing a grievous sartorial offense, wearing white shoes and carrying a white purse more than two weeks after Labor Day.

Others were willing to overlook the misstep. In November, Reno was named one of *Glamour* magazine's trend-setting Women of the Year, along with Justice Ruth Bader Ginsburg, Surgeon General Joycelyn Elders, American Red Cross president Elizabeth Dole, poet Rita Dove, screenwriter Nora Ephron, jockey Julie Krone, and others.

Within days of the signing ceremony for the Brady bill, the White House put out word that Clinton was considering a much broader gun-control plan. His first step was to order a study of a national gun-licensing system, which Reno assigned to her Office of Policy Development.

Reno, of course, had been advocating such a system for years. She saw it in simple terms: "I think it should be at least as hard to get a license to possess a gun as it is to drive an automobile."

And if safety on the road means drivers must prove proficiency behind the wheel, why shouldn't gun owners be required to prove that they can safely handle a firearm? she asked. An NRA gun-safety course would be just fine.

Early in 1994, the administration also proposed raising the fee for a three-year federal gun dealer's license to six hundred dollars. That fee had been just thirty dollars since 1968, although a provision in the Brady law hiked it to two hundred dollars. Treasury Secretary Lloyd Bentsen called six hundred dollars a far more realistic assessment, based on the costs connected to tightened regulations, including additional inspections and computerized record keeping. But he admitted the higher fee also could convince as many as two-thirds of the dealers to forfeit their licenses.

Since Congress would have to pass the second hike, the NRA immediately began working against it. The NRA charged that raising the fee would increase the cost of a gun, thus denying poor people their Second Amendment right to keep and bear arms. Reno's response: Baloney. Owning a gun, like driving a car, is a privilege, not a right.

Public sentiment was clearly on Reno's side. Polls showed overwhelming support for the new Brady law and the assault-weapons ban. That began to sink in with business owners. Wal-Mart announced that it would stop selling handguns.

Most impressively, even firearms manufacturers began to reconsider some of their business practices in light of the changing political climate. Winchester, a legendary name in the gun business, decided to halt manufacture of its much-criticized Black Talon bullets in late December. The hollow-point bullets for high-powered guns are designed to expand on impact with a target. So sharp were the bullet's hinged edges that they were said to pose a danger to doctors trying to remove them during emergency-room surgery.

Lawmakers on Capitol Hill had talked of banning such bullets or, as proposed by Senate Finance Chairman Daniel Patrick Moynihan, imposing massive taxes on them to discourage their sale. Under Moynihan's plan, the tax revenue collected would be used for emergency-room health care.

When Winchester announced its move, its representative said, "This action is being taken because Black Talon ammunition is becoming a focal point for broader issues that are well beyond the control of Winchester."

Reno's emphasis on prevention and early intervention solidified her role in the long-running debate within the Clinton administration over the best strategy to counter drug trafficking. During his campaign, Clinton criticized the Reagan-Bush approach, which amounted to military-style assaults on cocaine growers in Peru, Colombia, and other source countries, combined with far-flung interdiction efforts off borders and coastlines using ships, planes, trucks, even radar-equipped blimps.

Despite billions of dollars spent on direct U.S. efforts and support for police forces in Latin countries, the flow of cocaine and other drugs was hardly stemmed, as evidenced by the price and purity of drugs on the streets of American cities. Many drug-policy experts complained that Bush had his priorities wrong, spending two-thirds of the drug war budget on interdiction and law enforcement versus one-third on treatment and education.

Clinton promised that he would wage a "smarter" fight, but his first year's budget largely continued Bush's spending pattern. And a revised strategy that "drug czar" Lee Brown submitted in October 1993 was panned by Democrats as well as Republicans.

Brown, whose office had been trimmed from nearly 150 staffers to 25 under Clinton, advocated treatment in the United States and crop eradication in source countries. He proposed virtually eliminating the U.S. military's role in interdiction, although the Coast Guard and other agencies would still patrol.

Reno agreed that the cost of interdiction wasn't worth the results, but critics questioned whether it was smart to virtually quit. Reno and Brown touted Clinton's health-care reform plan, which would offer drug treatment to all who wanted it.

Hackles went up when Surgeon General Joycelyn Elders, the blunt-spoken former director of public health in Arkansas, responded to a reporter's question by suggesting that drug legalization should be studied. Reno was among the first to distance the administration from Elders's off-the-cuff comment, saying she would never support legalization, having seen the devastation caused by crack cocaine and other addictive drugs. White House representatives said Elders was not stating Clinton policy.

Reno's major contribution to the drug war was an unsung venture into unfamiliar territory: foreign affairs. She consulted privately with justice ministers from Colombia, Mexico, and a host of other nations on drug enforcement, interdiction programs, extradition treaties, and other matters. She carefully prepared for each meeting with experts from the Justice and State Departments and the National Security Council.

Her meeting with Colombian Attorney General Gustavo de Greiff took place on November 18, exactly two weeks before Medellín cocaine cartel leader Pablo Escobar was killed while trying to flee police. Escobar had escaped from his own custom-designed prison on July 22, 1992, and the Colombian government had been chasing him since.

At his meeting with Reno, de Greiff urged American patience with the struggle to defeat the wealthy cartels. "We expect the United States to understand our policy and appreciate the tremendous sacrifice endured by the people of Colombia in the international struggle against drug trafficking," he said.

After Escobar was killed, it was revealed that U.S. military intelligence had been helping Colombian police trace phone calls and otherwise track Escobar's movements for months. Reno congratulated the Colombians, but most analysts predicted that Escobar's death would have little impact on the flow of drugs to the

United States. His cartel had long ago been eclipsed in power and wealth by a cartel based in the city of Cali.

The fight against crime may engage world leaders and national legislation, but to Reno it is just as important that each American take the time to care. To make that point, she often recounts the story of a teenager she met early in her tenure as Dade state attorney.

"Unannounced, a lady dragged her thirteen-year-old daughter into my office and said, 'My daughter isn't going to testify.' I said, 'Wait a minute. Who are you? What are you talking about?' And she said, 'My daughter was a witness to a mugging, and I'm afraid for her, and I'm not going to let her testify.'

"Well, the daughter had been walking home from school. She was behind an elderly lady. Suddenly, a car screeched to a halt, a person jumped out, knocked the old lady down from behind, grabbed her purse and took off. The young woman got the last four digits of the license tag, called 911, and the car was picked up a couple of blocks away.

"The old lady couldn't see who had hit her and so could not testify. The young lady picked out the person immediately. He had a record. He belonged in prison. And I explained that we were not going to be able to see justice done if she didn't testify. The thirteen-year-old turned to her mother and said, 'Mama, I've got to do it. It's the American way.' "

As America's most visible combatant in the war against crime, Reno proclaims from her bully pulpit the message that Americans must take personal responsibility for their communities. She sees her own role just as clearly—to build cooperation among federal, state, and local governments in solving problems the public wants addressed.

Epilogue

The First Year: A Summing Up

Janet Reno began her second year as the nation's top cop politically battered and bruised but unbowed. The tragedy at Waco, political maneuvering on the crime-control bill, and backwash over the Clintons' involvement in the Whitewater Development Corporation affair had taught her some hard lessons on the ways of Washington. But there was never a time that the nation didn't know where she stood on the causes of crime, on gun control, and on the qualifications of career lawyers in the Justice Department.

At the end of her first year, Reno believed she was doing the right thing with her impact on the debate about crime, violence, and crime prevention. She, indeed, had led police chiefs, prosecutors, and the American Bar Association toward a rethinking of their priorities, especially involving children and youth. She had forged new alliances with other federal agencies involved with public health, housing, education, and worker training. She had inspired women, especially, to seek new roles in traditionally male spheres of political power.

But she had fallen short in influencing the congressional debate on the anticrime bill; she had bitten off more than she could chew by challenging the television industry on its violent programming; and she had largely failed to tame the Justice Department's massive bureaucracy—a daunting task, given its ninety-three thousand em-

311

ployees. She continued to have trouble finding and keeping top-level executives. She lost her first deputy attorney general and associate attorney general and still hadn't installed directors at major divisions like Civil Rights and Environmental Crimes. Webb Hubbell, caught in a dispute over billings with his old law firm, quit unexpectedly on March 14. Reno was terribly saddened to lose him.

Of the exultant throng that greeted her first speech at the Justice Department, some are disappointed at the pace of change. Many career staff members pinned their highest hopes on this idealistic crusader. Though changes have come, they've been slower than some have wished, given Reno's penchant for analysis and deliberation.

On the personal front, she lost weight—too busy to eat, she says—and didn't see enough of family and friends. Her trips home to Miami have been few and short, just a day for Thanksgiving and a weekend at Christmas. She misses spending time with sister Maggy and her family.

But Reno shows no signs of a slump. As she took her lumps in the press, Reno expressed real relief that the media mythmaking that had welcomed her to the cabinet had clearly run its course. In fact, when critical articles appeared, Reno found herself reassuring others that she wasn't upset. The longest and toughest appeared in October in the *New York Times*. But its hyperbolic headline—"Doubts on Reno's Competence Rise in Justice Department"—wasn't supported by the story itself.

The morning the article appeared, she recalled, "Everybody called me and said, 'Are you OK?' I hadn't read it yet, so I took it, and I looked up at the top and I started reading it veeerrrry carefully. And I braced myself and I opened it up [to the continuation inside] and I read it more carefully. . . . I got to the end, and I called Phil Heymann—he'd been worried—and I said, 'The *Miami Herald* was fifteen times worse to me for fifteen years. I expect much worse.' "

She was delighted with a piece that ran in the *Washington Post* that examined the highs and lows of her image. The December 21 article by media writer Howard Kurtz was headlined, "Janet Reno,

Hung Out to Dry? How the Media Put Her Through the Spin Cycle."

Kurtz wrote, "The media have a way of launching public figures into the stratosphere and then yanking them back to Earth without a parachute. In what has become a classic Washington ritual, the press pack has suddenly opened fire on Reno, often using anonymous quotes for ammunition."

Reno referred to the article at her weekly press briefing two days later as "the marvelous *Washington Post* story" and asked reporters, "Please, please, whatever you do in the ensuing months, don't put me through another spin cycle."

She still ranked at the top with *People* magazine. In its end-of-the-year issue, it named her one of the twenty-five most intriguing people of 1993, along with singer k.d. lang, the Clintons, and other celebrities. But, in a nod to objectivity, the magazine noted, "Lately her luster has dimmed."

Indeed, it was a wearier and wiser Reno who began her 1994 season. She's still got her legendary spunk, her flashes of the righteous, buck-stops-here law-woman who puts principle before politics. That's the Reno who shouldered blame for the Waco debacle, who reached out a hand to Lani Guinier, who flushed out secretive federal bureaucrats by rescinding a Reagan-era rule that encouraged agencies to withhold records rather than open them to the public. Henceforth, Reno had ordained, a "presumption of disclosure" would exist in response to requests under the Freedom of Information Act, with exceptions only for materials involving national security.

But she faced a formidable string of issues. Many aspects of the crime bill had to be resolved, including the "federalizing" of so many crimes that Chief Justice William Rehnquist worries that they will clog federal courts. It was time to conclude the complicated investigation into financial improprieties by Dan Rostenkowski, the powerful Illinois congressman and Clinton supporter. That probe appeared to expand in December with allegations that he had padded his congressional payroll with the friends and relatives of political allies, who did no work.

But the most sensitive case of all, one that forced Reno to repeatedly defend her principles against many in Congress and the media, led straight to the White House. The propriety of the Clintons' financial involvement with the Whitewater Development Corporation, dating back to 1978, triggered for Reno a basic issue about investigative credibility.

It was a complicated case with several interesting wrinkles: The Whitewater vacation-home development was tied to the fifty-million-dollar failure of Madison Guaranty S&L, a savings and loan institution in Little Rock, Arkansas, that was owned by friends of the Clintons. Hillary Rodham Clinton and her law firm had once represented Madison Guaranty S&L. And the Clintons' files from the deal had been removed from Vince Foster's office in the White House shortly after his suicide. The Clintons' lawyer negotiated a subpoena for those records that kept them from public view.

For months, Republicans accused the White House of a cover-up, in which Reno was colluding. But Reno refused to yield to calls for the appointment of a special prosecutor, preferring to leave the investigation to the trio of career Justice Department fraud prosecutors led by Donald B. Mackay, once appointed a U.S. attorney in Illinois by Richard Nixon. She reasoned, "If I appoint a special prosecutor, it's still my prosecutor, and there will still be questions about that person's independence. If I'm going to be responsible for the outcome of an investigation, then I want to make sure that it's done the right way."

And the right way, she was convinced, was leaving it to "career prosecutors who have worked for several administrations and who have real experience in federal prosecution."

Clinton promised to cooperate with that investigation, but when the White House delayed in turning over the president's files, the clamor for Reno to intervene rose to a fevered pitch.

Republicans, led by Iowa Representative Jim Leach, the top minority member on the House Banking Committee, were careful not to assail Reno's integrity but argued that any Justice Department employee depended for a paycheck on Reno, who worked for Clinton, creating the appearance of a lack of independence.

Many editorial boards backed the Republicans, including the *New York Times* and the *Washington Post*. In a January 7 broadside headlined "Janet Reno's Shameful Delay," the *Times* said Reno "seems hellbent on sacrificing her reputation to the White House's effort to contain the Whitewater Development flap."

Reno countered that anyone she appointed would be just as inherently beholden to her. She wanted Congress to reenact an independent counsel law, under which a panel of federal appeals judges would make the selection, removing control of the investigation from the attorney general and the Justice Department.

She had testified in favor of the statute in May 1993, a historic first. Previous attorneys general had objected to the law, saying it infringed on Justice Department powers. But Reno argued that an independent investigator could be necessary to preserve public confidence in government. And she got support from the *Los Angeles Times* editorial board, among others.

The earlier independent counsel statute had expired in 1992, unmourned by many Republicans who saw independent counsels as a constant aggravation for Republican presidents. The most embarrassing investigation was the Iran-contra probe led by former federal judge Lawrence Walsh, whose seven-year investigation cost about forty million dollars.

Minority Leader Robert Dole labeled Walsh's investigation a "witch hunt," and his Senate allies insisted on cost controls and other oversight for future independent-counsel investigations before the Senate voted 76 to 21 to extend the law in November. The House didn't vote until early 1994, after closing off a Republican attempt to use independent counsels to investigate allegations against members of Congress. Interestingly, Dole was among those now clamoring for an independent investigation of a Democratic president.

Finally, Clinton saw his domestic agenda threatened by the Whitewater controversy. He capitulated in mid-January and directed Reno to appoint a special counsel. Reno reluctantly agreed, stating, "Sometimes we have to go beyond what is generally appropriate simply to assure people that we have gone the extra mile."

Reno picked as her special counsel Robert B. Fiske, Jr., a former U.S. attorney in New York City who was originally appointed by a Republican president but continued to serve under a Democrat. "I said I was looking for someone who would be fair and impartial, who has a reputation for integrity and skill, someone who would be ruggedly independent, and I think Mr. Fiske fits that description to a T," she said.

Fiske, who once had been a candidate for deputy attorney general during the Bush administration, proved his independence by immediately declaring in response to a reporter's question that he planned to interview both the president and the first lady under oath. Reno, standing beside him, did not blink.

She had expected the question to be asked, and she knew how Fiske would answer it. And no, she said, she hadn't discussed the appointment of her independent counsel with the president or anyone else at the White House.

If Clinton hadn't given in, how long would Reno have held out on a point of principle? No one knows, but the incident emphasized the difference in their styles—and in the demands of their jobs.

Clinton's agenda was locked up by Whitewater; the issue consumed more newsprint each day, eventually leading to the resignation of White House counsel Nussbaum on March 5. Reno might have clung longer to principle, but legal arguments tend to get lost in sound-bite reporting.

Clinton is ultimately a pragmatic politician. Reno has seen that pragmatism in his willingness to jettison Guinier when controversy threatened to slow his momentum on appointments, and in his prompt surrender to the right wing when Reno's stance on a complicated child pornography issue proved a hard sell.

Yet Clinton reiterated his support for Reno during an appearance on Larry King's CNN show on his first anniversary in office (January 20). Clinton spoke forcefully when King asked if Reno would be staying in the cabinet.

"I think she's terrific," the president said. "You know, I told her when she was hot as a firecracker with the public and the press—I was joking with her once—I said, 'Janet, you go up and you go down in this business. And if you stay here long enough, you'll take a few licks.' And she's taken a few licks.

"But she has an enormous feel for simple justice, which is what I think people want in the attorney general. She's got a steel backbone, and she understands what really works. None of us are perfect. We all make mistakes. But, boy, she goes to work every day and really tries to do what's right for ordinary Americans."

"So she's staying?" King asked.

"If it's up to me, she is," Clinton said. "I think she's done a fine job."

And Clinton concretely demonstrated his support when he proposed a 24 percent increase for the department's budget—to $13.65 million—a hike greater than any other agency's.

Nonetheless, there could come a time when Reno's commitment to principle is such that she could simply quit and go home. After all, at her swearing-in, Clinton told her, "You proved to the nation that you are a strong and independent person who will give me your best legal judgment—whether or not it's what I want to hear. That is the condition upon which you accepted my nomination and the only kind of attorney general that I would want serving in this cabinet."

Speculation is the wont in Washington, and the speculation about Reno's future is constant. Some of the smart money is betting that Reno will be appointed to the supreme court—either because Clinton figures she would be a popular and thus easily confirmable choice, or because he will tire of her outspoken independence and want her out of his cabinet before he's up for reelection in 1996.

Her name even surfaced in a *U.S. News & World Report* article speculating on the retirement of Justice Harry Blackmun. Reno's selection would have a certain logic, given that Blackmun is the most outspoken opponent of the death penalty on the high court.

But many close friends believe that Reno would reject a Supreme Court berth. She has never served on the bench, and she passed up several opportunities to apply for appointment to judgeships in Florida, including to the state supreme court. She would be likely to consider herself unqualified for the nation's highest court.

Fans back in Florida would like her to return to the state and run again for political office. In late 1993, she was touted by some Democrats as a strong candidate for either U.S. senator or governor.

Democrats needed a strong candidate to challenge Republican Senator Connie Mack in 1994. An archconservative, his popularity has discouraged most prominent Democrats from challenging him. When Reno's name was bandied about as an ideal challenger, a survey of 806 Florida voters in early October 1993 showed her favorability rating of 63 percent to be higher than Mack's at 58 percent. But Mack beat Reno in a head-to-head match, 47 percent to 31 percent with 32 percent undecided. Pollster Robert Joffee attributed these results to the inherent advantage enjoyed by an incumbent—and to the fact that Reno herself had expressed no interest in the race.

Reno's Florida prospects are also linked to the political fortunes of incumbent Florida Governor Lawton Chiles, a Democrat who retired from the U.S. Senate in 1989. Many analysts believed he might step aside after several tough years facing budget woes, tax hikes, Hurricane Andrew, and ever more violent crime, but Chiles and his lieutenant governor, Buddy MacKay, announced their reelection campaign in late 1993. Reno's next chance for the governor's mansion would come in 1998, the year she turns sixty.

Reno's former partners at Steel, Hector & Davis would like her to return to the firm; that is, they'd love her to attract new clients. There's little doubt that she would be an extraordinary rainmaker. And she could likely command time to pursue her commitment to public-interest projects.

In the final analysis, smart money says Reno's hometown ties are the only ones that bind. After all, she has vowed to return to her small stand of scrub pines and palmettos and the rustic house her mother built. "That's my home," she says simply.

Whenever she is asked about the criticism she's sustained, especially from those ubiquitous unnamed White House aides, Reno likes to quote Lincoln: " 'If I were to try to read, much less answer, all the attacks made on me, this shop might as well be closed for any other business. I do the very best I know how, the very best I can, and I mean to keep doing so until the end. If the end brings me out all right, what is said against me won't amount to anything. If the end brings me out wrong, ten angels swearing I was right would make no difference.' "

Reno adds, "It's probably good advice to everybody in public service."

INDEX

321